Toward
the French Revolution

Toward the French Revolution

Europe and America in the Eighteenth-Century World

LOUIS GOTTSCHALK

and DONALD LACH

with the collaboration of Shirley A. Bill

CHARLES SCRIBNER'S SONS · NEW YORK

Illustration Acknowledgments

Pompeo Batoni: *Portrait of a Young Amateur*, courtesy of The Metropolitan Museum of Art, Rogers Fund, 1903.

"The manner in which the American Colonies Declared themselves Independent of the King of England throughout the different Provinces, on July 4, 1776," courtesy of the Fort Ticonderoga Museum.

P. Menant: *Vue et Perspective du Château de Versailles, de côté de la lat*, courtesy of the Art and Architecture Division, The New York Public Library, Astor, Lenox and Tilden Foundations.

Hogarth: *Canvassing for Votes, plate II*, courtesy of the Prints Division, The New York Public Library, Astor, Lenox and Tilden Foundations.

American Prints; Paul Revere: *Boston Massacre*, engraving, courtesy of The Metropolitan Museum of Art, Gift of Mrs. Russell Sage, 1910.

Goethe: *Sorrows of Young Werther*, courtesy of The Pierpont Morgan Library.

Josepita Andrade: *The New Cathedral of Salamanca*, courtesy of The New York Public Library, Astor, Lenox and Tilden Foundations and Revue des Deux Mondes.

Paul Sandby: *Henry VII Gateway From Without*, courtesy of The New York Public Library, Astor, Lenox and Tilden Foundations and by gracious permission of Her Majesty Queen Elizabeth II.

Nobles sikhs, courtesy of The New York Public Library, Astor, Lenox and Tilden Foundations and The British Museum.

Turkish fetes, 1700, courtesy of The New York Public Library, Astor, Lenox and Tilden Foundations and Mehmet Önder, Undersecretary for Cultural Affairs, Ankara, Turkey.

To the Memory of
Bernadotte Everly Schmitt

Contents

Preface

Every age is an age of transition—from that which has gone before to that which is yet to come. If the period here considered as the eighteenth century (1715–1789) is more strikingly an age of transition than most (as historians are prone to think), it is not because, lacking a brilliance of its own, it acts merely as a shadowy passageway between two dazzling chambers of time. It is because historians can hardly avoid concluding (despite the logicians' warning against reasoning *post hoc, ergo propter hoc*), that in large part both the brilliance and the tarnish of the eighteenth century were caused by the Augustan Age of Louis XIV, Queen Anne, and their fellow monarchs (sometimes in reaction against that age, sometimes in direct heritage from it) and that both the triumphs and the defeats of the French Revolution were a harvest that matured from seeds sown in the preceding years of the century.

So the authors of this book will at times deal with the eighteenth century as if it were a thread in the skein of time leading from that which stretched out before it to that which stretched out beyond it. But this "longitudinal" approach will, in addition, be supplemented by an effort to expound the century "in its own setting"—that is, as understood and misunderstood by those of its own generations who saw events as if they were *proles sine matribus creatae*—self-generated, without ancestors or descendants. And at times, the authors will even venture to be didactic: to suggest parallels, to make comparisons and contrasts, and to point out a moral as well as to adorn a tale.

The authors first published the greater part of this book in their *Europe and the Modern World*, Volume I (Scott, Foresman and Company, 1951). For their consent to use the text of that volume freely the authors are deeply indebted to Scott, Foresman and Company.

A number of scholars helped us in the preparation of the passages of this book that have been adapted from the 1951 edition of *Europe and the Modern World*, Volume I. Our indebtedness to them was there indicated (pp. viii and ix), and we continue to be in their debt. Space limitations have necessitated a shorter index than the authors would have preferred. In the preparation of this book we have received most helpful advice and encouragement from Elsie Kearns and Mary Edlow of Charles Scribner's Sons' editorial staff, and we wish to express our gratitude to them. Finally we thank Professor Lester G. Crocker, of the University of Virginia, whose suggestions after reading the galley proofs of this book saved us from making some rather dubious statements.

Toward
the French Revolution

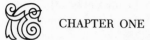

CHAPTER ONE

The Turn of a Century:
Europe and the East

At the beginning of the eighteenth century King Louis XIV of France was the example par excellence of the absolute monarch of Europe. Had this not been so, the chances are that the century would not have ended with a set of upheavals that long were regarded as the classical example of revolution. At the dawn of the century it was already evident that popular aspirations could gravely endanger a ruling dynasty. In the preceding century, in a series of civil wars known as the Fronde, which had darkened Louis' childhood years, the French, though repressed, had given rise to a kind of recurrent aristocratic rebel known as the Frondeur. The Czechs in Bohemia and the Magyars in Hungary also had made complications for the Habsburg rulers who failed to respect their local traditions. The English had beheaded one king and driven out another who believed that Englishmen's institutions could be shaped without their consent.

But as yet these bursts of resistance were linked with the anti-absolutist sentiments of the aristocracy, only at times shared by the gentry and the middle class. Defiance had not filtered down to the lower classes deeply enough to produce a fully self-conscious national solidarity. And in most of Europe, the trend of the times was against the aristocrats and in favor of absolute monarchy—especially in the great continental countries such as France, Brandenburg-Prussia, Russia, and Austria.

The consent of the governed was seldom sought, but probably the governed would generally have been on the side of strengthening the institution of hereditary monarchy. For the middle class wanted the centralization that dynastic control could effect and that the struggle for international power and commercial advantage made desirable; and the peasantry looked upon the great lords, the enemies of the king, as also their own oppressors. Even the so-called scientific revolution, the unprecedented advance of science and "natural philosophy" in the seventeenth century, played into the hands of the absolute monarchs, for it more often raised doubts about the validity of

1

the church's claims to intellectual supremacy than about the king's claims to sovereign power. New and unrecognized religions had arisen that the king might resent as heretical departures from the creed of which he was the temporal head. But they might work to his advantage, since they split the clergy and diverted attention from social and political issues to religious issues.

So, even though England's revolution was regarded by many Englishmen as "glorious" and even though Louis XIV's absolutism, at least in its later developments, was regarded by many Frenchmen as somewhat less than glorious (except perhaps in the realm of letters), it was the French model that was the more envied and emulated in Europe. Revolution in the name of a social contract was still, for the most part, a strange and offensive doctrine outside of Britain. The divine right of kings seemed a safer and more orderly principle of government at home and (though England had not fared badly) of victory abroad.

For victory abroad, the principle of balance of power had also in some ways justified itself. When they carried aggression too far, sovereigns like those of France, Sweden, and Turkey had been stopped in their tracks by coalitions of other powerful sovereigns, and each of the aggressors had emerged from the conflict somewhat chastened. Unfortunately for the much sought prospect of peace, the balance of power was attained only by strengthening some of the weak, and out of the coalitions arose new potential aggressors—England, Brandenburg-Prussia, and Russia, for example. The talons of some of the old powers—the Dutch Provinces, Spain, Sweden, and Turkey—were definitely trimmed by 1720, but France and Austria still retained enough sharpness and vigor to remain in the struggle for power. Together with Britain, Prussia, and Russia, they would engage in a sort of five-cornered struggle that was to become the major feature of world politics in the ensuing century.

Another major feature of the ensuing century was to be the controversy among the thinkers of at least the Western world regarding the nature of sovereignty. Did it belong to the head of the ruling dynasty (*si veut le roi si veut la loi*)? Or did it belong to the people (*vox populi vox dei*)? Or was it somehow divided between the two? And if divided, how divided? In seventeenth-century England the issue had been settled by force—the English civil wars and the Glorious Revolution.

To John Locke, already famous as a philosopher and champion of tolerance, had fallen the role of apologist for that revolution. His

Two Treatises of Civil Government, in tune with the naturalistic philosophy of the day, posited a prepolitical condition—a state of nature. This was

> a state of perfect freedom [for men] to order their
> actions, and dispose of their persons and possessions as
> they think fit, within the bounds of the law of nature . . .
> a state also of equality, wherein all the power and
> jurisdiction is reciprocal, no one having more than
> another.

This state of nature was not for Locke, as it had been for Thomas
Hobbes, an earlier writer, a state of anarchy and chaos. On the contrary:

> The state of Nature has a law of Nature to govern it,
> which obliges everyone, and reason, which is that law,
> teaches all mankind who will consult it that being all
> equal and independent, no one ought to harm another in
> his life, health, liberty, or possession.

Civil government arises, Locke assumed, when men in a state of nature combine to formulate a social contract and appoint some authority to enforce what natural law and reason dictate, thereby guaranteeing to all who enter the contract the full exercise of their
natural rights. Beyond this function governmental authority should
not extend.

From this major premise, Locke concluded that if any government should fail in preserving men's natural rights or should infringe
upon those rights, a revolution is justified. Contrary to Hobbes, who
had sought to justify royal sovereignty and had only reluctantly admitted the justification of anything resembling a popular uprising,
Locke considered the government at least as strictly bound by the
contract as were the people. Sovereignty for him resided in the people, not in a ruler above and beyond the contract: "The community
perpetually retains a supreme power of saving themselves from the
attempts and designs of anybody, even of their legislators, whenever
they shall be so foolish or so wicked as to lay and carry on designs
against the liberties and properties of the subject." Thus the uncere-
monious ousting of an English king in the Glorious Revolution became by Locke's reasoning a moral act vindicated by the royal viola-

tion of the social contract and based upon a higher law than that of mere men—the law of nature.

The English revolution and the theories of Locke were to have a wide influence in countries where a burgeoning middle class was beginning to view with alarm the restrictions imposed upon it by the prevalent system of absolutism, of aristocracy, or of both. In the next century France and the American colonies of Britain were to draw upon English precedents for ideas of revolution and the rights of man, and the English representative system of government was to become a working model for political aspirations abroad. England prospered conspicuously at the turn of the century. By 1714 she led all Europe in mining and metallurgical industries; her overseas commerce was steadily increasing, and she had become a first-rate colonial power. Furthermore, in a country whose middle class helped to make decisions, the old controls of government over industry gradually relaxed, and British foreign policy was increasingly shaped by the desire to secure commercial advantage. All these things the middle classes elsewhere looked upon with envy. Thus in subsequent decades Britain was to provide not only a philosophy of revolution but also a good example of middle-class activity in politics.

The apparently greater prosperity in Britain in the eighteenth century seemed to suggest a moral to liberal observers in absolutist countries. They were prone to conclude that there was a necessary connection between Britain's prosperity and her system of government. That reasoning is doubtful, since recent investigation leads to a different conclusion: that industrial progress in England surpassed that in France more vividly before the English Civil War, when both countries had been governed by largely similar systems, than afterward. Britain's industrial superiority in the eighteenth century is therefore attributable only in part, if at all, to political factors, and those factors were only indirectly associated with its type of government. Among these were the advantages derived, as we shall see, from continuing successfully to resist French domination of Europe, and from doing so largely by fighting abroad, at the same time that France was being exhausted by the ambitions of its rulers on the European mainland.

The English revolution introduced a new element into the dynastic rivalries of Europe. Through most of the seventeenth century, England had remained on the periphery of European politics, absorbed in her own civil conflicts. Though she intervened from time to time in major international crises, fought three wars against the Dutch, and was not above interfering in the internal affairs of other nations, she was no leader in continental conflicts as she had been in the days of Queen Elizabeth I. From the Glorious Revolution on, as the power of Spain and Holland declined, rivalry between France and England became more and more the dominant theme of European international politics, a rivalry stretching far beyond the shores of Europe to India in the east and the Mississippi Valley in the west. It resulted in a series of worldwide wars—fought on all the known seas and continents—sometimes named "the Second Hundred Years' War." These wars were not to be settled conclusively until 1805, when the Battle of Trafalgar was finally to determine that British maritime and colonial ascendancy would outstrip French competition.

One of the most bitterly fought phases of the Second Hundred Years' War became known as "The War of the Spanish Succession" (1701–1714). The immediate cause was a dispute over who should succeed the ruler of Spain—a Bourbon prince, of the family that reigned in France, or a Habsburg prince, of the family that reigned in Austria, both almost equally related to the childless ruler. Despite all the efforts made to settle that dispute before hostilities might commence, Louis XIV maneuvered to put his grandson Philip of Anjou upon the Spanish throne. Whereupon a Grand Alliance including Austria and England was formed to preserve the balance of power that would otherwise be upset by the Bourbon control of both France and Spain. By the treaties of Utrecht (1713) and Rastatt (1714) the big powers of the Grand Alliance won the greatest advantages. Although the Spanish throne and the Spanish colonies were conceded to the Bourbon prince, Louis' grandson Philip, it was only on condition that the thrones of Spain and France would remain separate forever. Austria was compensated by the acquisition of Milan, Naples, and Sardinia in Italy and of the Spanish Netherlands (now known as "the Austrian Netherlands" and later as "Belgium"). Britain received Newfoundland, Nova Scotia, and the Hudson Bay Territory in America from France, and the Rock of Gibraltar and the island of Minorca from Spain. By a separate treaty, Britain was also granted the *Asiento*, a special and highly remunerative contract for British merchants.

The lesser allies of England and Austria also received their awards. The former dukes of Savoy were now permitted by international agreement to take the title of "king"; and, having been awarded the island of Sicily at Spain's expense, the reigning duke took the title of "king of Sicily." A few years later he was able to arrange with Austria an exchange of Sicily for Sardinia and thereby became "king of Sardinia." The king of Sardinia thus became one of the most prominent rulers among the heads of the several disunited Italian states, and the heads of the house of Savoy were marked for a leading role in Italian political developments. The remuneration of the United Dutch Provinces (generally but incorrectly known as Holland) for their losses in the war was the confirmation of a defensive line known as "the barrier fortresses" along the border between the Belgian provinces and France. Since the Belgian provinces were now the Austrian Netherlands and the Dutch were permitted to garrison the barrier fortresses, the United Provinces seemed well protected against further French aggression. Other territorial adjustments benefited Portugal in South America and Brandenburg-Prussia in the Rhine Valley. In addition, Frederick, the Hohenzollern elector of Brandenburg-Prussia, in return for his support of the Grand Alliance, had been allowed to take the title of "king." Since West Prussia was still part of Poland, and he owned only the eastern part and was sovereign in that part, he took the title of "Frederick I, king *in* Prussia," rather than "king *of* Brandenburg-Prussia." By adding some Rhenish lands to his holdings at the close of the war, Frederick preserved the family tradition that each Hohenzollern ruler enlarge the state. On his death, Prussia was a potential rival to the Swedes on the Baltic, to the Dutch on the Rhine, and to the Austrians in northern Germany.

Most of the territorial changes by the treaties of peace were at Spanish expense. Thus the once-proud Spanish empire was humbled. Her outlying possessions in Europe were lost, and the British in Gibraltar and Minorca occupied Spanish soil. Spain still, however, controlled a vast empire in the New World, Africa, and the Philippines.

The treaties of Utrecht and Rastatt created a new international order. Since the former ruling family of Spain had been the Habsburgs, the threat of Habsburg domination of Europe was definitely ended with the partition of the Spanish dominions. In its place arose the threat of Bourbon domination, which, however, the treaties tried to meet. By obliging Louis XIV's grandson Philip (now Philip V of Spain) to renounce all claims to the French throne, the treaties attempted to forestall a future union of the two Bourbon houses under one crown. French overseas power was clipped by the cession of important colonial areas to Britain, which thus embarked upon the course of ousting the French from North America. Both Spain and France lost out in the centuries-old struggle for control of the congeries of states in the Italian peninsula, which temporarily fell under the domination of the Austrian Habsburgs; and in the competition for the lordship of the Belgian Netherlands, Austria was likewise temporarily recognized as the victor. Austria was thus able to act as a counterpoise to the Bourbon alliance of France and Spain on the Continent, and Britain served similarly on the seas and overseas.

During the war England (including Wales) and Scotland had decided to form a union with one ruler, one parliament, and one flag— the "Union Jack"—and, while retaining their separate churches (Presbyterian in Scotland and Anglican in England) and their separate laws and legal administrations, to become one country, thereafter to be known as "Great Britain." The treaties of Utrecht and Rastatt also signalized the growth of Great Britain as a world power, though one more interested in commerce and colonies than in continental possessions. Commercial advantage dictated the acquisition of Gibraltar and Minorca in the Mediterranean, and colonial rivalry dictated the acquisitions in America. The airtight mercantile system of the Spanish empire in America was impaired by two important commercial concessions to Great Britain. The *Asiento* permitted merchants to export several thousand slaves a year to Spanish America, giving them a temporary monopoly of the Spanish slave market, and grudgingly conceded that each year one British vessel of five hundred tons' displacement might anchor in the harbor of Porto Bello, Panama, presenting British merchants with a legal wedge by which to widen the opportunities for smuggling. The war combined with mutual commercial interests to effect a closer rapprochement between England and Portugal, expressed in the Methuen Treaty (1703), named after the English ambassador at Lisbon. The Methuen Treaty was abrogated only in 1836, thus becoming one of the oldest unbroken reciprocity treaties in history. By making Portugal dependent on Britain as a market for her wines and a source for her textiles, the Methuen Treaty initiated the growing influence of Britain over Portuguese affairs. The association thus begun accounts for the Portuguese dependence upon English wool and for the English taste for port.

The Dutch Provinces, originally the moving force in the alliances against Louis XIV, fared indifferently in the peace settlements. Except for their losses to England on the North American continent, their vast colonial empire had not actually diminished during the seventeenth century but now was eclipsed by larger, more populous, and stronger powers. In a three-cornered fight with England and France, the Dutch had had to choose one of their competitors as an ally against the other, and a marriage alliance of the most influential Dutch family, the House of Orange, with an English princess had resulted in their choosing England. As British might grew in the eighteenth century, Britain appeared more and more like a protector of the Dutch royalists, advocates of an hereditary crown for the House of Orange, than an ally of the Dutch republic.

The acquisitions of two smaller states, Brandenburg and Savoy, brought into prominence two new continental seekers of power. Because of the skillful part played by the Hohenzollern rulers in the wars of the French king, Louis XIV, and the Swedish king, Charles XII, Brandenburg-Prussia became a significant factor in the European equilibrium, a contender against Austria for leadership among the numerous German states within the loosely knit Holy Roman Empire and a potential threat to Polish safety in the east. Savoy was growing conspicuous among the Italian states. Each was destined in the nineteenth century to play a stellar role in making unified and powerful nations out of separate and disorganized states. In the Rhine Valley, the Hohenzollern possessions became a direct neighbor of Holland, and in the course of time Prussia was to share France's and Britain's concern with Dutch internal affairs. The treaties of Utrecht and Rastatt thus had an impact upon world politics that was decisive long after the Age of Louis XIV.

While the War of the Spanish Succession was going on in western and central Europe, on the high seas, and overseas, in eastern Europe a war that came to be known as the Great Northern War (1700–1721) was also taking place. It was essentially a fight for control of the Baltic Sea, precipitated by a coalition of the rulers of Russia, Denmark, Poland, and Saxony (then one of the leading principalities within the conglomerate Holy Roman Empire) against the young and untried King Charles XII of Sweden, the dominant power on the Baltic at the time. Before the war was over it had involved the German states of Hanover and Brandenburg-Prussia against Sweden as well as Turkey against Russia, thus widening the scope of the war to the Black Sea.

The Great Northern War was ended by the treaties of Stockholm (1720) and Nystadt (1721), which put an end to Swedish domination in the Baltic and to Sweden's career as a great European power. Sweden received large sums of money for the cessions of territory but perhaps not enough to compensate for her loss of prestige. Of her outlying possessions she retained only Finland and a small piece of Pomerania, on the southern coast of the Baltic. The Baltic ports of Bremen and Verden were given to Hanover, another of the larger states within the Holy Roman Empire, and most of western Pomerania was ceded to Brandenburg-Prussia. The Saxon duke, whom Charles XII had temporarily ousted, placing his own candidate, Stanislaus Leszczynski, on the Polish throne, was again recognized king of Poland, as King Augustus II.

Of the other powers for which Swedish supremacy in the Baltic had been a constant menace, Russia was eventually to be the most important. Until the end of the seventeenth century, Russia had been a sort of semi-Asiatic hinterland of Europe. It was forced and cajoled at last into the European orbit by an energetic Romanov ruler, Peter the Great. Peter's policy of "westernization" was based on several motives. For one thing, he admired western industrial techniques and political organizations and sought to bring western methods and institutions to Russia. Simultaneously he developed Russia's interests in eastern Siberia and the Far East—a kind of Russian overland mirroring of western overseas expansion. He also determined to push Russia's frontiers toward the Baltic, seeking "a window to the west." Another motive was his desire to make himself absolute at home, an aim that fitted neatly into his policy of westernization, since absolutism was the prevailing form of government in the west.

By the Treaty of Nystadt the ambitions of Tsar Peter on the Baltic Sea were crowned with success. He received Karelia, Ingria, Estonia, and Livonia, thereby making Russia Sweden's successor as master of the eastern shores of the Baltic. St. Petersburg, which Peter made his new capital, was a symbol of his success. Palatial buildings designed by Italian architects on the French model arose out of the swamps of the Nova delta at the head of the Gulf of Finland to house his westernized government. Russia was now in fact the easternmost country of Europe as well as the westernmost country of Asia. Even if she retained much of her unique culture and tradition, she had, nevertheless, become a factor to be reckoned with in occidental politics. In Baltic competition, Prussia and not Sweden was to be her future rival, though the Black Sea remained a Turkish lake.

The last great resurgence of Turkish power in Europe had taken place during the latter half of the seventeenth century. Spurred on

by an able line of viziers of the Kuprili family, the Turks had penetrated the Danube Valley to the gates of Vienna. But they were
thwarted at the Habsburg capital by the armies of King John Sobieski
of Poland, and after 1683 they were forced slowly to retreat to the
southeast. The Ottoman Empire (Turkey) never took the offensive
again, and until its modernization in recent times, it steadily lost territory and prestige.

In an effort to follow up their successes, the Christians of
Europe under Pope Innocent XI and the Holy Roman emperor
launched a Holy League against the Moslems, which has sometimes
been called "the last crusade." Even the "heretic" Tsar Peter the
Great cooperated in this prolonged drive to force the Turkish invaders back into their Asiatic homeland. The crusade against the infidel,
however, was obliged to share Christian Europe's attention with the
conflicts of Russia and Sweden in northern Europe and with the rivalry of France, Austria, and England in the west. Constant bicker-
ing among the Holy League's members delayed its advance until the
end of the century and presented to the Turks a splendid opportunity to rehabilitate themselves materially and morally for the eventual onslaught.

In 1699, the Turks finally sued for peace and signed the Treaty
of Karlowitz. By its provisions they agreed to surrender their former
conquests north of the Danube and thereby enabled all of their previous conquests in Hungary to be reunited to the Habsburg realm.
The political and military significance to the Habsburgs of the Karlowitz arrangement was greater than at first appeared, for the eclipse
of Ottoman power in the Near East was accompanied by a decline of
Louis XIV's and France's prestige and influence in the west. More secure than at any time since the Ottomans first menaced central
Europe in the sixteenth century, the Habsburgs after 1699 could
afford to pay less attention to their eastern borders while preparing
to strike out more aggressively toward the west.

The Moslems of eastern Europe were less menacing now not
only because of their military defeat but also because of the multitu-
dinous internal problems that beset their Sublime Porte. The Turks
had been strong and frightening conquerors only so long as they
could preserve their soldierly spirit and their military organization.
Like other conquerors, however, they soon lost their enthusiasm for
battle and even relaxed their vigilance in the foreign territories under
their control. The sixteenth-century despotism of Suleiman the Magnificent was succeeded by an easy-going absolutism that retained the

autocratic forms but little of the energetic spirit sometimes associated with despotism, and only sporadic efforts now imparted glory to the still vast empire. Degeneracy was particularly apparent in the central government. Lacking the ability to control their advisers, the weak sultans who succeeded Suleiman were soon controlled by them. Educated in seclusion, the latter-day rulers took but little interest in the actual direction of affairs. The bureaucracy, the provincial governors, and the chiefs of the armed forces ruled in the name of the sultan but without reference to his decisions.

The decline of the sultan's position during the seventeenth and eighteenth centuries was reflected by the transformation in character of the dominant class known as the "Ruling Institution." Originally comprising a body of slaves, dependent exclusively upon their master, the sultan, and subject to his bidding, the Ruling Institution became a self-perpetuating organization. Since it included the officials of the sultan's household, the royal advisers, and the standing army, with the passing of time it divided into numerous semi-independent units. This division of the Ruling Institution aided the shift in the Ottoman state toward hopeless decentralization. Slaves, who originally had been the only ones admitted to the Ruling Institution, were joined after 1637 by free Moslems who wished to share in the spoils.

Probably the most important section of the Ruling Institution was the janissary (infantry) unit of the standing army. The janissaries were particularly important at times of disputed succession to the sultanate, when their weight often was enough to secure the throne for one of the more fortunate candidates, and each succession crisis enhanced their influence. In the course of years their numbers increased. Not more than 14,000 in Suleiman's time, the janissaries in 1700 numbered almost 100,000, including Moslems and non-Moslems. Nevertheless, they still constituted a closed caste of unruly bandits, who existed by preying upon and terrorizing the countryside. Most firmly entrenched in the European possessions of the Porte, they were universally feared among the common people.

With the admission of Moslems to their ranks and the decline of central authority, the janissaries relinquished the institution of celibacy. Thereafter they subdivided into a number of hereditary fighting units willing to sell their services to the highest bidders— sometimes even to the enemies of the Porte. Ravaging, pillaging, and living upon the farmers, the janissaries came to be regarded in Europe as almost the worst of the visitations inflicted upon Christendom by the Moslem infidels. The sultan, on the other hand, frequently found the privileged janissaries useless and at critical moments had to call out the spahis, a feudal levy of cavalry supplied by the Moslem aristocrats. Although efforts were made to organize a military force along modern lines, not until the Greeks achieved their independence in 1829 did such a force come into being, and then the insubordinate janissary corps were finally dissolved.

Decentralization brought other changes in its wake. Persia effected its independence in 1735 under an aggressive leader named Nadir, who the next year took the title of "shah." The provincial governors of Egypt, Greece, Rumania, and other parts of the far-flung Ottoman possessions became virtually autonomous rulers. Almost the only unifying element remaining in the Turkish system was the devotion of the ruling elements to the Moslem faith. Even in religion, however, the traditional divisions became deeper, unswerving devotion to the Koran became less common, and the Turks, like their contemporaries in Europe, became ever more interested in worldly achievements.

The degeneracy that characterized Ottoman politics during the eighteenth century did not extend to all aspects of Turkish culture. The great cities of western Asia, such as Constantinople and Mecca, rivaled Paris and London in the brilliance of their social and intellectual life. Poets, musicians, and architects were handsomely patronized by the court. The Moslem ban on printing was removed in 1727 for all Arabic and Turkish books except the sacred Koran. Widespread dissemination of Turkish literature thereafter inspired European students to inquire more carefully into the languages and the traditions of the Moslem world. The wealth of imaginative Arabic literature also became more generally available.

The majority of Moslems did not accept unquestioningly the brilliant cultural life of the cities. Radical departures from custom were greeted in conservative quarters by open antagonism. In the middle of the eighteenth century appeared a reforming sect of "old Arabs" called the "Wahhabis," followers of Ibn Abdul Wahhab. They believed, somewhat like the contemporary Pietists and Jansenists of the West, in the literal interpretation of their holy scripture. They protested openly and vigorously against the Turkish failure to uphold the old Mohammedan doctrines, against the introduction of the printing press, and against the degeneracy of Mecca, the holy city. For two centuries the Wahhabis were to carry on their agitation, which sometimes took the form of holy war (*jihad*) against unbelievers at home or abroad. Support for their uncompromising zeal was widespread, and the Wahhabis quickly succeeded in checking the enlightenment of the cities of western Asia.

No strong middle class developed among the Turks, and Turkish industry continued to be limited to local crafts and small establishments. Trade with Europeans was mainly in the hands of Jewish, Armenian, and Greek subjects of the sultan. Many of the Turks possessed extensive holdings in land and were ready to play their part as landlords, but they left commerce and banking to the lesser peoples of the empire. The failure to appreciate fully the importance of foreign trade rapidly became one of the empire's most serious weaknesses. This weakness increased as the European countries, profiting from the opening of new sea routes to the East and the West, were more and more enabled to ignore the trade routes of the Mediterranean and the trading cities of the Levant. The Ottoman Empire of the eighteenth century was thus speeding downhill economically as well as politically and culturally.

The Moslem world, stretching west from the Pacific islands across Asia and East and North Africa to the Atlantic Ocean, had little to offer to Christian Europe during this period. The Arabs of Spain, Africa, and the Levant had already made their greatest contributions to western culture when the Far East, which had previously contributed much, began to contribute more. The Turks, for their part, took from Europe, except for its lands and its children, very little and gave very little. In fact, the Ottomans acted as a barrier between East and West, not, as once was believed, because they meant to interfere with European trade with Asia, but because they tried to profit from it exorbitantly without a corresponding effort in commercial enterprise. Turkish milking of the overland trade between East and West diverted commerce to the sea lanes. Even the sea lanes, especially those of the Mediterranean, were infected by "Barbary" (i.e., North African Arab) corsairs. The interior of Africa south of the Sahara was largely a "dark continent" to other peoples, although some of the Black peoples had developed a high level of art, learning, commerce, urban culture, and government and had frequently become converted to Islam. Christians and Arabs knew little beyond the harbors and estuaries of the coastal regions, where some of them had made settlements and traded, largely in slaves.

Loosely, the term "East Indies" has been used to designate India, Indochina, and the Malay Archipelago, but more strictly it refers to the last region—the world's largest group of islands, including today the autonomous states of the Philippine Republic and the Republic of the United States of Indonesia. Only in our own day have these Malayan islands become free. The Philippines were part of the Spanish empire until 1898 and then were ceded to the United States of America. They acquired independence in 1946. The Indonesian islands remained almost exclusively Dutch until in 1949 the recognition of the Republic of the United States of Indonesia made the hitherto Dutch colonies a sovereign state. Centuries of commercial, religious, and imperialist rivalry among Portuguese, Spanish, Dutch, French, and British (not to mention later contestants like the Americans, Germans, and Japanese) led to the reluctant recognition that the outcome of successful European colonization is likely to be a native nationalism and a repudiation of European political control.

In India the Hindu majority, although equally fearful of proselytizing, was not at first so hostile as the Moslems to Christianity, since it believed that Christianity would be crushed by the zealous resistance of Mohammedanism. When this belief proved to be unfounded, however, the Hindus joined the Moslems in opposition, warning their coreligionists that the "gospel" was an important feature in the European formula of successful penetration. Nevertheless, Hindus and Moslems alike were impressed by the learning of the Jesuit missionaries more than by the firearms and gold of the merchants. They remained, however, much more sympathetic with the Jesuits' intellectual accomplishments than with their religious arguments, and so far as is known, no Indian emperor ever seriously considered conversion to the teachings of Rome. The Protestant missions sent out from England to India were no more successful than the Catholics. No large body of India's population ever became Christian. To this day only about 12 million out of a population of nearly 500 million are Christians.

To the Europeans, contact with the non-Christian cultures of the East presented a challenge. In their letters and reports to Europe, the Jesuits praised, sometimes to the point of extravagance, the arts, crafts, and literature of the Hindus. Common merchants from Europe were forced to admit the superiority of certain Indian crafts and products and introduced expensive oriental commodities to the European market. Even unsophisticated Europeans were thus obliged to come to the startling realization that a great civilization, which was old when Imperial Rome fell, was still largely intact, vital, and in some ways more advanced and productive than the contemporary European-Christian civilization. Greatly impressed by the ethical principles of Hindus and Moslems alike, more thoughtful Europeans began to realize that many inhabitants of the world had lived a comparatively moral and satisfying existence with only meager, if any, knowledge of Christ and the Christian religion. Eventually that realization was to have serious repercussions upon European theology and philosophy.

Although resentful toward the Christians of Europe the Moslems, the Hindus, and other religious groups of the Indies and India were easily engaged in commercial dealings. The groups of Europeans in eastern Asia, however, were smaller than those in the western Asiatic areas. Hence they were too weak to force concessions and were at first obliged to ask for favors. On the other hand, the eastern Asiatic peoples were disunited, and their animosities made it easier for the thin population of Europeans to establish themselves, since they quickly learned that they could play one rival faction or ruler off against another. Maritime Asia and India were not to be effectively exploited, nevertheless, until the age of steam made possible the wholesale transportation of materials and men over the long stretches of land or ocean separating the subcontinent and the islands from Europe.

The rise of the United Provinces and England as sea powers in the early seventeenth century was followed by the organization of their great East India companies. Each of these two commercial organizations was granted a charter by its government entitling it to a monopoly of the trade between its homeland and the lands of the Orient. From the outset the Dutch organization was a joint-stock company in which the investors shared (in proportion to their respective investments) in the profits or losses of each voyage. Not long after its founding, the English enterprise was also transformed into a joint-stock company. Because of huge profits divided among a large number of investors, these trading companies enjoyed considerable public and governmental support. Their charters were reviewed from time to time, but as they could show almost uninterrupted prosperity, they were granted ever greater concessions and more vigilant protection. In the early eighteenth century the Austrians founded a company at Ostend (in the Austrian Netherlands); a Swedish company appeared soon after; and in the middle of the century Frederick the Great succeeded in forming a Prussian company.

The chartered companies drew revenue from several sources. Having succeeded the Portuguese in the East Indies and India, the two northern European countries, England and Holland, shared the spice trade and access to the luxury goods of the East. "India" ink, Chinese silk, and Japanese lacquer ware became important commodities in western markets. As time went on, the variety of oriental exports multiplied, and merchants in London and Amsterdam added porcelains, wall hangings, and rich brocades from the East to their stock. India's cotton goods, especially calico (so called because first imported from Calicut in 1631), were also in demand; and this demand became insistent enough to figure in the rapid transformation of the English textile industry in the next century. Tea from Ceylon and India was particularly popular among the English, and tea drinking eventually became an inveterate national habit.

The Dutch, meanwhile, learned to drink coffee, first introduced in the West by the English. Taken by the Dutch from Arabia to Java and the other Spice Islands, the coffee plant flourished in the Indies (as well as, eventually, in Dutch Guiana in South America). Indeed, the Dutch were soon able to export large quantities of it from the East, and in American slang all varieties of coffee are still referred to incorrectly as "Java." By the end of the seventeenth century, the coffeehouse was a familiar institution in London, and in France and elsewhere on the Continent the café was fast becoming "the poor man's club" and the center of political debate and literary gossip.

Although the products of the East were in great demand in Europe, few European commodities appealed to the Asians. Gold and silver from the Americas were often exchanged for oriental goods by Spanish merchants, but the northern Europeans, having less precious metal, found it more difficult to maintain a balance of trade and payments. Lacking commodities to market in Asia, the English and the Dutch helped to pay for their purchases by "invisible" exports and services. Using their superior ships and their greater maritime skill to advantage, they profited by engaging in the carrying trade between the numerous oriental countries. This legitimate enterprise was supplemented by a system of piracy whereby Europeans preyed upon vessels of both oriental and occidental origin.

Although the English at first challenged the Dutch effort to build up an East Indian empire in the islands, they began after the Restoration of 1660 to concentrate upon the relatively uncontested subcontinent of India. They were not left in peace there for long, however. In 1664 Jean-Baptiste Colbert, King Louis XIV's enterprising financial superintendent, organized the French East India Company with the object of participating in the lucrative eastern trade. This company's first acquisitions were in India, where it established in 1668 a trading post at Surat. Six years later it purchased the town of Pondichéry, upon which French trading and political activities centered. Shortly afterwards the French extended their activities east to Siam, where troops of Louis XIV endeavored unsuccessfully to win control of the city of Bangkok. By the end of the seventeenth century the stage was set in southeastern Asia for a bitter Anglo-French struggle—the Asian phase of the Second Hundred Years' War.

We are accustomed to think of Japan as the most progressive of the oriental nations. The rapidity with which it emerged from isolation in the nineteenth century to become in the twentieth one of the most advanced world powers in technology and one of the most fearsome in military and naval might could hardly have been guessed by any of the few Europeans who visited the Japanese islands in the first half of the sixteenth century. For over three hundred years, as neighboring peoples succumbed, to a greater or lesser degree, to European encroachments, the Japanese remained practically united, isolated, and intact. When finally they too permitted a restricted importation of European influences to their shores, it was from their east (America), by way of the Pacific, as well as from their west (Europe), by way of the Indian Ocean, that these imports were to travel.

Because of their close association with their missionaries, Spanish and Portuguese traders were under suspicion and were therefore badly treated by Japanese officials. The English meanwhile had found that trade with Japan was not sufficiently attractive and therefore did not try to retain the early foothold they had won. By the third decade of the seventeenth century, the Dutch, willing to carry on trade without benefit of clergy, had become the only Europeans permitted to trade in Japan, and even they were subject to ludicrously strict regulation. They were virtually imprisoned in Nagasaki harbor, from which they were permitted to carry on a carefully supervised commerce. The Japanese themselves were simultaneously discouraged from trading with foreigners. They were not allowed to leave the country for any reason whatsoever; those who had lived abroad were forbidden to return; and the building of oceangoing ships was prohibited. Aside from the Dutch, the only foreigners permitted to do business with Japan after 1640 were a limited number of Chinese.

The drastic measures taken by the early Tokugawa shoguns helped to spell the virtual isolation of Japan from the rest of the world. As a practical political measure, the hermetical sealing of Japan against alien influences seems to have justified itself in one sense at least—it probably helped to preserve the Tokugawa rule until 1868. For the general welfare of the Japanese nation, however, it was perhaps essentially unwise. Before its self-imposed enclosure, Japan was only slightly behind the western nations in material advancement. But by the end of the Tokugawa era, Japan culturally and economically was still much the same as it had been in 1600, whereas many of the western nations had meanwhile undergone an amazing transition from agricultural to industrial economies. Japan had won political stability, but only by binding her people down in every aspect of life within a system designed, above everything else, to preserve the status quo. That system was not to be successfully challenged until the nineteenth century.

More confident than the Japanese rulers of their own prestige and power, the Ming dynasty of China and its successors were less zealous in excluding foreign influences from their dominion and deliberately encouraged trade with other peoples. Nevertheless, the Chinese succeeded in keeping their culture mostly uncontaminated by alien customs and manners until the nineteenth century.

As has happened frequently in Chinese history, the danger from without was intensified by instability within. The domestic economy was swiftly becoming dislocated because the depressed and hungry peasantry had revolted against the short-sighted and burdensome measures of the landlord-dominated "literocracy." Taking advantage of Peking's preoccupation with its internal difficulties, the northern tribes increased their pressure upon intramural China. The Manchus, the best organized of the tribal warriors, combined their efforts with those of numerous malcontents within China. After more than three centuries of rule, the Ming rulers were forced to relinquish their "mandate from Heaven" and to abandon the "Dragon Throne." In 1644 the last of the desperate Ming dynasts committed suicide, but pacification of the south was not accomplished until 1685.

The Manchu conquerors displayed remarkable forbearance and a surprising degree of political acumen in their handling of the conquered Chinese state. Despite their eagerness to invade the cities of China, the Manchu tribesmen committed but few outrages. Realizing that the stability of their regime would depend largely upon public support, they did as little as possible to disturb the normal routine of life. They confirmed the Ming law code, preserved the existing tax measures, and continued the time-honored system of examinations for officeholding. Although Manchus were injected into the official-dom at strategic points, the old offices and customs of government were carefully retained. Manchu troops were stationed at strategic cities but were required to be as unobtrusive as possible. Chinese continued to hold office, to serve in the armed forces, and to enjoy rights equal to those of the Manchus. By moving carefully, the con-querors succeeded in disturbing "All under Heaven" only slightly. The Manchus therefore retained the "mandate from Heaven" until the Revolution of 1911.

The Manchu emperors, like all emperors of China, were consid-ered so august that they were not referred to by name. Their reigns were given distinguishing titles instead. Fortunately for the Manchus, the first of their rulers were able administrators. The K'ang-hsi reign (of Shêng Tsu), which began in 1662, was the second of the Ch'ing dynasty. Tolerant of foreign learning and benign in his attitude to-ward the western traders, the emperor was one of the most enlight-ened rulers of his day. He completed the pacification of the country. The German philosopher Gottfried Wilhelm von Leibnitz in the *Lat-est News from China* (1697) characterized him as "the Louis XIV of the East."

The end of the resistance to the Manchus in China brought marked advantages to the European maritime powers also. When the country was finally pacified, the K'ang-hsi emperor opened the coun-try's ports for trade. At first, the Portuguese and the Dutch profited most from this traffic with the Chinese merchants. Soon the British and the French joined them. The increase in the number of partici-pants in the China trade at Canton was so rapid that measures for their regulation became necessary. In 1702 the imperial government appointed an overseer of trade, to whom it granted a complete com-mercial monopoly subject to a full and strict accountability for the conduct of the Europeans.

Just when it seemed that all was going well, the situation of the Jesuits in China was compromised. Early in the eighteenth century, a religious controversy arose that endangered the status of all western Europeans in the "Middle Kingdom." Coreligionists accused the Je-

suits of permitting Chinese converts to practice the "pagan rites" of
Confucianism and of translating, inaccurately and with malice afore-
thought, the Christian term "God" into the Chinese terms *T'ien*
(Heaven) and *Shang Ti* (Supreme Ruler). This accusation placed the
Jesuits on the defensive. They claimed that the rites in question were
civil or political and not religious.

Because the Jesuits were already involved in disputes over
dogma with Jansenists and Cartesians in Europe, the papacy dispatched a special legate to investigate the situation in Peking. Meanwhile, the K'ang-hsi emperor had endorsed the validity of the Jesuits'
stand and had virtually offered them his protection. The papal curia,
however, decided that many of the "Confucian" ceremonies practiced by the Chinese and permitted by the Jesuits were, in fact, of a
religious rather than a civil or political character, and the Jesuits
yielded. Thereupon the "Son of Heaven" was outraged that they
should accept the decision of a foreign potentate rather than his own.

Thus, life became more difficult for the Jesuits. The emperor
permitted the anti-Christian elements at Peking and Canton to have
a freer run, and from 1717 onward numerous anti-Christian decrees
were published. Nevertheless, Roman Catholic and Russian Orthodox missionaries continued their Christianizing efforts in China. Despite persecution, the cause of Christianity in China survived.

Pioneers and adventurers continued, moreover, in the name of
the tsar, to explore Siberia's coastal region. Before the end of the seventeenth century, the Kamchatka Peninsula was opened up, and permanent settlements were planted on it. Moving southward from
Kamchatka, the Russian explorers found their way into the Kurile
Islands, the stepping stones between northern Japan and the Asian
continent. Some of them then attempted to enter Japan itself but
were severely rebuffed. Thereupon, Russian exploration worked
northward from Kamchatka into the Aleutians and finally onto the
North American continent. By 1728, Captain Vitus Bering, sailing
under orders issued four years before by Peter the Great, voyaged
between America and Asia through the straits that still bear his
name. He thus confirmed, as had previously been suspected, that
America and Asia were not joined by land. Within a short time, Russian vessels began to sail directly from Kamchatka to Alaska in the
persistent search for furs—one of the few commodities for which the
Chinese were willing to engage in trade. Thus the northern Pacific
area on two continents passed under the control of the tsars.

While the Russian explorers were opening the northern Pacific, their compatriots had been zealously seeking to find practical ways of trading with China. Several diplomatic missions were dispatched by Peter the Great in an unsuccessful effort to promote relations with Peking. In 1727, however, his successor was able to conclude the Treaty of Kiakhta with the successor of the K'ang-hsi emperor. In keeping with the Chinese policy of balancing "barbarian" with "barbarian," this treaty gave the Russians the right to send Orthodox priests to Peking; it also made trade relations between Russia and China somewhat more congenial than they had previously been. Camel caravan routes were now developed that crossed the Mongolian Desert and linked the two great empires in trade, much of which was smuggling. Russia thus became a prominent, though lengthy, link in the exchange of goods and culture between East and West. After 1727 a vast commerce, both legal and illegal, between Russia and China enriched the subjects of both states. Exchanging Siberian furs for Chinese porcelains, ginger, tea, and silk, some of the merchants of the Eurasian state made particularly splendid fortunes.

Meanwhile, the western Europeans had been deprived of their trade privileges and had proved willing to resort to the illicit but profitable trade in opium. The great influx of Chinese goods into western Europe had remained possible only so long as the feelings of the K'ang-hsi emperor remained friendly toward Roman Catholic missionaries. But the western traders at Canton, who had basked in the imperial favor toward the Jesuits before the Rites Controversy, began early to feel the reflected wrath of the "Son of Heaven." The appointment of a responsible overseer of trade at Canton in 1702 foreshadowed tighter regulation of foreign commerce in the south. Fifteen years later, upon initiating a series of anti-Christian decrees, the Manchu government returned to the Ming policy of restricting trade to Canton. In 1720 a merchants' guild (*co-hong*) replaced the overseer of trade at Canton, acquiring his exclusive trading privileges and assuming his responsibility for the conduct of foreigners. For a long time thereafter, the China trade was subjected to vigorous restrictions, and the traders themselves were closely watched and strictly limited in their activities.

In Europe, at the beginning of the eighteenth century, the Rites Controversy led to the publication of many works on China and Confucius. The divergent accounts of the Confucian rites published by champions of the conflicting Catholic orders whetted the appetite of the "enlightened" thinkers of Europe for more information. It has been suggested that the knowledge that Europeans acquired of the Chinese merit system of examinations contributed significantly to the western system of competitive examination for civil service positions, which began to appear in the seventeenth and eighteenth centuries. Although these influences were based upon information transmitted to Europe by competent missionary scholars, the use made of it was often sentimental or polemical and without regard to or full understanding of oriental conditions. Deists and *philosophes* were eager, among other things, to show that a non-Christian people to whom Revelation had not been vouchsafed had nevertheless developed a healthy and respectable morality. In Germany, Leibnitz and Christian von Wolff studied Chinese thought and found in it a commendable philosophy, based upon human reason. In France, Voltaire, Quesnay, and other *philosophes* learned as much as they could about the oriental world in order to sharpen their arguments about the universal nature of "enlightened despotism." The "Chinese sage" became almost as much a literary stereotype of the eighteenth century as the "noble savage."

Art objects from the oriental countries also exerted a considerable influence upon European craftsmen, architects, and painters. Imitation not only of Chinese but also of Indian and Japanese "oddities" became a vogue of the eighteenth century. European craftsmen worked diligently to make successful imitations of Indian textiles, Japanese lacquer, and Chinese porcelain. Indian princes, Japanese goddesses, and Chinese mandarins were used as decorative motifs on European-made porcelains and on drawing-room tapestries. In England, especially, gardens were carefully designed in the Chinese style of careless grace. In the famous palaces of France and Germany special chambers were set aside as display rooms for highly prized products of the Orient, where collections of jade and ivory carvings, silk and cotton cloth, brilliantly colored glassware, lacquered boxes and furniture, cloisonné vases and table tops, paper and silk wall hangings, or delicate porcelains would excite the visitor's admiration and envy as he drank different varieties of Chinese tea.

So far the East had given to the West more of cultural value than had been received in return. It was somewhat sobering to European minds that great philosophers, soldiers and rulers, fine cities, beautiful buildings, an impressive literature, and respectable systems of ethics and theology were to be found among peoples who had known little or nothing of Jerusalem, Athens, and Rome. It was somewhat frustrating, too, that they could not be conquered, like the

American Indians, by handfuls of conquistadors but, on the contrary, did not hesitate to exclude and expel alien intruders or to extend them only a haughty welcome. Europeans were to discover one day what these strange developments portended. The eastern people were not destined, like the Indians of America, to disappear before or to be absorbed or submerged by the Europeans; rather, adopting only part of European culture, they were to resist full domination and eventually, in our own time, to recover, for the most part, a fuller sovereignty. Meanwhile the Far East, India, and the West were to learn much from each other, the gravest lessons coming in more recent centuries.

In Europe a literature of protest and of social consciousness had become a prominent part of intellectual activity in the closing decades of Louis XIV's reign. In France the growing misery, as the cost of war in distress, taxes, and lives mounted, could not be entirely concealed even by an officious censorship. Several prominent men of affairs proved willing to run the risk of royal displeasure by calling attention to the suffering that Louis' quest for lands, glory, and power had brought to France. In England, practically untouched at home by war, the hardships were less felt and protest was less vehement, but opinion was more free, and voices were raised in criticism of governmental policies and social abuses. Everywhere, as the carnage mounted, a desire for peace arose.

A revealing instance of the differences in English and French political development is the contrast produced by the relatively free press in England and the licensed press in France. While newspapers and periodicals of every description prospered in England after 1695, in France all political papers except the official *Gazette de France* and a few provincial papers were suppressed, and in 1700 only three periodicals, devoted to literature, science, the theater, and other popular but nonpolitical topics, survived. As a result, a large French contraband trade in books grew up. Printed or alleged to have been printed abroad, books and periodicals purveying political information and opinion were smuggled into France and sold by "bootlegging" methods. Writers got into the habit also of circulating their manuscripts clandestinely. If sufficiently interested, readers made copies so that several copies became available and are still to be found, some of them yet unpublished, in French libraries. Manuscript, or "hand," newspapers (*nouvelles à la main*) circulated in the same fashion. As might be expected, a native political press flour-

ished also in mercantile Holland and was strictly forbidden in aristocratic Spain.

In England Joseph Addison and Richard Steele, the satirist Jonathan Swift, whose *Gulliver's Travels* is still a widely read satire, and
the narrator and pamphleteer Daniel Defoe, whose *Robinson Crusoe*
is a lasting children's classic, all excelled in the new, easy-to-read
prose style. Although some of Swift's best work was to come after the
wars of Louis XIV, before 1715 he had published his *Battle of the
Books* (1704), which showed that the quarrel of the Ancients with the
Moderns then raging in France also involved English men of letters,
with Swift on the side of the Ancients; his *Tale of a Tub* (1704) poked
fun at religious formalism and casuistical learning. Before 1715
Defoe was perhaps most distinguished for his *Essay on Projects*
(1698) and *Shortest Way with Dissenters* (1702), in which he advocated a wide program of reforms and reduced intolerance to an absurdity.

The Revue (edited by Defoe), *The Tatler* (edited by Steele), and
The Spectator (edited by Steele and Addison), were all founded at the
beginning of the eighteenth century. They were periodical essays
rather than magazines but were forerunners of the modern journal of
opinion. Each issue of *The Spectator* and *The Tatler* contained a short
essay on a literary or social topic or a mild satire on contemporary
manners or persons, preaching good conduct and gentlemanly behavior. Their popularity was immense in England, and they were widely
read and imitated in other countries.

In France Jean de La Bruyère's *Characters* (*Les Caractères*,
1688) is sometimes said to be the first effective appeal to the lay social conscience. This book held up various types of persons of his day
to ridicule, particularly the aristocratic sycophant and the fortune
hunter. Some of La Bruyère's most vehement words express his resentment of the hardships of the poor:

> One sees in the countryside wild animals, males and
> females, dark, livid, all burnt up by the sun, crouching on
> the ground, which they dig and stir with invincible
> obstinacy; they have something like an articulate voice,
> and when they rise to their feet, they reveal a human
> face; and in fact, they are men. They retire at night into
> their lairs, where they live on black bread, water and
> roots.

This picture of the French peasant was written about the middle of Louis XIV's reign, when to the normal hazards of poverty and famine had been added the unbearable taxes levied to support a lavish court and costly military ventures, the burden of quartering soldiers in private homes, and forced labor on roads used increasingly for military purposes. A large part of the peasantry had never been well off. They lived close to the margin of subsistence, too poor and too tired to be anything but ignorant, too inarticulate to express their dissatisfactions except in jacqueries, sporadic and unorganized rebellions. La Bruyère was one of the first French men of letters to speak of their misery.

Amid the general adulation of Louis XIV, other critical voices were raised. They came most conspicuously, however, not from the peasantry or the middle class but from aristocrats who resented the new absolutism and longed for the old days when the aristocracy had had a fuller share in the government and had acted (so they sometimes claimed) as a buffer between royal power and the people. Among them was a great military engineer, Marshal de Vauban, who had observed the inequalities among the people while constructing fortresses along the frontiers of France. Although he believed in absolutism, he was deeply concerned with the welfare of the masses, whose labor he regarded as the foundation of national wealth. In his *Proposal of a Royal Tithe* (*Projet d'une dîme royale*), written in 1698 but not published until 1707, he protested against the unjust distribution of taxes and, in particular, the exemptions and privileges of the upper classes. He estimated (probably too loosely):

> Nearly one-tenth of the people is reduced to beggary and, in fact, actually does beg; of the remaining nine-tenths, five are in no position to help them because they are themselves very little removed from the same unfortunate condition; of the remaining four-tenths, three are greatly distressed and embarrassed by debts and lawsuits, and in the [last] tenth there are fewer than a hundred families, and I believe it is true that there are not ten thousand families, large or small, that can be said to be really well off; and if you excluded businessmen, . . . those whom the king supports by grants, a few merchants, etc., I am certain that the rest would be a small number.

He advocated the abolition of most existing taxes and the substitution of a royal tithe or *dîme royale*, a tax of 10 percent on all incomes, peasant, aristocrat, and merchant alike. His book was suppressed by Louis as too critical of the existing regime and has greater value as a historical document than it had as a contemporary influence. Vauban died in disgrace and—it was said—of a broken heart.

But most of the critics, being noblemen, wanted social innovation less than a restoration of old institutions—a renewal of aristocratic power through the revival of the Estates General. One such critic was Archbishop Fénelon. An aristocrat by birth and sentiment and a believer in divine right, he nevertheless felt that Louis' policy lacked a genuine regard for the popular welfare. He believed that a paternalistic king should share with the aristocracy a solicitous attention to the needs of the people. "Never forget that kings rule, not for their own glory, but for the good of the people" was his admonition to the young hero of his narrative *Télémaque* (1699). The book, probably designed to instruct his pupil, the dauphin of France, in the art and ethics of governing, contained much oblique criticism of Louis XIV's reign. Louis' militarism was sharply condemned: "The evils of war are even more horrible than you think. War wears out a state and always endangers its very existence, even when the greatest victories are won." He contrasted the grandeur of the royal Château of Versailles with the sorry condition of the country at large: "Which is more praiseworthy, a beautiful city of marble, gold and silver, with a neglected and barren countryside, or a cultivated and fertile countryside with a modest city of simple manners?" Louis' strict mercantilist policies too were attacked by Vauban and Fénelon, as well as by other writers, including the rising school of economists known as the "Physiocrats" (of whom we shall say more later).

When the treaties of Utrecht and Rastatt finally restored peace to Europe after one of its most costly wars, the desire for concerted action to prevent future wars was widespread. Once more the map of Europe was redrawn on lines intended to be permanent. Once more sovereigns and subjects turned to the tasks and the hopes of peace. The desire for a universal system of law had received classical expression in the seventeenth century in the works of Hugo Grotius (d. 1645) and Samuel von Pufendorf (d. 1694), both of whom had argued that reason demanded cooperation among rulers to promote the welfare of their peoples and had propounded a system of international law.

In battle-scarred France the Abbé de Saint-Pierre, who had been a secretary at the peace conference at Utrecht, published in 1713 his *Plan of an Everlasting Peace.* He suggested a confederation of princes as a framework for preventing war. This confederation, composed of deputies of the Christian rulers of Europe, was to stay in continuous session, to enforce both domestic and international peace, and to preserve the status quo by force of arms. War was to be renounced as an instrument of national policy. Far in advance of his time, Saint-Pierre also wanted to "make commerce between Christian nations perfectly secure, free, and constant." Anticipating the free-trade doctrines that later grew up in Britain, he declared, in the face of contemporary mercantilist opinion, that commercial relations, if they were to last, could not be beneficial to one nation at the expense of another but must clearly be of benefit to all concerned. His book reflected the yearnings of a war-ridden generation for permanent peace but had little practical effect. In the early eighteenth century, despite the aggressions of Louis XIV, the need for collective action for peace did not seem so compelling as it was to become in our day, when warfare has become more nearly total.

European society at the beginning of the eighteenth century was in some regards much like that of earlier centuries. The great intellectual, religious, commercial, and geographical revolutions of the preceding eras had effected important social changes, but for the most part the outward forms seemed the same, no matter how profound the internal modifications. Except in a few republics, society was still topped by a king and his court; the clergy was still given the place of highest venerability; the nobles, especially the military nobles, still enjoyed the most privileges and the highest honors and offices; the middle class still resented its social inferiority and strove to overcome it; most of the population by far was made up of peasants; and the poor of the cities were largely negligible and, in any case, generally neglected.

The king claimed to rule "by the grace of God." He was the head of the national church. He was usually the chief personality in shaping his people's culture and institutions. He nearly always proposed to weld his dynastic state into a unified and uniform nation with himself as its puissant ruler. In countries like France, the full growth of royal absolutism in the latter part of the seventeenth century was the outcome of a long process. In Prussia, on the other hand, it was rapidly created by a few rulers; and in Russia, its achievement had been so swift that it amounted to a kind of autocratic revolution.

"One king, one law, one faith" was the ideal of eighteenth-century absolutism. It was an ideal only imperfectly achieved in even the most absolute of states. Local traditions, practices, and institutions were confirmed by ancient treaties and charters and still had to be respected; religious dissent was to be found in almost every state and led to doubt of the ruler's supremacy in church matters; and powerful groups such as the nobles, the clergy, and the guilds persisted in stubborn defense of their traditional or chartered privileges. Nevertheless, in many states of Europe the broad aims of absolutism had been achieved to a striking degree. Internal order was maintained; religious uniformity was enforced with the king as head of the church; and the resources of the state were increased and better marshaled through royal regulation. Sometimes these ends were considered desirable in themselves for the greater welfare of the monarch's realm, but often they were sought only as a means of competing favorably with other states in the continual struggle for international superiority in commerce and war.

Relations with other states were of paramount concern to the eighteenth-century monarch, and a government's international power and prestige were to a great extent determined, as they are today, by the relative efficiency of its army on the field of battle. For that reason, as well as for the maintenance of a ruler's power at home, military force was an important instrument of his authority. Seldom, however, did the king count upon a citizen soldiery. Professional armies made up of men who had been soldiers all their lives and knew no other trade were officered by noblemen who considered military service their highest calling. If enough nationals could not be induced, cajoled, or pressed into the royal army, whole military units were always available for a price in Switzerland, Germany, and elsewhere. These well-equipped, well-trained mercenaries were a familiar feature of the eighteenth-century army, replacing or supplementing older systems of feudal levies, recruitment by officers, and privileged military castes.

Battles were numerous. It was a period in which war followed war, with only brief intervals of peace, involving constant drains on royal treasuries and consequent burdens upon the middle and lower classes as well as the king and the aristocracy. Although absolutism generally meant domestic peace and order, it tended to sharpen dynastic ambition. A king who was autocratic might go to war all the more readily because he was easily able to command the military resources of a well-regulated state. Nevertheless, warfare in a period of horse-drawn transportation was necessarily limited in the numbers and areas directly involved and so meant a drain upon only a part of an unoccupied land's resources. "Total war" was still mostly unknown.

Of the king's subjects the courtiers were the most dashing. Their influence varied from one state to another, but in general their glamour was great and their power considerable. Court nobles had many social privileges. Many offices and occupations were open only to them, and they retained generous exemptions from taxation and the right to levy seignorial dues upon the peasantry. They were still rich as landlords and important as military, ecclesiastical, diplomatic, and civil officials. Young courtiers, as members of a hereditary official class, were frequently well trained for their anticipated posts in the army, the government, or the church. Sometimes the nobles were also highly appreciative patrons of the arts and letters, science, and philosophy. But their political power and authority had of late been endangered by the increasing clamor of king and middle class for power and authority. Many an ancient scion was now more a hereditary parasite than a vigorous participant in the government's affairs.

Not all nobles were courtiers. Some were too proud or too poor to go to court and become henchmen of the king. They remained on their estates—the squires of England, the *hobereaux* ("sparrow hawks") of France, the Junkers of Prussia—cultivating their lands, superintending their own affairs, and playing the local lord when they could. In their own provinces they often had great prestige, which was enhanced if they occasionally visited court or went off to the wars. While their national fame was less than that of the great absentee landlords who lived at court, they were frequently better liked or respected among the peasants on their lands, when they were not petty tyrants or skinflints.

At a time when wealth was measured largely in land, the economic power of the landowning aristocracy was still great. The aristocrat's political importance, however, was gradually being overtaken, in Western states at least, by the growing power of the middle class—the merchant, the professional man, and the industrial entrepreneur. In France, that power was still at the disposal of absolutism; in England, it had been enlisted to overthrow absolutism. In France, commerce and industry advanced largely under royal initiative and within the mercantilist system of royal control, and the merchant or manufacturer was dependent on the king's good will in running his business. In England, on the other hand, the crown granted private monopolies to individual entrepreneurs, who were then fairly free to manage their affairs as they saw fit. They thus developed an independence of royal favor conspicuously lacking in France.

The peasant in some ways paid for the wars, the elegant court, and the elaborate government of his ruler. The peasantry generally made up about three-quarters or more of the population. Cities rarely contained more than a hundred thousand, and the largest, London and Paris, had only around a half million. The city artisans and the "proletariat" (which at this time meant "low," "vulgar") seldom had enough property to pay taxes. Although in some countries, like France, they had begun to organize rudimentary labor unions (*compagnonnages*), such associations were frowned upon by the law and were more like clubs for mutual aid and camaraderie than for collective bargaining. The new middle-class merchants, industrialists, and bankers paid huge taxes, but these groups were not numerous; and as taxes were frequently on land and agricultural commodities, and as privileges and exemptions reduced the large landowners' tax load, it was the peasantry as a class who, though each individually paid little, collectively paid by far the greatest share of the taxes to state, church, and feudal lord.

Respect for the political power of the common man was seldom a characteristic of eighteenth-century statesmen. Writers or reformers might sometimes show a becoming moral indignation at the common misery, but the peasants were not a revolutionary force. A busy king could afford to be paternalistic about them in a leisurely fashion, for the Bible taught him that "the poor always ye have with you." They were a perpetual but not pressing problem and bore their burdens as best they could because they had no means of avoiding them. They moved within the framework of a stratified society and an absolute state, and if they sometimes protested against it, the rare peasants' uprisings, in France disdainfully called *jacqueries*, were usually frustrated and did little to alter their conditions or to shape institutions and the course of empires. It was the more articulate and powerful upper classes—the aristocracy, the middle class, and especially the kings—who were the decisive influences in designing the early modern cultural pattern.

Nevertheless, the generally passive relationship of the common man to the land, to his betters, and to the intellectual, political, and religious currents of the time was significant in the movements and trends of his day. The peasants' precarious livelihood depended upon the soil they tilled. Some of them were freeholders; some were tenants; some were sharecroppers; and some were serfs. By the beginning of the eighteenth century there was considerable variation in different parts of Europe in the relation of the peasant to the land.

In France the seignorial system still generally prevailed, with its usual peasant holdings, its primitive methods of cultivation, its common ownership of pasture and woods, and its obligations owed to the lord. But despite the persistence of many seignorial obligations, an increasing number of peasants were acquiring certain proprietary rights in their lands. Subject to the dues and rights claimed by the lord, such peasants were free to use the produce of their property as they wished and to sell the land or will it to their heirs. This trend toward peasant proprietorship became so clearly marked even before the French Revolution that, with the eventual abolition of the seignorial system, France acquired and long retained an agricultural economy largely based on small proprietary holdings. The tendency to purchase even a conditional property right in a piece of land was especially characteristic of the enterprising peasantry in the more fertile areas of France. In the less fertile areas, serfdom tended to survive uncurtailed or to change to *métayage* (sharecropping). By either of these institutions, the landlord was assured of labor, and the peasant was fairly certain that, no matter how unfortunate or shiftless he was, his lord's need for labor would provide him with subsistence.

In England, on the other hand, the more rapid growth of capitalism and the incentive of the profitable wool trade operated to break up the manorial system and to consolidate smaller holdings into large estates devoted mainly to sheep raising. The peasantry tended to become agricultural laborers rather than freehold proprietors, or to seek employment under the domestic system or in the small factories that were increasing in numbers. A class of freeholders known as the "yeomanry" maintained itself for some time after the decline of the manorial system, but by the end of the seventeenth century it was gradually dying out, its holdings being purchased by the wealthier classes. England became a land of large estates and tended to remain so until after the First World War.

In middle and eastern Europe the aristocratic basis of land ownership and the system of large estates at the beginning of the eighteenth century were even more pronounced than in England. Except in southwest Germany, the peasantry lost status and sank to serfdom. In eastern Germany, Poland, Russia, and the Austrian domains, the landowning aristocracy retained on their own estates the semifeudal authority that in the west had been undermined by the gradual increase of monarchical power. In addition, the comparative absence of commerce and industry tied the peasant closely to the land. The lowly status of the peasants on huge estates owned by Prussian Junkers, Russian boyars, and Hungarian magnates was to persist into the twentieth century.

All over Europe the gulf between upper and lower classes had tended to grow wider in the seventeenth century. Yet this development did not take place everywhere to the same extent. In England, for example, many of the gentry were as ignorant and provincial in manners and attitudes as the lowliest farmhand. Nevertheless, even in England the lower classes were expected to keep their place. It was only in capitals and palaces, where the wealthy middle class frequently penetrated the ranks of the aristocracy by marriage and prestige, that rigid class distinctions might become at all obscured.

Several trends increased the barrier between upper and lower classes. One was that the rich became richer, and their manner of living became more and more lavish. Whereas in medieval times the nobles suffered many of the same hardships that the commoners had had to endure, the seventeenth-century and eighteenth-century aristocrat, and the well-to-do merchant too, became more and more noted for their luxurious mode of living. They wore fine clothes, gave sumptuous banquets, gambled, drank imported wines, attended balls and theaters, traveled to foreign lands, and patronized poets and scientists. Whereas the lord had once lived side by side with the peasants on his estate, he now frequently lived a different life from that of the lowly tiller of the soil. In France and to some extent in England, many nobles literally moved in another world. They were absentee landlords. They resided at court or in the cities and often neither knew nor cared what was happening in the provinces.

A second trend that tended to set the lower strata more apart from the nobility and the middle class was the growth of a rank of wage earners. Both on the farm and in the small shop the impersonal employer-worker relationship was replacing the cooperative manorial enterprise and the master-and-assistant relationship of the guild system. This change was still rare on the Continent, but in England it was becoming rather common. Something like one half the English population were farmhands who owned no land. A class of agricultural laborers was growing up whose interests were often antagonistic to those of the employer on whom they were dependent.

A third trend was the increase in the hiatus between the educated and the ignorant. The educated were the clergy and, as a rule, the nobility and the wealthy or professional middle class. The mere ability to read and write put them in touch with a whole world of ideas and knowledge that was utterly foreign to the illiterate peasant, whose education rarely went beyond learning his catechism by rote from the parish priest or vicar. Even among the literate, there were wide divergences, for though belles lettres were now customarily written in the national tongue, science and scholarship were still often expressed in the international language, Latin, and were expected to become the property of only the initiate. Among the educated, new ideas in religion and philosophy and new scientific discoveries were doing much to modify old patterns of thought, while the lower classes, only indirectly affected by the intellectual ferment, believed and acted as their parents had. This period between the Middle Ages and the Industrial Revolution, when new ideas were rapidly colliding with old ones but were largely a monopoly of those who could buy and read the expensive books in which they were set forth, was characterized by a most marked cultural lag. Those who worked for a living lagged far behind those who had money and leisure.

But though the upper and the lower strata of society were growing farther apart, contemporaries in both classes were probably unconscious of the trend. Class cleavage was generally accepted as the usual order of things. If the peasants rebelled occasionally, it was rather in protest against specific grievances than in favor of abstract rights or class equality, and their rebellions effected little reform. The rate of social change, though increasing, was still so slow that rarely did one expect to do things differently from a preceding generation. Local custom determined how a man would farm his land, usually dictating a three-year rotation of wheat, grain or vegetable, and fallow, and (sometimes fortified by laws restricting certain employments to certain classes) indicated what trade he would follow—usually that of his father. A woman generally accepted the traditional pattern as daughter, sister, wife, housekeeper, and mother.

In the beginning of the eighteenth century only the higher circles of urban society experienced a great fermentation, and even among them it was likely to be intellectual or political rather than social or economic. It involved religious, artistic, and literary criteria and the problems of royal prerogative and aristocratic privilege. Rarely was lower-class participation in government suggested or a more equal distribution of property proposed, and when a few daring agitators or writers advocated equality, they were looked upon as extremists and won little following. Nevertheless, among the propertied—court, aristocracy, and middle class—the primarily political fermentation was at the close of that century to lead to a great struggle for power, in which were to be involved grave social and economic implications.

 CHAPTER TWO

The Turn of a Century: The Americas

The last wars of Louis XIV had been intercontinental wars. They had been fought in Africa, South America, India, and North America as well as in Europe and on the high seas. Hence their outcome helped to shape the destiny of non-European peoples. Some of those peoples, passing from conqueror to conqueror as spoils of war, changed rulers. Furthermore, their participation in the colonial phase of the Second Hundred Years' War taught them some military, diplomatic, and political lessons that forced them to a more rapid maturity. Perhaps most important to the overseas territories was the new pattern of European power that grew out of the treaties that ended the wars. As Sweden, Denmark, Spain, Portugal, and the Dutch Netherlands lost standing, leaving France and England the major contestants for supremacy, the new European balance of power meant important changes in the Americas.

Several formerly significant colonial powers ceased, in the first part of the eighteenth century, to have direct influence upon the North American continent. Holland and Denmark retained areas only in the West Indies and South America; Sweden disappeared entirely from the American scene; England remained the only Protestant nation on North American soil; Spain, now ruled by a Bourbon dynasty, had less reason than before to fear the French; and the two Bourbon, Catholic dynasties had a common enemy in Britain, which had grown formidable by her colonial victories at Dutch and French expense. Meanwhile, by virtue of having been affected by the civil war and the Glorious Revolution within the mother country, as well as by her international conflicts, the Anglo-American colonies were developing a self-assurance and solidarity that was lacking in the carefully superintended colonies of Spain and France. What had once been a many-cornered struggle for dominion in North America thus was to become essentially a two-cornered one with Protestant Britain on one side and Catholic France, aided by Spain, on the other.

Although the great majority of British colonists wrested their living from the land, an ever-increasing minority turned their attention to such other pursuits as trapping, fishing and whaling, lumbering, shipbuilding, and manufacturing. Some of the very geographical conditions that hampered farming in New England stimulated a more diversified economy. Its rocky hills were covered with rich forests; its waterfalls, which hindered transportation, offered power for mills; and its deeply indented coastline, which cut up the farming areas, provided excellent harbors and an abundance of commercially valuable fish. As a result, New England soon developed the most varied economy of all the Atlantic seaboard regions. The middle colonies could also boast good harbors, such as New York. Their waters abounded in oyster beds and fish, and the land was heavily timbered.

Hardy fishermen brought back to American ports much greater quantities than could be consumed at home. As a result, a brisk export trade developed. Fish shipped to Spain were exchanged for fruits; fish that went to the West Indies paid for sugar and molasses. The profits from the fish and carrying trade were used in part for purchasing manufactures in England. The fishing industry was confined principally to New England; and it is estimated that in 1765 it employed some 10,000 men, that its product was annually worth about $2,000,000, and that 350 vessels were carrying the fish to Europe and the West Indies. The Puritan devotion to both "God" and "Cod" was to provide an easy rhyme for later cynics.

An allied industry was whaling, which the New Englanders also pushed to extraordinary lengths. The whalers of Nantucket and New Bedford pursued the sperm whale from Brazil to the Arctic, and by 1774 at least 360 ships plied the whaling trade. Whale oil and spermaceti were needed for soap, lamps, candles, and cosmetics, as was whalebone for stays.

New England's ships, of course, required chains, anchors, spikes, and nails, while the farmers' agricultural implements also needed iron. Fortunately, almost every colony possessed iron ore and virtually unlimited charcoal resources. As a result, numerous iron works sprang up in New England, the middle colonies, and Virginia and Maryland. At first the ironmasters turned out bar iron for domestic purposes only and shipped pig iron to English mills, but as time went on, rolling and slitting mills were established, and nails, guns, iron tools, and agricultural implements were turned out in increasing quantities. By 1750 the growth of the American iron industry worried British manufacturers to the point that Parliament was led to pass a statute encouraging colonial ironmasters to produce pig iron for British use but preventing them from manufacturing it at home into hardware, tools, and implements. Colonial manufactures continued, however, to increase in spite of these restrictions.

This ever-increasing flow of commodites from farms, plantations, fisheries, mines, and forests hastened the rise of colonial commerce. Opportunities abounded for enterprising merchants and shipowners to reap quick profits in coastwise and ocean commerce. Several triangular routes of trade became famous. The merchantmen of New England and the middle colonies might carry American raw materials such as grain, meat, lumber, and fish to southern Europe, where they would take on in return wine and fruit, which they would then transport to England and exchange for manufactured goods, which they would bring back home and sell at a considerable profit. Or the American commodities might be shipped to the West Indies in exchange for sugar, molasses, and other tropical products, some of which would be reshipped to England in return for manufactured commodities. A brisk, although outrageous and sometimes murderous, trade involved the shipment of rum to Africa in return for slaves, who were then sold at profiteering prices in the West Indies, where the ships would take aboard sugar, molasses, and other West Indian products for sale in the colonies or England. In the direct transatlantic trade between America and Britain, the southern colonies had the lead. Their imports and exports were double those of all the other colonies because, on the one hand, the British demanded the staple products of the South and, on the other, the South lacked manufacturing facilities, with consequent dependence upon imports from Britain.

Exports from the northern colonies such as fish, meats, and cereals were less welcome in Britain than southern tobacco, rice, and indigo, for the northern products competed with domestic products while the southern ones did not. Besides, the British shipowners bitterly resented the heavy inroads that New England vessels were making, both by lively smuggling and by legal means, into their carrying-trade profits. And so there gradually developed an increasing economic friction between Britain and New England—largely because their climate, products, and pursuits were sufficiently similar to make them highly competitive.

Economic relations between Britain and the southern colonies, on the other hand, were much more cordial, for climate, products, and pursuits were dissimilar, and the commerce that developed between them proved extensive and mutually advantageous. The southern colonies relied almost entirely upon a staple-crop economy, especially tobacco in Virginia and rice and indigo in South Carolina and Georgia. When Jamestown was first settled, the London Company had sent over Dutchmen and Poles to begin producing tar, pitch, turpentine, and potash. Later, ironworks were set up on the James River, and Italians were imported to manufacture glassware. But to no avail. The imported craftsmen found life among alien English and hostile Indians too much for them. By the 1630's Virginia ceased to be considered a potential industrial area and turned to the cultivation of tobacco.

Just as the agriculture of the northern colonies achieved a high degree of self-sufficiency, so their trade and industry became less and less dependent upon British commerce. In London, mercantilists and empire builders alike were to do their utmost to enforce a "navigation system" that by law obliged the importation of finished products from England. But the abundance of resources at hand, the aggressiveness and ingenuity of the colonists, and the time and money expended in long ocean transportation conspired with newer theories of trade to raise doubts regarding this mercantilist philosophy. Each infant industry as it grew increased the desire for economic and, consequently, for political emancipation from English dictation.

A highly romantic and profitable industry in colonial days—one that declined with the passing of the first frontier—was the fur trade. The pelts and skins of beaver, otter, mink, and fox received high prices in European markets, and the first cargo that the Pilgrims had sent back to England in 1621 was composed largely of pelts. Most of New England's furs were brought in by the Indians, who exchanged them for beads, metal knives, hatchets, cloth, whiskey, and trinkets— and the White traders reaped rich rewards by the exchange. The Dutch West India Company had promoted trade energetically in the Hudson Valley, and after the English conquest of New Amsterdam (renamed New York), the region continued to yield furs in abundance until the end of the seventeenth century. Nor was the trade confined to the northern and middle colonies. Furs valued up to £30,000 used to leave the harbor at Charleston, South Carolina, year after year.

With the increase of population and the accompanying decrease of fur-bearing animals, trappers and traders had to move westward in search of pelts. Pushing up to the Mohawk and into the Ohio Valley, they were confronted by French muskets. Rival trapping, trade, and territorial ambitions helped to bring on the battle for empire between France and England. Somewhat ironically, the trade that had so much to do with kindling the war was already declining as a colonial industry.

Britain was deficient in lumber, needed for numerous civilian purposes and even more for the wooden ships of the proud Royal Navy. The New England forests, however, were dense with spruce, cedar, and white pine—the last so important in the fashioning of spars and masts that royal agents would mark the largest trees with the "broad arrow" that signified their being reserved for the navy. The other colonies also had forests of soft and hard timber, excellent for constructing houses, wagons, household utensils, furniture, staves, barrels, and many other things now made, at least in part, of other materials. From the forest, too, came tar, pitch, turpentine, and other "naval stores," upon which shipbuilding was dependent. Sawmills sprang up along the newly settled banks of the rivers, and the colonists soon were turning out finished and semifinished lumber products for local, English, and West Indian markets.

Because of the abundance of lumber and naval stores, the colonies soon turned to the specialized industries of shipbuilding. New England took the lead. The industry was aided by the quantity of materials at hand, the accompanying growth of the fishing industry with its demand for sturdy vessels, and the English Navigation Laws, which forbade colonial trade in any other than English and colonial ships. Colonial New England's heyday of shipbuilding was reached between 1700 and 1735, when her ships plied all the seas. She constructed twice as many vessels as the colonies in all the other sections combined. At the outbreak of the American Revolution, almost a third of the 7,694 ships engaged in Britain's trade had been built in colonial shipyards.

The English colonists, who thus frequently found economic well-being in America, had brought with them a deeply ingrained political tradition. For generations prior to the founding of English settlements in America, Englishmen of the upper classes had enjoyed certain liberties and had participated in enacting laws in Parliament. While the early Puritans of the Massachusetts Bay Colony were defying hunger, disease, winter, and the Indians to found a new community, their kinsmen in England had risked neck and property in fighting the absolutism of the Stuarts and in preserving their hard-won constitutional prerogatives. The victory for parliamentary government at home meant the preservation of the Englishman's political rights in the colonies as well.

Society in the English colonies, despite the recent influx from other countries, remained in its essential cultural forms predominantly English. The majority of settlers were of English stock and had transplanted to their new home their language, laws, religious concepts, literature, and systems of education. Their basic social-class structure and even their amusements, fashions, art, and furniture had first evolved in England. But these English institutions were modified in the colonies by new factors. A culture that was basically English in 1607, 1620, and 1630 developed through gradual natural processes to where, in 1776, it had become distinctive and "American."

A dominant note in colonial society was its more fluid family relationships. In a vast majority of cases, to be sure, a strong domestic tie resulted from a family's exploitation of their land in common, and such ties were reinforced by the English family system, with its common-law principle that the father was the head of the household legally and economically. The Old-World family rigidity, however, was softened by New-World economic conditions. America offered cheap land and many new occupations to lure children away from their parents' roofs. As a result parental domination became less binding.

Furthermore, in a land brimming with economic opportunities, the class restrictions that had determined a family's status in England tended to disappear. An indentured servant might become a landlord. The son of a blacksmith might become an ironmaster. A penniless Franklin might become a man of means. A backcountry farmer's boy like Thomas Jefferson might marry a wealthy man's daughter. In a new and rich country a son had no need to follow in the footsteps of his father or to be content with his family's station in life. For that matter no family needed to stay where they did not prosper, since greener pastures beckoned elsewhere.

The average colonial family was large. Some diaries and family Bibles record names of from fifteen to even thirty children. But if the colonial mother had many children, she did not live in a shoe and generally she knew what to do. Everyone in the family worked on the New England farm, and children were an economic asset as workers and as a sort of insurance in old age. While father and the boys labored in the fields, the womenfolk prepared meals, worked at the cheese press, washed and mended clothes, and made soap. Everyone had his task on the farm, and the parents considered work not only necessary from an economic standpoint but also the best molder of character for their children. In the South, where slaves did most of the hard work, more time was devoted to social amenities among the leisure classes.

The high rate of birth was accompanied, unfortunately, by a high mortality among families. Many women died at a tragically young age, the victims of frequent childbearing. Infant mortality may have averaged as high as 40 per cent. Infant mortality and the high death rate among adults in America, as in Europe, were largely due to existing superstition and to ignorance of hygiene and proper medical care. Even in cases of measles or smallpox the doctor might prescribe some remedy like Venice treacle, an extraordinary concoction that included vipers, opium, white wine, licorice, St. John's wort, spices, red roses, and some twenty other ingredients. One bright spot in this gloom of medical ignorance was a campaign for smallpox inoculation in Massachusetts under the leadership of Cotton Mather (d. 1728), who had read about the use of this process among the Turks. In 1721–1722, Dr. Zabdiel Boylston first introduced this innovation, and it was gradually adopted despite strong opposition. Boylston's contribution saved many lives, for smallpox had previously taken a terrible toll in New England.

Colonial family life had its distinctly bright side. Although the first houses of the colonists were crude, flimsy affairs capable of standing up but a few years, with the passing of the Indian menace and the increase of prosperity more spacious and comfortable homes were erected. In New England the farmhouses were solidly constructed, with heavy oak timbers and a double sheathing of clapboards. In the middle colonies the houses were generally built of stone and duplicated European models. In the tobacco country the typical house in the seventeenth century was a rectangular frame building with a shingled roof and a chimney at either end. As greater wealth accumulated, planters and the richer city dwellers copied contemporary English architectural styles, and the popular Georgian mode was incorporated into the colonial designs, often with excellent and attractive results.

An indispensable feature of the colonial home was the large fireplace. The American winter was more severe than the European. In an age devoid of furnaces and also of stoves (except among the Germans of Pennsylvania) and dependent upon wood for fuel, the fireplace had both to heat the home and to cook the food. But in neither farmhouse nor town house did the fireplace do an efficient job of heating during the winter months. Warming pans had to be used to take the shock out of going to bed in cold bedrooms. Baths in the winter were infrequent. Such drainage as existed ceased to work altogether because the rare plumbing was frozen. Bundling was accepted among betrothed couples as a means of keeping warm while courting. Winters were so hard in the ill-heated New England houses that one can easily sympathize with John Adams' wish that he might hibernate from autumn until spring.

The interior decoration of colonial houses differed according to region and social status. In New England the farmer's house contained furniture, kitchen utensils, and tableware that were homemade and functional, and ornamental, if at all, only incidentally. The Boston merchant and shipowner could afford silver plate, imported linens, and carved woodwork. The homes of the richer southern planters in the eighteenth century were lavishly, even extravagantly, furnished, frequently with objects brought from Europe. The inventory at the death in 1763 of one South Carolina planter showed the furniture in the "best chamber" to be worth £195, that in the dining room £126, and that in the parlor £135. His linen was worth £127 and his silver plate £600. Even without an allowance for the difference in money values between that day and this, these figures add up to over $4,000—a goodly sum for a deceased's furniture, clothing, and dishes. Allowing for the depreciation of the dollar since that day, the figure might easily be considered in the general range of $40,000 in current purchasing power. At the beginning of the eighteenth century, in the colonies as in Europe, china replaced pewter among the genteel. The more fastidious also took up the new-fangled habit of using forks—sometimes referred to as small instruments "to make hay with our mouths." In one respect—the absence of plumbing—the mansions of the wealthiest resembled the hovels of the poorest. Stationary bathtubs were not common until over a century after the colonial period had ended. Until then a movable tub was placed in the choicest position in the house and filled by hand with hot water. It was an arduous process that was not indulged in every day.

While food was more abundant in the colonies than in Europe, diets varied with place and occupation. In New England the farmer provided most of his own edibles. Fruits and vegetables were plentiful and were very often preserved by the farmer's wife. Meats included beef, pork, and mutton, and those living near rivers or on the coast could enjoy fresh fish. Because of the lack of refrigeration the winter diet tended to be monotonous, relying as it did upon salt meat and fish. The New England farmer had to buy his salt, molasses, spice, tea, coffee, and rum. Cane sugar was a luxury to most of the rural folk, who sweetened their meals sometimes with maple sugar or honey but generally with molasses. The heavy outdoor life of the farmer and his quest for diversion encouraged him to turn to his table, where he ate heartily. And he washed his food down just as heartily with draughts of various alcoholic concoctions. Punch, beer, and cider were consumed in amazing quantities by New Englanders, and while the wealthier also drank imported Madeira, claret, port, and other wines, the poorer people managed to buy rum—most of it distilled in New England. According to one contemporary judgment, the rum was "so bad and unwholesome that it is not improperly called 'kill-devil.' " At gala banquets toasts expressing noble sentiments to great men were frequent. In the 1780's when Lafayette was entertained by the merchants of Newport, the bill for alcoholic beverages indicated that the amount provided must have been staggering. By that time it was customary to drink thirteen toasts on public occasions, since thirteen (the number of states) was regarded as a lucky number. In the South the poorer people lived to a great extent on hominy, corn bread, pork, and rice. The planters could boast of sumptuous tables and placed a wealth of meats, seafoods, and dairy products before astonished European travelers. Pies, puddings, fruits, and nuts topped off the heavy repast, and the guest had to be strong-headed to rise steady—if not sober—from the table littered with decanters and empty bottles of choice Fayal, Madeira, and Rhenish wines, imported from Portugal and Germany. So universal was drinking at this time that it is not surprising that "Gen'l Washington notwithstanding his perfect regularity and love of decorum could bear to drink more wine than most people." Even in the midst of war Washington would sometimes dine for an hour or more.

The dress of the average farmer was plain and durable. While the northern farmer might have a suit of "Sunday best" (which in many cases was even willed to his son), his daily attire usually consisted of homespun, perhaps with leather breeches. In the summer months adults and children would often go barefoot, except to church. The modest southern farmer dressed himself in no more stylish a manner than his northern neighbor. The moneyed classes, however, decked themselves out in the most lavish and fanciful finery.

Fashions were dictated in Europe. Fashionable gentlemen wore tight-fitting breeches, lace-trimmed shirts, richly brocaded coats, powdered wigs, gold-headed canes, and either fine leather slippers with silver buckles or riding boots. Fashionable ladies would follow the London styles, which were said to reach the colonial cities in America before the provincial cities of Europe. Sweeping and colorful dresses trimmed with gold lace and fur were worn by the belles of North and South. Farthingales and crinolines were generally preferred for formal occasions, but the hoop skirt was coming in, adding to the demand for whalebone and wire as well as for cloth. Expensive jewelry, long bodices, high coiffures, fans, and snuffboxes adorned the American beauty of the wealthier classes as conspicuously as her European contemporary. Differences in costume marked differences in wealth much more clearly in colonial times than in our own day of ready-made and store-bought clothing.

The colonies did not lack amusement, among either the southern planters or the New England Puritans. Although the first legislature of Virginia had passed strict laws against gambling, drunkenness, Sabbath-breaking, and "excess in apparell," inhabitants of that province, along with Maryland and colonies to the south, nevertheless indulged heartily in racing, hunting, dancing, and card playing. Cockfighting was exceedingly popular in the South, as was horse racing. So was dancing, even in New England, although Boston had prohibited the teaching of dancing in 1685. The colonists took their dancing seriously and displayed unflagging vitality in the course of an evening. For example, a wedding at Norwich, Connecticut, was the occasion of seventeen hornpipes, forty-five minuets, fifty-two country dances, and ninety-two jigs! Dancing by couples was relatively unknown.

Colonial court records indicate that heinous offenses such as homicide and theft were fairly uncommon. Vagrancy was likewise effectively discouraged. But other crimes, even in straitlaced New England, were not infrequent, and the guilty were subjected to harsh and utterly unsympathetic treatment. It was an age when, in Britain and the colonies alike, the death penalty could be invoked for acts then considered crimes, some of which, like petty theft, would be considered only misdemeanors today. Actually colonial courts were more lenient than their counterparts in Britain, largely because the colonies had abundant resources and insufficient labor—a man's life was too valuable to be snuffed out casually when he could be sentenced to forced labor.

In Massachusetts in the eighteenth century severe penalties could be invoked for more crimes than in the South. Although the Puritans were no longer hanging persons for witchcraft, still murder, treason, so-called unnatural vices, and, religious offenses brought stern retaliation from New England courts. Mutilation, branding, and whipping were common punishments and might be administered for a variety of offenses. Sometimes the authorities would order a guilty prisoner to be "set up by the heels in the stock" or to "stand in the pillory" with a sign on his head telling of his offense. Women whose language or tirades had given offense might receive duckings. In the South the law was especially hard on slaves, as can be seen in the slave codes of Virginia, the Carolinas, and Georgia. As a general rule, the slave's diet was simple, his clothing meager, and his housing primitive. While some masters were humane, the slave was a chattel and in the eyes of the law not a person; sometimes he was subject to extreme measures of correction.

The colonial church was an institution at once social, religious, and intellectual. The vast majority of farmers were deeply religious, and that was the case regardless of the colony in which they lived. Naturally the strength of the various sects differed from place to place. Congregationalists flourished in most of New England, Baptists in Rhode Island, Dutch Reformed in New York, Quakers, Lutherans, and other sects in Pennsylvania, Catholics principally in Maryland, while Anglicans found their stronghold in Virginia and the South. Despite sectarian differences, all these churches exercised a profound influence upon their respective adherents.

The colonial farmer was usually a devout, God-fearing Christian who attributed his largely unpredictable fortune to the inscrutable wisdom of Providence. The southern farmer was as deeply religious as his counterpart in New England, and the Sabbath would find both in their respective pews, listening to equally long sermons on similar subjects. The farmer put up gladly with such heavy-handed didacticism, for the minister was probably not only sincere and forceful, he was also likely to be the most learned man in the community. When one recalls how unlettered were the inhabitants of the backwoods settlements which in numerous instances were founded by immigrants who had endured heavy sacrifices to win freedom of conscience, the role of the colonial church can be better appreciated.

The church not only gave the farmer's family religious counsel, it gave them social stimulation and even political direction. To work on the Sabbath was a serious offense in colonial days, and pleasure-

hunting on Sunday was condemned in Puritan New England, although more lightly countenanced in Virginia. However straitlaced a
particular community might be, the churchyard was invariably the
place for farmers, close by the graves of their kith and kin, to talk
over crops and weather, and for their wives to gossip together, and to
discuss fashions, children, household problems, and neighbors. Inside
the church the congregation's political concepts would be molded,
however imperceptibly, by the minister, who often, in New England
at least, was one who had broken irrevocably with the authoritarianism of the Church of England and who therefore preached a doctrine of religious and civil freedom.

At the end of the seventeenth century, the clergy had ruled the
intellectual life of America no less than that of Europe. Protestantism
had substituted the infallibility of the Bible for the infallibility of the
church, and the desirability of being able to read and understand the
Scriptures had given a strong impetus to education. The clergy, as intellectual leaders, wrote weighty tracts on intricate theological subjects, such as original sin and predestination. The Puritans in England and New England alike had attempted to establish theocratic
societies within a rigid and narrow framework that frowned upon religious toleration and political freedom. But in both regions the experiment of a Bible commonwealth had fallen before the onslaught
of new historical forces. For one thing, the increase of English trade
and the new prosperity to be found in America tended to shift men's
search from spiritual to secular rewards.

The American colonies did not possess the same intellectual advantages as the European centers. Libraries, universities, printing
houses, journals, academies, and other media of communication were
newer and rarer. Yet the very freedom of the New World's environment urged the colonists to rebel against clerical authoritarianism.
The frontier did not encourage unquestioning acceptance of the doctrine that salvation was only for the faithful and the elect; rather, it
gave strength to the democratic belief in equality of opportunity—
even the opportunity for salvation. Political self-determination implied freedom in spiritual matters. Men began to evaluate their religious as well as their political and economic beliefs from the standpoint of natural laws, with the result that the new spirit of
rationalism permeated America as well as Europe. It was no mere coincidence that when the British colonists felt called upon to justify
their revolt from Great Britain, as they were to do in 1776, they
should seek their justification in "the Laws of Nature and of Nature's

God." Decades before the signing of the Declaration of Independence, Americans were turning imperceptibly but irresistibly from a miraculous to a rational interpretation of the universe and from a theocratic to a democratic social philosophy.

At no time had the influence of the English government been absent from the founding and evolution of American colonies. The crown had granted charters to trading companies and proprietors and had specified the territories that each might settle, as well as the division of lands and the type of government under which the settlers were to live. Furthermore, the Royal Navy struggled to maintain a clear passage across the ocean, while its armed forces successfully fought against such enemies as New Netherland and New France and kept the Spaniards well to the south. The crown both protected and encouraged colonial commerce, and although its mercantilistic system was one day to prove too constricting and burdensome, it assisted the economic activities of the infant colonies at a time when assistance was most needed.

True enough, the Spanish and the French colonies in the New World were also the recipients of unceasing governmental attention. But New Spain and New France suffered from an absolutism that stifled initiative on the part of the colonists and enforced stultifying colonial policies such as forbidding non-Catholics to emigrate. The French and the Spanish colonists were not allowed to participate in making their own laws, levying their own taxes, or choosing their own governmental officials. Instead, their rulers chose royal governors, who carried out their mandate without brooking any interference from the colonists. Such paternalism not only proved on occasion to be inefficient and corrupting; it was all too successful in stunting the growth of self-government and independence in New Spain and New France. On the other hand, Anglo-American self-reliance was the logical outgrowth of political action taken by the English crown itself.

At the close of the seventeenth century, the political structures of the Anglo-American colonies differed in detail, but they possessed basic institutions in common. Each had a representative assembly, and this assembly was elected by property owners and taxpayers. To vote in Massachusetts, a man had to own real estate yielding forty shillings a year, or else (since landed property was regarded as a surer guarantee of interest in the commonwealth than other forms of wealth), he must possess other properties whose value amounted to at least £50; furthermore, until 1684, he could not vote unless he was a member of the established Congregational Church. In Virginia a farmer was eligible to vote only if he owned at least fifty acres of land or else twenty-five acres on which stood a house twelve feet square (i.e., somewhat more than a rude log cabin). The vote in South Carolina was at first restricted to members of the Church of England possessing fifty acres or a personal estate of £10. And so it went in every colony. Only free males, of course, could vote.

Admittedly these suffrage restrictions worked the greatest exclusion upon the urban artisan class, who owned little or no property. In the city of Philadelphia, for example, suffrage restrictions disfranchised about nine-tenths of the male residents. In the colony of Massachusetts, on the other hand, the great number of small farms made some four-fifths of the men eligible to vote. In actual practice, however, it is doubtful that more than half of the adult men in Massachusetts ever voted—largely because great numbers of them came from classes in England or elsewhere that never had voted.

The colonies established still higher property qualifications for membership in the representative assemblies. In New Jersey a man had to own at least one thousand acres of land before he was eligible to sit in the assembly. Thus, through the various suffrage and office-holding restrictions, the pre-Revolution governments of the colonies were definitely controlled by the propertied. Nevertheless, the number of persons eligible to vote and who actually voted in all of the Anglo-American colonies was exceptionally high for that day, and the colonists acquired an experience with representative government that was then unusual.

To offset the growing power of locally elected legislatures, the crown had strengthened its position by taking over colony after colony and making them royal provinces. Their executive power thus passed into the hands of governors appointed by the king. Virginia had been the first colony to be so transformed; it became a royal province by 1624. By 1776, Georgia, the two Carolinas, New Jersey, New York, New Hampshire, and Massachusetts had likewise become royal provinces. In Maryland, Pennsylvania, and Delaware, the proprietary system continued in effect until 1776, and their governors were not chosen by the assemblies but by the proprietors. Only Rhode Island and Connecticut retained the right to elect their own executives throughout the colonial period. And so there evolved in British America three different types of governmental authority: royal power expressing itself through governors appointed by the

British crown; proprietary interest mediating between the crown and the colonists; and self-government championed by local assemblies. In England, the "imperialists," as those who favored the close supervision of the separate parts of the empire were sometimes called, looked with growing suspicion upon the growth of local autonomy, especially in Rhode Island and Connecticut.

Where there was a royal governor, he had sweeping powers, reflecting his position as the representative of the crown in the colony. He controlled the military forces and was the head of the highest court in the colony. He could grant pardons and issue reprieves. He enforced both the English laws, as they affected the colony, and the laws passed by the colonial legislature. He summoned, adjourned, and dissolved the general assembly. In addition, except in the case of Massachusetts (where the council was chosen by the assembly) and of Rhode Island (which had no council), the governor, whether chosen by king, proprietor, or people, appointed the members of the council. The council acted both as the upper house of the legislature and as an executive advisory body. As a rule, its members were recruited from wealthy and influential families and could be relied upon, because of their social position and desire for political favor, to act as a brake upon the actions of the lower house.

The representative assembly, however, was not without its measure of strength. For it controlled the purse strings and, like the British Parliament, soon discovered that high-sounding royal threats had invariably to give way before the counterthreat of withholding funds. The assembly would demand that money grants be approved annually and that the treasurer responsible for their payment be appointed by the assembly itself. Thus money might not be forthcoming if certain previous conditions were not met. Just as the financial powers of the House of Commons eventually helped to make it dominant in British government, so the money powers of the representative assemblies in the colonies aided in making them preeminent in domestic affairs. In this way, a large degree of local independence had actually been won by the Anglo-American colonies before the outcome of the American Revolution made it an acknowledged fact.

Although, in the course of decades, the thirteen colonies individually acquired a knowledge of self-government, only gradually did they come to appreciate clearly the wisdom of intercolonial planning and action. A lack of understanding of their common problems, local suspicions, slow transportation, and bad communications combined to keep them isolated. Common dangers did, however, suggest the

desirability of local cooperation. New England delegates met from
time to time until 1685 to discuss common problems, particularly defense against resentful displaced Indians, but the decline of the Indian menace brought in turn a decline, and eventually an abandonment, of collective action for defense.

A greater danger than the Indians to the Anglo-American colonies came from the territorial aims of France in North America.
When Louis XIV made the Huguenots a persecuted minority within
France, they would gladly have hewed homes out of the wilderness
to escape religious persecution in France, but they were forbidden to
emigrate. As a result of the home government's short-sighted colonial
policy, New France (Canada) lost a potentially excellent population.
The French who did emigrate preferred at first to go to the more
congenial West Indies, where, by 1665, France held fourteen islands
containing over fifteen thousand Whites and about as many Black
slaves. At that time, the total White population of Canada was estimated at three thousand.

Louis' able minister Jean-Baptiste Colbert assumed direction of
French colonial policy in 1667. He appreciated the value of New
France and introduced new ideas and new blood. He ended company control in 1674 and placed the country under royal administration. A permanent French settlement was finally established on the
Gulf of Mexico in 1699. France in the eighteenth century could
claim a continental empire extending from the northern extremity of
the St. Lawrence to the southern extremity of the Mississippi.

France was to lose this empire to Britain and the faults of
French colonial policy largely explain this loss. The exclusion of such
refugee groups as the Huguenots prevented New France from ob-
taining a population sufficient to settle and defend its vast area.
Moreover, the French crown, like the Spanish and the Portuguese,
tried to establish a seignorial system by granting high-sounding titles
and huge tracts of land to nobles. The lands of these *seigneurs* were
worked by their tenants, the *habitants*. The *seigneurs* were generally
quite poor themselves and had to work in the fields with their tenants. Although it was not uncommon for the *habitants* to marry the
seigneurs' daughters, the French land system suffered from an important limitation—the absence of free land. Land was unavailable
to the small worker because the *seigneur* monopolized it.

The "hardy pioneer" was thus no more a product of the French
than of the Spanish system. The tendency of the French government

to centralize power in the hands of royal French officials discouraged the kind of local initiative that flourished under the English colonial system. Besides, England as a maritime power gave greater attention to her navy and overseas empire, whereas France, though also strong on the seas, as a great continental power looked primarily to her place in Europe and to her land armies. Thus the British pioneer gained a confidence and a self-starting quality that the French pioneer, for all his sturdiness, was likely to lack.

Canada abounded in rich lands waiting to be cleared. Yet, since the seignorial system, except in isolated cases, would not permit the free gift of land to pioneers, the more spirited of the population were tempted to try their fortune at fur trapping instead. Agricultural production was further hindered by the lack of adequate communications and the absence of large markets, for Europe was mainly interested in importing tropical produce from areas farther south. As a result, labor in New France tended to be hard, and poverty to be commonplace.

Toward the end of the seventeenth century, the French population of New France nevertheless increased rapidly. A total of three thousand in 1665 became fifteen thousand in 1700 and eighty thousand in 1763, when Canada fell to British conquest. The increase was due principally to the growth of native-born families, for immigration accounted for a much smaller number than it did in the neighboring British colonies. Consequently, in the race for manpower in America the French fell behind. Yet today, their descendants number between three and four million. They have not only dotted the pleasant St. Lawrence Valley with tranquil villages and made Montreal (despite a large English-speaking minority) the second largest French-speaking city in the world, but have also emigrated in large numbers south of the border to become an important element in the population of New England.

The French colonial influence in North America did not end in Canada and New England, however. The Great Lakes area and the Mississippi Valley were explored and dotted with sparse, widely separated settlements. New Orleans was founded in 1717. Various business ventures were organized to bring colonists to this region, named Louisiana after the French kings. Its crops, such as tobacco, rice, indigo, cotton, and, later, sugar, were more certain of a ready market in Europe than those raised by the Quebec *habitants*. Black slaves were introduced in large numbers, radically changing the pattern of both the agriculture and the social life of Louisiana from that of Quebec.

Yet the population did not increase rapidly. The settlers had to contend with river floods, yellow fever, and hostile Indians.

In the territory lying between New Orleans and Quebec, the social amenities were few and the hardships and dangers of the frontier great. Farming was hindered by the crudeness of tools and by the lack of fertilizer. Warfare with the competing English and the apprehensive Indians was frequent. While the surpluses of wheat were quickly transported by *bateau* down the Mississippi to New Orleans, upstream voyages were slow and cumbersome. Fur trading was a profitable pursuit in this territory, and French trappers became familiar with the Wisconsin and Illinois scene. Smuggling of goods across the Spanish borders was likewise remunerative.

Many modern American cities and leading American families owe their origin to the pioneering efforts of the French in the middle territory. The numerous French place names scattered throughout this area—including St. Louis and Detroit—still testify to the daring and far-flung roving of French missionaries, trappers, and explorers. The population, however, proved far too thin and spotty to build up the permanent empire that planners in Paris had dreamed would extend from the mouth of the St. Lawrence to the mouth of the Mississippi. But if the French empire was doomed to failure on the North American continent, it persisted in the West Indies and Guiana, and the French cultural contribution to the North American scene, as in Quebec and New Orleans, has been a permanent one.

The Spanish had built and fortified a vast empire in North America by the time their rivals began. Back in 1565 they had founded on the east coast of Florida the small post of San Agustín— known better as St. Augustine—and Florida struggled along thereafter as a Spanish colony, changing hands once or twice, until finally annexed by the United States in 1821. Spain's activities along the Florida-Carolina frontier were designed principally to block further English advances rather than to establish starting points for further imperial thrusts.

During the seventeenth century New Mexico was another sphere of the Spanish attempt at colonial expansion. The attempt faltered, not for lack of interest, but because the promise of treasure failed to materialize, the land proved arid, the distances from Mexico City too great, and the Indians too hostile. Furthermore, the church and civil officials quarreled regarding authority, and the governors all too often proved incapable, greedy, and cruel. Despite the fact that missionaries went where the soldiers went and sometimes preceded them, the Indians were exploited shamelessly, and the sale by one governor of the proud Apaches as slaves to miners was an important cause behind the great Indian revolt of 1680. The Apaches killed 400 Spaniards in the territory, and the remainder, about 2,000, were driven to what is now the southern border of the state of New Mexico. The Indians, however, did not remain united, and by 1696 the Spanish civil and ecclesiastical authorities regained control.

As early as the end of the sixteenth century Spain possessed an imperial area approximately twenty times her own size, containing (in 1574) about two hundred Spanish towns and about 160,000 Spanish settlers. The Spanish monarch owned two colonial kingdoms in the New World—New Spain and Peru. The first consisted of the mainland north of the Isthmus of Panama, the West Indies, and what is now Venezuela; the second, of all territory south of New Spain save for Brazil, which belonged to Portugal. The king ruled his colonies through the Council of the Indies, which had come into existence as soon as Spain's colonizing energy had made clear the necessity for a special colonial agency. Its duties were primarily political—to formulate legislation, to select officers for the colonies, and to act as a supreme court for important colonial cases. The king possessed another efficacious agency in the Casa de Contratación. This was a sort of board of trade, which looked after the monarch's mercantile interests by promoting and controlling colonial commercial ventures and by operating a *casa*, or trading house, at Seville as a depot for colonial imports and exports.

The kingdoms of Peru and New Spain each had a viceroy, appointed for a short term but eligible for reappointment. The viceroy was checked by a council (*audiéncia*), which was also the supreme court. All officials of importance were appointed by the crown, and these offices were likely to go to the highest bidders. Colonial self-government was confined to election by the towns of local councils, but these councils exercised power only over matters pertaining to the policing and general well-being of the locality. The colonists had no voice regarding taxation. They had to pay to the crown poll taxes, customs on imports, and excises on goods exchanged within the colonies. In addition, the king received rich revenues from the sale of monopoly rights to trade in certain natural products and in slaves and was entitled to a fifth of all gold and silver mined.

The Spanish colonies, in keeping with the prevailing concepts of economics, were dominated by the mercantilist system of tight royal control. In return for imports from Spain of wines, olives, figs, oil, iron, quicksilver, dry goods, etc., the colonists exported gold and silver, sugar, drugs, cacao, vanilla, and other native products. Trade was strictly limited to Spanish vessels and merchants. In fact, for over two centuries (1503–1718), in order the better to regulate and protect colonial trade, all American shipments had to be made to and from Seville, and American trade with the Philippines was restricted to Acapulco. A few other ports such as Veracruz and Porto Bello were permitted to engage in intercolonial commerce. Later these restrictions were relaxed, but not before a large smuggling trade had sprung up between the Spanish colonists and English, French, and Dutch traders. Never did the British government impose such heavy economic restrictions upon its thirteen colonies as the Spanish crown imposed on New Spain and Peru. Eventually these restrictions played a large role in ruining Spain's overseas empire, for the bureaucratic monopoly of the Casa de Contratación smothered the home merchants' initiative while the imposition of heavy taxes and customs duties heightened the colonists' dissatisfaction and desire for independence.

Nevertheless, during the sixteenth and seventeenth centuries the Spanish colonies had waxed rich and developed a variegated society. The majority of colonists engaged in farming. Groups of settlers would establish a pueblo—or town—to which a grant of some four square leagues (about eighteen thousand acres) would be given. The small settler would be accorded a building lot inside the town, and outside the residence area he would receive a modest plot of land to grow grain, plant a garden and orchard, and pasture his animals. The cities of Spanish America sprang from such origins. Where the towns remained small, there developed a farming class of Spaniards who intermingled with the local Indians and imported Black slaves. *Creoles* (American-born Spaniards) and *mestizos* (part Spanish, part Indian) as well as *mulattoes* (part White, part Black) have since become significant parts of the population of Latin America.

The social and economic predominance of the *Peninsulars* (natives of Spain) in the colonies was hampered by the fact that only Catholic Spaniards were allowed entry. This policy was part of the Spanish king's desire to bar other Europeans and heretics. But this exclusion had a double effect upon the fate of the Spaniards in America. It drove Protestants, Jews, and non-Spaniards to settle colonies to the north—colonies that became ever more populous and thus increasingly menacing to Spanish control of the New World. At the same time it confirmed the scarcity of Spaniards in the colonies, encouraged intermarriage or extramarital relations with Indians and Blacks, and thus increased the proportion of mestizos and mulattoes.

The large estates, or *encomiendas,* owned either by the clergy or by aristocratic laymen, were spectacular cultural centers and important political and economic units. These estates were worked by the forced labor of the exploited Indians or by purchased Black slaves. On these estates would be raised several important colonial export crops such as vanilla, cacao, indigo, and cotton. The Spanish also introduced cattle, horses, sheep, mules, and hogs, and the breeding of livestock became a source of much wealth. By the eighteenth century the hides of Guadalajara, Mexico alone were valued annually at 400,000 pesos. To translate that sum into current American dollars is not easy, because money values are complicated by many variable factors: by populations, by resources, by methods of production, transportation, and marketing, by quantities of money and credit in circulation, and by stability of governments. But at a rough estimate, 1 peso would buy in the eighteenth century about as much as $2 to $5 or more would today of certain staple commodities. Hence 400,000 eighteenth-century pesos would be worth at least $1 or $2 million today. Colonists who engaged in the hide business, it would seem, could expect to make good profits.

On the other hand, the colonists were not allowed to raise products like olives, grapes, flaxseed, and hemp, which were reserved for Spanish cultivation and were exported to America in Spanish ships along with such other government monopolies as wines, figs, iron, quicksilver, dry goods, and certain manufactured articles. Manufactures were permitted to the Spanish colonies only if they did not compete with home industries. Mexico City, for example, became a center for the manufacture of fine carriages.

Industry was, however, the exception rather than the rule in Spanish America. Next in importance to agriculture ranked mining. This was the most dramatic aspect of Spanish colonial economic life and the source of greatest riches to the king. At first precious metals came from robbing temples and graves, but gradually systematic mining was introduced. The silver mining town of Zacatecas is a case in point. One mine alone for a long time netted a daily profit of 1,000 pesos (roughly from at least $2000 to $5000 or more). In another, in the eighteenth century, 600,000 pesos were earned in one week. Still another produced a half million in six months. The king's share over a period of two centuries averaged over 250,000 pesos a year, and that of the owners around 2 million. The output of the mines in the New World is believed to have increased nearly ninetyfold between 1500 and 1750.

The influx of precious metals from the New World into Europe had important economic effects. Before the sixteenth century, not enough gold and silver were mined in Europe to take care of the growing trade requirements, with the result that precious metals had been drained off to pay for purchases from the East. The hundreds of millions of dollars in gold and silver that poured into Europe from America, beginning around 1500, profoundly affected European life. It produced what has sometimes been called "the Commercial Revolution." Hard and ready money increased, making trade more mobile. The increase of cash also furnished Europe with sufficient capital to embark on large-scale commercial and manufacturing ventures. Larger ships had to be constructed to carry the increased commerce.

Kings had fuller exchequers from which to finance their dynastic and imperialistic schemes. This increase in currency and commerce stimulated the growth of banking and credit facilities and thereby did much to lay the foundations for the rise of modern capitalism. By making money easier to get and hence "cheaper," it also introduced a general tendency for prices to rise. This tendency, too, often worked in favor of business enterprise, since the entrepreneur had less reason to fear loss from falling prices, but it worked a hardship on those whose incomes failed to keep pace with the fairly steady upswing of prices. The wealth that Spain received from the New World was thus a source at once of economic strength and weakness. Nor was it an unmixed political blessing.

When the English defeated the Armada in 1588, Spain's mastery of the seas was forever destroyed. Although she kept most of her overseas empire until the nineteenth century, she was powerless to prevent other countries—notably England—from planting settlements in the New World and encroaching upon territory staked out for Spain by papal decree, Spanish missions, and Spanish *presidios* (or garrisons).

Whereas the English and the Dutch generally treated the Indians as savages who should be either expelled or exterminated, the Spaniards, like the French, had a more enlightened policy. True enough, they exploited the labor of the Indians no less than the other White settlers did, but they made efforts also to protect native workers from patent abuse. The piety of the crown and the zeal of the church combined to save as many Indian souls as possible. The excellent mission system developed in Alta California was perhaps the finest of the Spanish social agencies. The monks taught their charges good farming techniques, irrigation, and the construction of buildings, and encouraged them in sewing, weaving, leather work, and pottery making. This preservation and Christianization of the Indian, together with his intermarriage with his conqueror, made the Spanish colonial system unique in the New World. More even than the French, the Spanish settler in America intermingled his blood and his culture with the Indians'. The results have been permanent. Indian ancestry and tradition were and continue to be common in all parts of Spanish America. Sometimes, as in the bigger cities, they are forced to yield predominance to European influences, but in the villages and remote areas they are still largely unaffected or affected only superficially. Rural Spanish America is still largely Indian, with a veneer of Catholic and Spanish culture.

In the West Indies, plantation work proved so hard as to decimate the Indians in the years immediately following Columbus' voyages. Consequently, for the first time Black slaves had been imported to the islands in 1503, several years before they reached the continent (1510). After that the Spanish king granted a contract to slave traders, who paid large sums for that right—the *Asiento*. Smuggling occurred as a result of a curb placed upon the number of slaves legally imported. It has been estimated that the Spaniards brought in an average of about three thousand Blacks yearly between 1550 and 1750. Forced labor was thus characteristic of the large plantation, or *hacienda*. Since much of Latin America was arid and since irrigable land was limited, physical conditions favored a system of labor by strictly supervised gangs of Indians or Blacks. As already noted, the development of the "hardy pioneer" and "rugged individual" was thus not facilitated as much as it was to be in the English colonies.

A crowning achievement of Spanish colonial intellectual life was the founding of schools and universities. The church took the lead in giving instruction to both the Spanish and the Indian inhabitants. In 1551, eighty-five years before the founding of Harvard College, the first school of higher learning in the English colonies, two universities were established in the Spanish colonies: at Mexico City, in the viceroyalty of New Spain, and at Lima, in the viceroyalty of Peru. Altogether, seven Spanish-American universities were founded before the end of the seventeenth century. They were patterned after the Catholic-Spanish tradition of the University of Salamanca. Later (1773),

the Royal Academy of the Beaux Arts was founded in Mexico City
and gave free instruction in painting, sculpture, and architecture.
Long before that time, Spanish baroque architecture had been transplanted to the New World, and Latin America had begun to make
unique and rich contributions in the various arts. The famous cathedral of Mexico City, which took over two hundred years to complete,
still stands as a lasting testimonial of Spain's cultural and religious influence in Latin America.

Brazil was assigned by papal demarcation (1493) to Portugal
when the rest of the Western Hemisphere was awarded to Spain.
Brazil's story closely resembles that of the Spanish empire in America. Mercantilism, exploitation of Indians, Black slavery, and Jesuit
missionaries brought similar effects, desirable and undesirable. Huge
royal grants encouraged a kind of New-World "feudalism" and, as in
the Spanish colonies, led ultimately to the centralizing of power over
the proud landlords in the hands of royal governors. Cities like São
Paulo and Rio de Janeiro developed as strategic, commercial, cultural, religious, and political centers.

The close association of Portugal with Spain from 1580 to 1640
encouraged the Dutch to rival Portugal in this vast region washed by
the mighty Amazon and Orinoco, and Dutch Guiana was founded. In
the seventeenth century, treaties between the English, French, and
Dutch completed the creation also of an English Guiana and a
French Guiana to the diminution of Dutch Guiana's size. European
languages and cultures—or what has sometimes been called Euro-
peanization—have persisted in these and many other areas where
European political preponderance once prevailed.

 CHAPTER THREE

The Struggle for Empire (1714–1763)

By the eighteenth century Europe was less isolated from the rest of the world and less provincial than in medieval times. Her commerce reached around the globe to places that had earlier been unknown, and her colonial ties not only spread European civilization abroad but closely knitted her interests with those of far-off lands and peoples. Rivalries once purely dynastic and intra-European were becoming more conspicuously commercial, national, and world-encompassing.

Along with Europe's expanding horizons its wealth also expanded, and as the riches poured in from east and west, they slowly helped to change the fabric of the old European society. Some of these changes will now engage our attention. We shall find the ancient Habsburg-Bourbon rivalry, about which so much European political history had revolved, giving way to Anglo-French rivalry for overseas dominion; and Austria, divorced from her alliance with Spain, devoting her major attention to maintaining her hegemony in central Europe against the new threat from Prussia. We shall see that at the very time when kings were trying to perfect their respective systems of absolutism, an insistent clamor for political liberty and popular participation in government was gradually undermining the institution of hereditary absolute monarchy. Furthermore, the middle class, having steadily grown in power and influence through preceding centuries, became less ready to ally itself with kings and more ready to challenge the predominance of the nobility in society and politics. The new vogue of naturalism, interacting with the new scientific knowledge and the rising sway of secular influences, combined more and more with the growing restiveness of the middle class and other dissatisfied groups to produce a critical and reforming spirit. Finding themselves hampered by old institutions and traditions, the middle class became more convinced than ever that the world should be made over so as to be of greater benefit to a larger number of those who lived in it.

In spite of these trends, the traditional political and social structure—the Old Regime—was to remain essentially intact in most of
Europe for the first three quarters of the eighteenth century. The
gathering spirit of reform was directed at modifying existing institutions rather than overthrowing them. The elimination of aristocratic
and clerical privileges, the abolition of serfdom and slavery, greater
equality in taxation, the ascendancy of reason in human affairs—such
rectifications were the aims of the "enlightened" eighteenth-century
reformers, for few men believed in the violent overthrow of the constituted authorities or in the political and social equality of all mankind. The Old Regime was not yet ready to crumble; some of its best
—certainly some of its most colorful—days still lay before it. Yet in
this period the latent weaknesses of the regime began to show patent
symptoms and were eventually to bring about an unmistakable collapse and the cataclysm of the French Revolution.

While Europe was learning to adjust to the new international
order fashioned by the treaties of 1713–1714 and 1720–1721, new
domestic arrangements were taking place inside the leading European countries. Frederick I, who had been the first of the Hohenzol-
lerns to bear the title of "king in Prussia," was succeeded in 1713 by
his son, Frederick William I. Anne, who had followed her cousin and
brother-in-law William III as the ruler of England in 1702, died in
1714 and was in turn followed by her German second-cousin George
I. And in France the seemingly interminable reign of Louis XIV
came to an end in 1715, allowing his five-year-old great-grandson to
replace him as Louis XV. Thus Prussia, the power whose rise in central Europe was to be a major source of international readjustment
on both sides of the Rhine and of the Vistula, and France and England, the two powers whose Atlantic and overseas rivalry was to determine policies on both sides of the Channel, found themselves
guided by new and inexperienced hands.

In Prussia the change was least marked. Ascending his throne
just before the War of the Spanish Succession came to a close, Frederick William continued the domestic and foreign policies of his
predecessors. He further centralized and fortified the Prussian bureaucracy by introducing a closer cooperation of financial, legal, and
administrative officials and a stricter regulation of local government,
business, industry, and finance. To the mercantilist philosophy that
prevailed in his day, he added the precept of paternalistic relations
between the monarch and his people. This new mercantilism, which

found expression in the king's stern personal control over his subjects and his emphasis upon an efficient and rigorously trained administrative personnel, later became known as *cameralism*. The term is derived from the Latin word *camera*, which means "chamber" or "office" and, in this connection, referred to the patronal management of royal properties. Cameralism spread from Prussia to the rest of Germany and became a factor in the ultimate development of that respect for authority and for state regulation of private life commonly regarded as characteristically German. Frederick William created professorships of cameralism at the universities of Frankfurt and Halle, where prospective civil servants listened to lectures on the problems of administrative science in a paternalistic state.

In keeping with his paternalistic policy Frederick William built up a strong standing army. Though Prussia's population was probably no more than 2,500,000 at the time, he maintained a force of 83,000 men. Theoretically this army was raised by a process of "enrollment" that amounted to universal military conscription (probably the first peacetime effort in that direction by a modern state), but the number who were exempted, obtained substitutes, or escaped was great, despite the boasted efficiency of the Prussian bureaucracy. Even so, it formed a huge and well-trained army, which was to give a good account of itself in the ensuing wars.

Frederick William tried to be a stern father to his people—and he sacrificed his son's happiness in the attempt. He undertook personally and gruffly to monitor his subjects' behavior. He created a crack regiment of Potsdam Guards—giants recruited from all over Europe at great cost and drilled with a carefulness that was exceeded only by the precautions taken to guard them from risk in battle. He left to his son and heir a strong army, a full treasury, a centralized and prosperous state, and an enviable prestige in international diplomacy. Nevertheless, few bonds of affection united that son to his father. The boy had shown an unprincely taste for music and literature and had once tried to run away from home. For this "desertion" he had been punished by being forced to witness the execution of a friend who had helped him in his attempt to run away. Eventually this unsoldierly prince was to become known as "Frederick the Great."

In Britain the accession of George I resulted from a predictable political adjustment. Anne's reign, filled though it had been with the tensions attendant upon fighting a long and costly intercontinental war, had also been preoccupied with the question of the royal succession. By the Act of Settlement of 1701, the English Parliament had repudiated the claim to the crown of James II's Catholic son and had fixed the succession to the throne in the Protestant house of Hanover, descended from King James I through his granddaughter Sophia, electress of Hanover. The Parliament of Scotland, after some hesitation, accepted this Act of Settlement upon deciding (1707) that the two countries should thereafter form one combined country known as "Great Britain." When Anne died (August 1714), having been predeceased by Sophia of Hanover, Sophia's son George, already elector of Hanover, became also George I of Great Britain. Great Britain thus remained Protestant and united, but only by accepting a foreign ruling house (the Hanoverian) that divided attention between its new British realm and the German country of its origin. Louis XIV and his successors, still hoping to affect Great Britain religiously and politically, continued to give aid and comfort to Anne's half-brother, known to his followers, the so-called Jacobites, as "James III" and to his opponents as "the Old Pretender."

The death of Louis XIV was not unwelcome to many of the French people. As the body of the once-glorious Sun King moved to its final resting place, jeers and curses followed it in some quarters, where the evil that he had done by his intolerance, wars, and taxes had made a more lasting impression than his fostering of the arts, literature, science, industry, and national prestige. Louis himself realized before he died, having been the most powerful king in Europe for seventy-two years, that he had made unforgivable mistakes. According to Voltaire, to the handsome five-year-old boy who was to be his successor, Louis XIV said on his deathbed:

> You are soon to be the king of a great kingdom. What I would chiefly recommend to you is never to forget the obligation you are under to God. Remember that you are indebted to Him for all that you are. Try to preserve peace with your neighbors. I have been too fond of war. In this do not follow my example any more than in my too expensive manner of living. Get advice on everything. Try to find out what is best, and always take care to pursue it. Help out your subjects as much as you can, and do what I have been so unhappy as not to be able to do myself.

To the people of France the accession of the charming Louis XV was a welcome change from the austerity and rigor of the Grand Monarch in his old age. Louis XV was soon called the *bien-aimé* (the well-beloved) and for a long time remained so to his people. But, being a mere child, he had to have a regent. Louis XIV, who had himself succeeded to the throne at the age of five, had tried to forestall the well-known evils of a regency such as had befallen France during the childhood of his father and again of himself. By creating a council of relatives and trusted officers of the crown, he had hoped to avoid the weakening of the royal position by intrigues among the nobility. But immediately upon the Sun King's death, his will ceased to prevail. The Duc d'Orléans, Louis XIV's nephew, with the support of some other nobles and the Parlement of Paris, all of whom hoped to regain some of their lost prestige by this maneuver, made himself sole regent.

The new reigns in Prussia, Britain, and France began at about the same time that new regimes were established in Spain, Belgium, and Italy. The Bourbon ruler of Spain, Philip V, introduced a policy of friendliness toward France in place of the traditional Spanish alliance with Austria. In Belgium and Italy, on the other hand, Austrian influence now crowded out the ancient preference for Spain. At the same time, in the Holy Roman Empire the prestige that the electors of Hanover acquired as rulers of England enabled them to enter into the race for hegemony along with Austria, Prussia, and Saxony.

The coincidence of new reigns and regimes in so many European areas at once threatened the uneasy peace imposed by the treaties of Utrecht and Nystadt. A series of major problems, some quite hoary, others arising from recent developments, seemed to require joint consideration if a new war were to be avoided. Would Britain, France, or Spain control the seas and thereby the finest overseas empire? Would France and Spain fall to the same Bourbon heir? Would France be able to extend her boundaries northward and eastward to the Rhine? Would Austria or Spain predominate in Italy? Could Austria retain her control in the Empire? Would Sweden be replaced by Russia or by Prussia in the Baltic? Could Poland survive the joint pressure of her neighbors? Would the Ottoman Empire remain undisturbed in the Balkans? Would the Stuarts regain the crowns of Scotland and England? These questions were to crop up dangerously throughout the century. The treaties of 1713–1714 and of 1720–1721 had thus left almost as much unsolved as they had solved. The satisfied nations of Europe (Britain, France, and Holland) formed a Triple Alliance (1717) in order to preserve the Treaty of Utrecht, which the unsatisfied nations (Spain and Austria), hostile to each other as well as to the Triple Alliance, sought to upset.

Until 1721 the intrigues of the new Bourbon king of Spain, Philip V, and his minister Cardinal Giulio Alberoni to get for Philip's descendants some dynastic advantages in France and Italy made peace uncertain. In fact their maneuvering led to a moderate and fleeting war in 1718–1720. The resulting adherence of Austria to the Triple Alliance (thereby making it a Quadruple Alliance) forced Spain to desist from her dynastic intrigues. The only significant outcome of this conflict has already been indicated: the ruler of Savoy exchanged Sicily for Austria's Sardinia.

The diplomatic situation in western Europe, however, continued complex and dangerous. Recognizing the instability of peace, the five major powers of that area (Austria, Britain, France, Prussia, and Spain) adopted a novel plan. At Cambrai in 1724 the first international congress of the modern age to meet in peacetime was convened in an attempt to allay an explosive diplomatic situation. The congress was more notable as an innovation than as a success. For four years it tried to find pacific solutions not only to Philip's problems but also to those of the Habsburg Charles VI. For one thing, Charles wanted to create a Belgian East India company, thus inevitably rousing British, French, and Dutch opposition. At the same time, since he had no son, he hoped that all the European powers would accede to his proposal—the so-called Pragmatic Sanction—that his daughter Maria Theresa be permitted to inherit all his realm undisturbed. Cambrai eventually proved ineffectual, and a new congress was called at Soissons. But it was distinguished from its predecessor only by its short duration. Within a few months Soissons also proved futile, and the quest for allies (which had in fact not ceased during the congresses) became a free-for-all scramble.

Louis XV reached thirteen and was declared a major before the death of the regent. Even after the regent's death he was kept under tutelage, however, by an incapable prime minister, the Duc de Bourbon. To hold the young king under better control, Bourbon arranged his marriage, though he was only fifteen and "the handsomest youth of the kingdom," to Marie Leszczynska, the twenty-two-year-old, homely daughter of the poverty-stricken ex-king of Poland, Stanislaus Leszczynski. Bourbon had every reason to believe that the queen would be grateful and subservient to him for having found her so fine a match. But he was replaced the next year by the less grateful and subservient king, who chose the former royal tutor, the Bishop (later Cardinal) de Fleury in his stead. After the first eight years of marriage, Louis had little to do with Queen Marie, preferring the companionship of a succession of ladies who were formally recognized as court mistresses (three of them from one family) —among them able politicians like Madame de Pompadour and Madame du Barry. Nevertheless, his position as son-in-law of the ex-king of Poland soon involved France in intrigues over factious Poland's still-unsettled status.

In 1733, Augustus II, king of Poland and duke of Saxony, died, and the Polish throne, elective by the Polish nobility, became again a political football. Some of the Polish nobles supported Augustus' son, also named Augustus. As hereditary duke of Saxony, Augustus could bring German, and particularly Austrian, influence to bear behind him; Tsarina Anna of Russia also supported Augustus. Nevertheless, the majority of the Polish electors chose Stanislaus Leszczynski. To France that appeared a windfall—a means of offsetting the prestige of the traditional enemy, Austria, and winning an ally in eastern Europe by the fortuitous relationship of the king of Poland to Louis XV. Fleury, old and feeble, would have preferred to stay out of the quarrel, but when civil war broke out in Poland and Stanislaus was badly defeated by Augustus, French public opinion demanded that an army be sent to support the father of France's queen. Thus began the War of the Polish Succession (or Election).

Badly beaten in Poland, France undertook to attack Austria. A coalition for that purpose was easily created. Philip V of Spain (or rather his ambitious wife, Elizabeth Farnese) hoped to find good realms for his sons in Italy, especially since the birth of seven children to Louis XV had diminished his still-cherished hope of inheriting the French crown. The Bourbons of Spain were therefore ready to form a compact with the Bourbons of France against Austria; and the king of Sardinia, also hoping to gain at Austria's expense, soon joined it. All three members of this alliance had a common interest in securing power in Italy at Austria's expense. Hence, the War of the Polish Succession was fought primarily, not in Poland, but in Italy and the Rhine Valley.

By 1735 the French army had given so good an account of itself that Austria was ready to consider peace terms. It was three years, however, before the complicated Treaty of Vienna (1738) was for-

mally ratified. That treaty serves as a striking example of how in the
eighteenth century peoples and territories were shuffled around to
serve dynastic interests. Stanislaus did not regain Poland but was
compensated by being made duke of Lorraine, which on his death
(1766) was to pass to Louis XV. Philip V's son Carlos became king of
Naples and Sicily (the so-called Kingdom of the Two Sicilies); the
Bourbon family thus established a new dynasty in one of the most
powerful states in Italy and ruled there until Italy became a unified
nation in the 1860's. Emperor Charles VI was compensated by the
marriage of his daughter Maria Theresa to Francis, the hereditary
duke of Lorraine. Since Francis, however, had been displaced in Lorraine by Stanislaus, he was made grand duke of Tuscany, where the
last of the hereditary Medici family had died without direct heir.
France also promised to guarantee the Pragmatic Sanction. Thus the
Habsburgs were compensated for their loss of the Two Sicilies by
gaining control of Tuscany, and Charles was encouraged to hope for
the continued unity of his possessions under Maria Theresa and her
husband.

The period of negotiations from 1735 to 1738 that ended in the
Treaty of Vienna was not a peaceful one. Provoked by the frontier
belligerence of the Crimean Tartars in 1735 and led on by the desire
to recapture Azov and to secure the right to navigate the Black Sea,
Tsarina Anna of Russia attacked Turkey in 1736. That year Cardinal
Giulio Alberoni, once the molder of Spain's foreign policy under
Philip V but now earnestly engaged as an ecclesiastic in Rome,
pleaded for a united attack upon the Turks and for the establishment
in Europe of a nonsectarian, permanent diet to manage the territories freed from Turkish domination. But Russia proceeded to go on
alone. Austria, constantly eager to push the Turks farther back in the
Balkans, joined her the next year. Thereupon, the Swedish, fearful of
Russian success, and the French, still actually at war with Austria,
gave their moral support to Turkey. Turkey thus put up an unex-
pectedly vigorous resistance to the Austro-Russian forces. In 1739
Austria agreed to the Treaty of Belgrade. By that treaty she withdrew from her advances south of the Danube and the Save; and
those two rivers remained the boundary of Austria until the twentieth century. Russia also shortly made peace, acquiring only the port
of Azov, which was to become, however, a foothold for further conquests on the Black Sea coast. The peace settlement in the Near
East, roughly coinciding with the peace settlement on the Rhine and
in Italy, signified an enormous recovery of prestige and power by

France in European diplomacy. In 1740 Louis XV still commanded the affection of his subjects and the respect of his neighbors. Moreover, no major changes had been made in the intercontinental settlements contrived by the Treaty of Utrecht.

The year 1740 marked one of those fateful instances, with which the past of Europe is dotted, when chance determined that several significant figures should die at nearly the same time, thus bringing into the open a set of complications and crises that might otherwise have been kept under cover. Between the signing of the Treaty of Utrecht in 1713 and the year 1740 there had been several wars, but they had been relatively localized and costless. Now came a worldwide conflict, breaking up the stability created at Utrecht and leading to a new series of wars that was not to end until a new equilibrium was created by the Congress of Vienna in 1814–1815, after the collapse of the Napoleonic empire.

The chief antagonists in the new conflict were Prussia and Austria, which fought what appeared to be merely a contest for territory but were in fact engaged in a struggle that in a little more than a century was to end in Prussia's control of Germany; France and Austria, which, apparently fighting merely over the lands that lay between them in Belgium and the Rhine Valley, were actually involved in a test of their relative strength in Europe; England and France, which fought for predominance in territory overseas and commerce on the high seas, where the outcome of their race for imperial supremacy would be determined; and Russia and Prussia, which had become the chief competitors for control in the Baltic area. Sweden, fearful of the growing strength of both Prussia and Russia, felt obliged to follow the leadership of France. So did Spain, whose family compact with France became more binding as time went on, and so did Turkey, which shared with France an ancient enmity to Austria. France's international prestige was thus fortified by a string of alliances. Her favorable diplomatic position was only slightly offset by Britain's domination of the unstable aristocratic republic that had prevailed in Holland since William III's death and by the temporary ascendancy of Austria in Poland.

On the other hand, Austria's position was weak. The friendliness of Austria and Russia was unstable, for, though they had common potential enemies in Prussia and Turkey, they were also rivals for advantage in Poland and the Near East. Nor could the loyalty of Britain to Austria be counted upon to be much more steadfast, for, though both countries wished to keep France in check, especially in the Netherlands, they had very little else of common interest between them. Whereas Britain's major attention was pointed overseas, Austria's was fixed on Germany and the Balkans. The support of Austria's potential allies (i.e., Britain and Russia), therefore, could not be as confidently anticipated as could the hostility of her inveterate enemies.

Charles VI fully recognized Austria's weak position. For years he had centered his foreign policy upon getting international acceptance of the Pragmatic Sanction, hoping to bequeath all his hereditary property to his daughter Maria Theresa. Such a formal understanding appeared to be a wise precaution at a time when the succession of a doubtful heir might lead to intrigues, treaties of partition, and wars among rival dynasties. Nevertheless, although nearly every interested ruler in Europe had solemnly endorsed the Pragmatic Sanction, Charles' foresight proved futile. In 1740 three of the great powers of Europe acquired new rulers. The once browbeaten, music-composing, flute-playing, poetry-writing, French-speaking, anti-Machiavellian crown prince of Prussia succeeded his gruff and unpolished father in May as Frederick II and immediately showed that despite his weakness for music and literature he was hard of both heart and head. The rulers of Austria and Russia died within the same month (October), giving place to a woman (Maria Theresa) and a child (Ivan VI, infant grandnephew of Anna) respectively.

The fates, it seemed, could hardly have been kinder to Frederick. The two countries that stood most in Prussia's way—Austria in the Holy Roman Empire and Russia in the Baltic area—were immediately weakened by disputes of succession. Charles Albert, the elector of Bavaria, despite the Pragmatic Sanction, sought the Imperial throne, which Charles VI had hoped to secure in uncontested succession for Maria Theresa's husband, Francis; others laid claim to parts of the Habsburg estate. France openly supported the Bavarian elector. Russia, which might have gone to Austria's help, was itself involved in a court intrigue that was to go on for about a year and was to end only when Elizabeth, the attractive, indolent, but capable daughter of Peter the Great, took the throne by military force.

Britain had also accepted the Pragmatic Sanction, and Maria Theresa might have looked to it for help against her French-supported rival. Britain, however, was engaged in a maritime struggle with Spain that seemed bound to divert her attention from continental affairs. The British minister at the time was Robert Walpole—the first "prime minister" properly so called, since he dominated both Parliament and the cabinet and was permitted by the king (now George II) to determine policy. Walpole had consistently followed a program of domestic manipulation and international appeasement, but in 1739 he had reluctantly yielded to a popular outcry for war against Spain. The Spanish coast guard had been vigorously regulating the *Asiento* and other provisions for English trade with the Spanish colonies—so vigorously, in fact, that, according to Captain Robert Jenkins, it had cost him his ear when the Spanish guards had searched his vessel for contraband. "The War of Jenkins' Ear," as it was called, was now going on between England and Spain. Admiral George Anson voyaged around the world in 1740 to attack Spanish sea power and with alacrity preyed upon the Spanish galleon plying the route from Manila to Acapulco. Walpole could be counted on to avoid continental imbroglios.

Frederick easily perceived his extraordinary good fortune: Austria weak, her friends preoccupied, and France and Bavaria favorably inclined to him. Claiming not to be bound by his father's endorsement of the Pragmatic Sanction, Frederick dug up a title to a choice province of the Habsburgs—Silesia, whose possession would add a large, fertile, mineral-rich, German-speaking area to the growing Hohenzollern state. While the other opponents of Maria Theresa hesitated to unleash a general European war, Frederick invaded and captured Silesia. It soon became apparent not only that he had inherited from his frugal father a magnificent army but that he himself had an unusual gift for military strategy. Impressed by Frederick's success, the enemies of the Habsburgs hastened to join with him. A coalition of France, Spain, Bavaria, and (at first) Saxony soon drew up plans with Prussia for the division of Austria's territory.

At this point Austria experienced a turn in her fortunes. Walpole was forced to give place as the leading minister of Britain to the belligerent John Carteret, who not only wished to prosecute the war against Spain more vigorously but was anxious to diminish the prestige of France. Carteret immediately put Britain into the European conflict. With Britain, George II's continental possession, Hanover, and his ally, Holland, entered the struggle on the side of Maria Theresa. So did the king of Sardinia. Thus by 1742 three separate European conflicts—the Spanish-English, the Austro-Prussian, and the Franco-Austrian—had become one: the War of the Austrian Succession.

The war was fought on several continents. In America the French and the English clashed for control of the St. Lawrence basin. British successes there were offset by French successes in India. Through diplomatic maneuvering in Sweden and Denmark France kept Russia so preoccupied that only at the end of the Austrian War did Tsarina Elizabeth take part—and then only by a show of force, for the peace negotiations were by that time well under way. Frederick had twice withdrawn from the fighting, signing separate peace treaties by which Austria twice yielded Silesia to him; Scotland and England had had to endure an invasion by the Stuart pretender's son, "Bonnie Prince Charlie," in a futile Jacobite attempt to regain the British throne; the uninterrupted line of Habsburg emperors had been temporarily broken when Charles Albert of Bavaria was made Emperor Charles VII (1742) and ruled as such until his death in 1745; and between defeat and taxes, the popularity of Louis XV had disappeared.

The war involved several areas of campaigning in Europe, including Silesia, Saxony, Bohemia, Bavaria, Italy, Belgium, the Rhine states, Britain, and Holland. How far warfare had changed from the ruthless and unrestricted carnage of the Thirty Years' War (1618–1648) is illustrated by what happened at the Battle of Fontenoy (1745). Though the fate of the Netherlands hung in the balance, with English, Hanoverians, Dutch, and Austrians on the one side and French on the other (each about fifty thousand strong), at one point in the battle English and French guards conducted themselves as if on parade, marching with flags flying and drums beating until they were face to face. Then they cheered each other before opening fire. Legend even has it that their officers disputed who should fire first, each insisting upon that advantage (if indeed it was an advantage) for his opponents. At any rate the English fired first but lost the battle and retreated; each side had over seven thousand casualties. Armies were large and the percentage of casualties fearful, but warfare had become a professional soldier's business, conducted according to generally acceptable rules and seldom involving noncombatants directly, as it had in the seventeenth century.

The war in America was not equally costly. Louis XIV had already lost a large part of the French empire in North America that his ancestors had gradually built up for over a century, and the losses were continued by his successor Louis XV. The conflict called in Europe "the War of the Austrian Succession" was to be known in America as "King George's War," after George II of Britain. In a sense the British had become involved in this struggle chiefly because of colonial rivalry in America, which had led, among less dramatic events, to the alleged slicing off of Captain Jenkins' ear. The war itself settled nothing decisively in the Western Hemisphere, but it served to help the British colonies in America to mature. The success of a joint expedition from New England that captured the great French fortress of Louisburg on Cape Breton Island contributed particularly to that end. This fortress had sheltered privateers that raided New England commerce, and when, at the end of hostilities, Louisburg was returned to France, the colonists found a common bond in their mutual indignation.

The wars of Britain and France for colonial empire in America were paralleled in India, where internal discord furnished the European nations with opportunities and pretexts for intervention. Continuous hostilities between Aurangzeb, the religiously fanatic Moslem ruler of India, and the Hindus of the Mahratta (or Marathi-speaking) group of west and central India had divided the country hopelessly in the last half of the seventeenth century. To make the confusion worse, the two major religious groups (Hindus and Mohammedans) were also disunited internally. Following the death in 1707 of Aurangzeb, the last of the powerful Mogul rulers, the central authority at Delhi became continually weaker, and the local rulers, whether Moslems or Hindus, became correspondingly more independent. As the country divided into numerous hostile camps, the aspirants to power began to cast about openly for support from abroad. The Europeans were not the only ones to take advantage of India's disunity. Nadir Shah, the energetic ruler of Persia, invaded India in 1739 and plundered the Moslem city of Delhi. Thus, Asians, coreligionists of the Moslems, also hastened the foreign conquest of India.

Until 1744 the French and the British company in India, despite the increasing chaos, enjoyed a period of quiet growth and steadily increasing prosperity. Both organizations had been involved in the European financial booms and bubbles of the early eighteenth century, and both had managed to survive the crash that followed. The British, however, proved stronger in India than the French, for much the same reasons as had prevailed in America. In material resources and strategic holdings, the British company was considerably better off than its French counterpart. Moreover, the fact that Britain was not, like France, almost automatically embroiled in continental en-

tanglements made it possible for the British to concentrate more un-
reservedly upon their Indian ventures. Nevertheless, the French
steadily improved their foothold, and the British at Bombay, Madras,
and Calcutta observed with undisguised hostility the expanding activities of their rivals at Surat and Pondichéry.

After the outbreak of the War of the Austrian Succession in Europe, Joseph-François Dupleix, appointed governor of the French
colonies in India, roused the particular suspicion of the British when
he met with outstanding success in ranging the native rulers behind
the French. The war in Europe presented the British with a reason
for armed attack upon the French positions in India, and after a few
years of delay and preparation, actual hostilities commenced in 1744.
In the struggle that ensued, the French at first had the upper hand.
Persuaded by Dupleix, Mahé de La Bourdonnais, a free-lance sea
captain in the service of the French, attacked Madras in 1746 and
forced its capitulation. Dupleix and La Bourdonnais quarreled over
the spoils, however, while the British readied themselves for a revenge attack against Pondichéry. With the arrival of a substantial
British fleet in 1748, the French city was vigorously besieged. But the
War of the Austrian Succession ended in Europe while the siege was
still in progress, and so the contestants in India also agreed to a truce.
The siege of Pondichéry was lifted, and Madras was returned to Britain.

Despite the rehabilitation of the French military reputation at
Fontenoy, the French had endured defeats (as well as costly victories) in the War of the Austrian Succession and, deserted by Frederick, had proved unable to cope successfully with the Austrians in
Germany. By 1748 all sides were ready to make peace. At Aix-la-
Chapelle they accepted the status quo ante (the conditions prevailing
before the war), with the important exception that Frederick was reluctantly permitted by Maria Theresa to keep Silesia. Otherwise
eight years of war had brought very little change to three continents.
In France the phrase *bête comme la paix* (stupid as the peace) entered into current usage. Since the war had in fact been fought to determine whether Austria would be partitioned, the status quo ante
was a victory for Maria Theresa. But it had also shown that a calculating and able statesman presided over the councils of Prussia and
threatened Austrian hegemony in Germany.

The Seven Years' War (1756–1763) continued the War of the
Austrian Succession after an eight years' truce. The Treaty of Aix-la-

Chapelle had in fact settled nothing. Obliging Britain to return to France her conquests in America, and France to return to Britain her conquests in India, it had left undecided their recurrent struggle for naval and colonial supremacy. And while it had apparently recognized Prussia's predominance in north Germany by yielding Silesia to Frederick, his title to that area was insecure, since Maria Theresa planned to get it back as soon as she could. The interval of ostensible peace between 1748 and 1756 was, therefore, filled with preparations for war. In America the French and the British maneuvered for advantages. Likewise in India the formal end of the War of the Austrian Succession brought no cessation of the struggle for empire. On the high seas the British, without a declaration of war, captured hundreds of merchant vessels, and the French retaliated as best they could. The Seven Years' War thus became the first to begin in the overseas areas and then to spread to the mother countries in Europe.

In expectation of the renewal of the world-wide conflict, the European countries used the interval between wars to build up alliances. The new chancellor of Maria Theresa was Prince von Kaunitz, who had been Austrian ambassador in Paris and her representative at the negotiations of Aix-la-Chapelle. He had long been convinced that the natural enemy of Austria was not so much France as Prussia. Upon becoming chancellor and foreign minister in 1753, he endeavored to enlist Austria's traditional enemy, France, in an alliance against Prussia. Louis XV, however, long remained difficult to persuade.

Meanwhile, Britain's fear that she would become involved in an overseas war with France induced her to approach Austria and Russia for a renewal of their alliance. Her purpose was to secure a continental defender of Hanover against French attack. When Kaunitz hesitated, still hoping for a French understanding, and when Elizabeth of Russia made only partly satisfactory promises, George II's ministers approached Frederick himself, and Frederick, by the Convention of Westminster (January 1756), agreed to defend Hanover if the French attacked it. Thus Frederick assumed the guise of the defender of Germany against the non-German allies of the Habsburgs and, at the same time, secured a powerful and rich ally in Britain to offset the expected enmity of France and Russia.

The news of the Convention of Westminster persuaded Louis XV to take action, and the Treaty of Versailles (May 1756) followed. By its terms France and Austria, whose inveterate hostility over a period of centuries had been the hard core upon which European diplomacy had centered, now became allies. Kaunitz thus achieved his "Diplomatic Revolution." France and Austria acknowledged that Prussia was their major menace, while Britain was left free to concentrate her attention upon India and America.

Actual warfare had meanwhile been going on in America and India without the formality of a break in diplomatic relations or a ceremonial declaration of belligerency. The indecisiveness of King George's War (i.e., the War of the Austrian Succession) had made clear to the French and the English in America that their conflicts would be renewed, and sooner rather than later.

In North America the British colonists outnumbered the French. But their numerical superiority was offset by the fact that, whereas the French were strictly centralized and their actions coordinated, the British had made only rudimentary attempts at intercolonial co-operation. In an effort to derive fuller advantage from the friendliness of the Iroquois Indians and to stop provincial bickerings and rivalries, particularly over Indian problems and western land disputes, the British suggested an intercolonial conference. This conference was held at Albany in 1754 with delegates attending from Maryland, Pennsylvania, New York, and all the New England colonies.

One of the purposes of the conference was to bring the colonies under "articles of union and confederation with each other for mutual defense of his majesty's subjects and interests in North America in time of peace as well as war." The delegates agreed that a union of the colonies was "absolutely necessary for their preservation," and a well-known delegate from Pennsylvania, Benjamin Franklin, brought forward a notable scheme to effect such a colonial union. It called for a president-general and a federal council, which would maintain an army, levy taxes, control public lands, and take charge of relations with the Indians. Although this "Albany Plan" was adopted unanimously by the Albany Congress, the colonial governments were too jealous of their separate powers to accept it, while London was afraid that such a plan might lead to notions of self-sufficiency prejudicial to the interests of the crown. Although ultimately rejected, Franklin's plan for union was nevertheless actively debated among the colonials, and it incubated ideas put to excellent use in later years.

Even though the Albany Plan had met with a universally cool reception, Franklin himself was not surprised. "Every Body cries, a Union is absolutely necessary," he commented, "but when they come to the Manner and Form of the Union, their weak Noddles are perfectly distracted." Undoubtedly provincialism and local patriotism played their part in defeating the Albany Plan. Colonial legislators were unwilling to consider themselves anything other than members of their particular colonies or to surrender any portion of local autonomy and power to a central union. But the opposition was also grounded on economic objections. The shrewd colonists knew all too well that the mother country was interested in having them bear a larger proportion of the cost of imperial defense, and the Albany Plan contemplated this very obligation. The national debt in the 1750's had not yet become so serious a problem to the British government as it was shortly to become, but already the colonists had shown their hostility toward shouldering any portion of it.

The expected outbreak of formal belligerency, known in Europe as the Seven Years' War, came in 1756, but it was touched off by bullets fired two years earlier at the order of a young Virginian surveyor-soldier, George Washington, when his forces opened fire upon a French party in the wilderness of western Pennsylvania. Historians have ever since debated whether Washington, in so doing, committed a justifiable act of violence, but it is still more important that the act marked a change in world affairs. Whereas previous wars in America had been pale reflections of conflicts already begun in Europe, this war began in America and ultimately involved the European powers.

In America the Seven Years' War has become known as "the French and Indian War" (1754–1763). It began over the erection by the French of a series of forts in the Ohio Valley. The future expansion of all British colonies westward was jeopardized by this strategic move, and they joined with British regulars in meeting the grave threat to their advance. The defeat in 1755 of General Edward Braddock and his British regulars, unaccustomed to Indian tactics in the forests, not only hampered British military fortunes but also gave the colonial militiamen reason to doubt the superiority of British regulars when fighting in the New World.

French successes mounted as their redoubtable leader, the Marquis de Montcalm, inflicted one setback after another upon the British. But the tide changed when "the Great Commoner" William Pitt took charge of affairs in London. Pitt saw the war between Britain and France as a gigantic struggle for empire on a world-wide scale, and he mobilized Britain's full resources to that end. His energetic spirit was infused into Britain's war effort. Leaving the European phases of the war to be fought by his ally Prussia, he concentrated upon the campaigns in America. Louisburg was captured, as were several forts in the Great Lakes region and the Ohio Valley. Then, in 1759, General James Wolfe and 4,500 soldiers scaled the cliffs above Quebec City. They joined battle with the forces of Montcalm on the field known as the Plains of Abraham. Both commanders fell, but the British won the day, and with this victory France's fortunes in America were foredoomed.

When the Treaty of Paris was signed in 1763, Britain obliged Spain to cede Florida, and France to cede Canada and the territories east of the Mississippi except New Orleans. That city, together with all the rest of Louisiana, had already been granted to Spain by France as an inducement to agree to peace and was regarded as compensation for Spain's loss of Florida. France retained in the Western Hemisphere only her West Indian islands, French Guiana, and two small islands off the coast of Newfoundland, but she lost her North American continental empire permanently (except for a few years under Napoleon Bonaparte).

Despite British successes, the French and Indian War brought the inadequacy of the colonial system into full focus. Britain had begun her life-and-death grapple with France in the New World with her colonies neither united for action nor prepared for proper defense. The mother country had had to make use of the old requisition system. In 1757 the English colonies were told that they had only to levy, clothe, and pay the provincial soldiers, while London would otherwise provision and equip the men. The colonists were also promised compensation for any expenses if they were vigorous in raising troops. The results were, from the home government's view, highly unsatisfactory. The colonists did not regard the struggle wholly as their own. Only three of the colonies, Massachusetts, Connecticut, and New York, contributed anything like their proper share, while Maryland and Pennsylvania furnished practically nothing. In 1760 General Jeffrey Amherst complained that "the Sloth of the Colonies in raising their troops and sending them to their Rendezvous made it impracticable for me to move the Troops on as soon as I could have wished." Some of the colonies were more concerned with internal political problems than with prosecuting a war in which their entire future was at stake. Frequent quarrels arose regarding the length of service. By and large, the inadequacy of the requisition system served to convince British authorities that the colonies were incapable of defending themselves and that a system of centralized control for defense would one day have to be introduced.

But if the colonists were not keen about incurring heavy financial obligations in the prosecution of the war, great numbers of them were all too ready to profit by the conflict. Not only did the merchants continue to carry on their lucrative trade with the French West Indies but the French forces in Canada were actually provisioned with beef and pork from New England, New York, and Pennsylvania. Merchants and shipowners in Rhode Island carried on such a flourishing illicit business that Governor Francis Bernard of Massachusetts wrote home to the Board of Trade: "These practises will never be put an end to till Rhode Island is reduced to the subjection of the British Empire, of which it is at present no more a part than the Bahama Islands were when they were inhabited by Buccaneers." Colonial vessels were protected largely by the device of flag-of-truce passes, theoretically issued by colonial governors for the exchange of prisoners of war. Governor William Denny of Pennsylvania sold these passes in great numbers, eventually providing blank ones for £20 each. Ships from almost every American port were busily engaged in trafficking with the enemy, despite Pitt's outbursts against "this dangerous and ignominious trade" and the epithets of military and naval officers, who called these traffickers "traitors to their country." Pitt contended that because of this illicit trade the French were "enabled to sustain and protract this long and expensive war." The unhappy situation convinced the home government that upon cessation of hostilities, the entire system of colonial administration would have to be thoroughly overhauled.

The Treaty of Paris of 1763 made the British empire the largest colonial setup that had yet appeared, probably not excluding that of the Emperor Charles V in the sixteenth century. This empire had been won only at a heavy cost in men and money. The public debt had reached the figure of £140,000,000. That would be, at a rough estimate, the equivalent of several billion dollars in late-twentieth-century values, and there were no more than approximately 8 million people in all England, Scotland, and Wales to pay it. The need for new taxes seemed inescapable. The government in London felt that the struggle against French territorial threats had been waged for the welfare of the American colonists as well as for London's interests. Besides, the colonies were no longer so poor or so sparsely settled as they once had been. By 1763 their population, Black and White, had increased to about 2,500,000. This striking growth was due largely to the movement sometimes called "the Great Migration" of the eight-

eenth century. Many Germans, Scotch-Irish, Scots, Irish, Swiss, and
other Europeans had gone to start a new life in America, enlarging
the colonial cities and pushing back the colonial frontiers. The thirteen English colonies were obviously prosperous communities. The
British government saw no reason why they should be excused from
bearing their share of the expense of defending the empire.

But the colonists saw things differently. They had outfitted and
maintained 25,000 men during the struggle, and they did not relish
the prospect of assuming further burdens. To be sure, they had benefited greatly from the war, but the very benefits made them more
reluctant to pay its costs—at least at Britain's behest. The colonies
were now free of the menace of France and had less need to count
upon Britain's protection than ever before, especially if it were now
to be more costly. The "Great Migration" had brought in groups
which were not British, and in many instances these groups felt that
they had good grounds for resentment against Britain. And the
"Great Awakening," the amazing revivalist movement of eighteenth-
century America, had created a strong sense of solidarity among non-
conformist sects that had reason to question the supremacy of Angli-
canism and the Church of England. Events were shaping swiftly for a
momentous struggle to determine who would pay for what and how
much, and, even more important, upon whose decision. The struggle
was to end only when the colonists won complete freedom of Great
Britain.

Despite the Treaty of Aix-la-Chapelle in 1748, the hostilities of
Britain and France had not ceased in India any more than in North
America. Unable to compete commercially with the British, Dupleix
after 1748 used the limited military means at his command to intervene advantageously in India's internal dynastic wars. In the bitter
battles between the Moguls and the Mahrattas, he used his superior
fighting forces to support whichever side was willing to make him the
greater concessions. After several years of brilliant intrigue, the
French governor claimed to control through puppet rulers most of
southern India. Although this claim was certainly exaggerated, Dupleix's policy of intervention had been astonishingly successful and
foreboded ill for the future independence of India.

Dazed by the rapidity of Dupleix's successes, the British endeavored to follow his example. Robert Clive, a young English officer
destined to become one of the foremost empire builders in British

history, checked French progress by enlisting native support on the British side. It was not difficult to win the mercenary native rulers away from the French through bigger and better promises, intrigues, and threats or to hire Indians to serve as mercenaries in the British army (*sepoys*). Gradually, despite the fact that the British and French governments in Europe were formally on peaceful terms, the seething plots and counterplots in India erupted into open warfare.

In 1754, after several years of this undeclared warfare in India, Dupleix was suddenly superseded and recalled to Paris. Daring though his policy had been, it might have met with success had he managed to make his acquisitions self-supporting and potential sources of wealth. He had been confronted, however, by an enemy with greater material resources under the leadership of the bold and practical Clive. Dupleix's policy collapsed quickly after its initial successes. The French government now came to realize that its brilliant but erratic governor had pursued his own ambitions without due regard for the national interest and without reporting accurately on his own activities or those of the enemy. The pay of his troops in India was in arrears and his allies, bought with cash, had vanished when the British outbid him. The directors of the French East India Company were outraged by Dupleix's high-handed policy of borrowing money on the company's credit without proper authorization. French investors were troubled by the huge sums of money diverted from their pockets to finance enterprises in India that appeared fantastic or hazardous at best. Although Dupleix wrote lengthy tracts defending his actions in India, he remained without honor in his own country for the rest of his life. He was never able to recover a penny of the personal fortune he had risked in his India ventures and died impoverished in 1763.

Shortly after Dupleix's return to Paris, the nawab (viceroy) of Bengal sent a large force against the British in Calcutta. Since the small garrison in the city was no match for the nawab's army, many of the Europeans were evacuated by vessels in the harbor before the arrival of the attackers. Those who remained behind were captured after a feeble resistance and shut up in the Calcutta fortress's punishment cell known as "the Black Hole." One hundred and forty-six miserable prisoners were jammed tightly together into a small, poorly ventilated space on a sultry summer's night. With less than two square feet per person and only two barred windows to provide air, they struggled against suffocation, thirst, and trampling. Only twenty-three of them survived until the next morning. Outraged by this atrocity, the British, and Clive in particular, determined to recapture Calcutta.

In Europe, meanwhile, hostilities between France and Britain had been resumed in 1756. Despite the need for troops in other theaters, a sizable force was immediately dispatched from England to Bengal. Calcutta was quickly retaken, and in 1757 the nawab was forced to sign an offensive and defensive alliance with Britain. Clive, however, was not satisfied merely with the nawab's capitulation. Confident that the French could not take Madras or other important British settlements, he concentrated his attention upon dethroning the nawab and establishing his own puppet as ruler of Bengal. This he achieved by the Battle of Plassey in 1757, where a small force of sepoys and British trounced the larger force of the nawab, which was honeycombed with treason and apathy. Though not much of a battle, Plassey proved decisive. Owing his position to British support, the new nawab could do nothing but agree to the British demands. Plassey was the first important European military victory in modern times over an oriental potentate on his own soil. By this battle, in the British patriot Edmund Burke's ethnocentric phrase, "one of the races of the northwest cast into the heart of Asia new manners, new doctrines, new institutions." Clive's victory at Plassey established British supremacy in northeast India and virtually settled the outcome of the struggle with the French.

In 1758 France's military forces in India were placed under the authority of Comte de Lally, a military tactician of great reputation. He failed, however, to get along with his naval and civilian colleagues or to acknowledge the need for diplomatic intrigue in the conduct of war in India. Time after time he struck at strategic points, but with almost no success. Even though Clive was preoccupied by events in Bengal, Lally found it impossible to meet the expectations of the people at home.

Lally's position slowly became untenable as the British built up their naval power in the surrounding seas. Lacking funds and supplies, the French were forced to take the defensive. One by one, the French fortresses were reduced, until in 1760 the British, led actually though not nominally by the hard-driving Colonel Eyre Coote, stood before Pondichéry, the seat of French power in India. The French resisted siege for almost four months. Finally, with the aid of a powerful fleet that arrived opportunely, the British obliged the fortress to capitulate.

The fall of Pondichéry ended the French effort to control India. Although the settlement was restored to the French by the Peace of Paris of 1763, the company founded by Colbert was dissolved ignominiously less than a decade later, and the French crown took over the administration of the French settlements in India. Scattered and limited, they remained mostly under the colonial administration of the French government until recently, while control of the great subcontinent passed to Britain.

Open warfare did not begin in Europe until the fighting in America and India was well under way. Believing in the strategic advantage of the surprise offensive, Frederick II began the war by an attack upon Saxony (August 1756). Maria Theresa went to the defense of Saxony, and the Holy Roman Empire, of which Francis, Maria Theresa's husband, was the emperor, soon joined Austria. Much more serious from Frederick's point of view, Russia formed an alliance with Austria and France for the partition of Prussia. Attracted by the prospects of sharing in the spoils, Bavaria, the Palatinate, Württemberg, and Sweden joined the coalition. Prussia thus found herself almost completely surrounded by enemies and unaided except by the British and the Hanoverians.

Although Frederick's ability as a strategist and the thorough organization of Prussia for war proved equal to the emergency for a while, he and the Anglo-Hanoverians were defeated in several engagements and forced to take the defensive. Hard pressed on all sides by powerful enemies, Frederick nevertheless had the advantages of "inner lines"—that is, he could move his armies about within his own territories and, by covering short distances, could meet widely separated enemies. In that way he was able to defeat a French-Imperial army at Rossbach in November 1757 and the Austrians at Leuthen the next month. In both battles Frederick's force was greatly outnumbered—at Leuthen by about 82,000 to 33,000.

Frederick thus saved Prussia temporarily and won a reputation for military genius, but the outlook continued dark. In Britain, George II, much against his own inclination, was forced by public clamor to give William Pitt, "the Great Commoner," the leading position in his cabinet. Pitt arranged for a more effective Hanoverian army and a large subsidy to Frederick, but (as we have seen) he devoted his chief attention to maritime and colonial warfare. For Frederick, the years from 1758 to 1760 were difficult ones indeed. Despite several victorious battles, he lost Berlin to the Russians (1760).

What saved Prussia from the partition her enemies had planned was in part that they were equally spent. But also, in 1762, after a long illness, Tsarina Elizabeth died, giving place to the son of the preceding Tsarina Anna, Peter III, and his German wife Catherine. Peter was as intense an admirer of Frederick as Elizabeth had been an enemy. Furthermore, Catherine owed her brilliant marriage to Frederick's good offices. An influential group of Russian statesmen had long doubted that the destruction of Prussia and the corresponding strengthening of Austria would be good for Russia. Consequently, Russia changed sides, now becoming Prussia's ally. A court intrigue similar to several earlier ones that since the time of Peter I had determined who should reign in Russia soon removed Peter and made Catherine sole ruler. Prussia, however, continued to have nothing to fear to the east.

Meanwhile, under Pitt's watchful strategy, the war in America and India progressed favorably for Britain. The policy of Pitt to fight chiefly for empire overseas led to dazzling results. General Wolfe, though he declared he would rather have written Thomas Gray's mournful and melodious *Elegy in a Country Churchyard* (1750), captured Quebec, with the strategic results that have already been set forth. French attempts to invade England led only to the destruction of three French fleets and postponed for two decades France's challenge of British supremacy on the seas. In India, Clive and Colonel Eyre Coote with their small armies won the great victories which determined that the British and not the French would dominate India.

The death of George II and the accession of George III in 1760 seriously curtailed Pitt's program. George III not only did not favor the war but definitely wished to "be a king" and to determine his own policy. When it was learned that the French were ready to consider peace but were being offered only crushing terms by Pitt, public opinion veered to the king's side. France nevertheless might have yielded had not Charles III of Spain seen fit to join a new Family Compact (1761). This was in part the work of Comte de Choiseul, one of the few able ministers Louis XV permitted to serve him. At this turn of events, Pitt was forced to resign and Lord Bute became the chief adviser of the king. Britain continued to make new conquests—now at the cost of Spain in Havana and Manila. Thereupon

Spain refused to make peace until France assured Charles III compensation in Louisiana for his losses. Peace was not made until February 1763. Britain, France, and Spain signed a treaty at Paris, and a few days later Maria Theresa and Frederick signed another at Hubertusburg.

The Seven Years' War was probably the bloodiest, so far as the actual combatants were concerned, that had yet been fought in Europe. It cost around 850,000 lives, not counting deaths from disease and other indirect causes. French armies had numbered as many as 100,000 in a single battle. Only the wars of the Spanish Succession and the Austrian Succession could vie with it in the size of armies and the number of casualties.

The war ended in a humiliating defeat for France and Austria. France lost her empire on the North American continent and in India to Britain, which emerged as the chief colonial power of the world. Frederick at last obtained the definitive surrender of Silesia from Maria Theresa. Except for Spain, which yielded Florida to Britain and received Louisiana as compensation from France, the other European belligerents returned from the peace negotiations without territorial loss or gain. Prussia now stood forth as a world power destined to rival Austria for leadership in the Germanies.

On both sides of the Channel the peace was unpopular. In England Bute was hissed because he had gotten too little. Louis XV, whose recovery from an attack of smallpox during the War of the Austrian Succession had been the cause of popular thanksgiving and *Te Deums,* was now execrated for his sacrifice of French interests to Austrian and Spanish ambitions. Mounting taxes and the exorbitant cost of the war in blood and territorial cessions added to the dissatisfaction. Although his earlier mistresses had been tolerantly endured, now "La Pompadour," who seems to have been far more deserving than her predecessors, was hated because she mixed in politics and because it was believed that she influenced the king's decisions. As we shall soon see, strife with his own law courts and the writings of the group of social critics known as the *philosophes* rapidly increased the speed with which Louis' popularity waned.

One result of the Seven Years' War was the decision of Catherine II and Frederick II to continue to act together in international affairs. Their alliance soon revealed its general aims when Augustus III of Poland died and the whole Polish question was reopened. Frederick and Catherine candidly used their influence to place a Polish henchman, Stanislaus Poniatowski, discarded lover of Catherine, on the Polish throne (1764). A league of Catholic nobles—the Confederation of Bar—resentful of this foreign domination of their country, began to agitate for independence and constitutional reform. Young Casimir Pulaski (c. 1748–1779), one of its leaders, was to meet death as an American cavalry general in the war for American independence. Unfortunately these Polish noblemen who raised the standard of rebellion against a ruler imposed by foreign powers found little support among the peasantry, especially among the minority of Protestant and Orthodox peasants, who, with good reason, assumed Polish independence to mean also a reinforced Catholic establishment.

In its way, nevertheless, the defiance of Russia by the Confederation of Bar may be looked upon as an early manifestation of the revolutionary spirit that was to reach a riper stage in the final quarter of the century. In any event, it was in vain, for Catherine intervened with military force, claiming to be championing liberty and toleration. Polish Catholics now appealed to France. France did not care to intervene directly, but encouraged the Turks, ever fearful of Russian aggression, to make war on Russia. The Russians, however, were more successful against the Turks than the French had foreseen, and their success led the Austrian government to worry about the outcome of the international tangle. Things began to look as though Austria might have to take a hand to save both Poland and the Balkans from falling under Russia's control and thereby upsetting the balance of power in eastern Europe. A new general war might even have resulted had not Frederick, Kaunitz, and Catherine come to an agreement: Russia would be appeased and at the same time Prussia and Austria would be rewarded by each of the three powers taking a huge share of Polish territory.

Thus in 1772 occurred the first of the three partitions of Poland by which Poland was to disappear as a sovereign state, not to be restored until recent times. What was left of Poland after the first partition was a resentful but pitiable second-rate power. Prussia, both East and West, now became entirely a Hohenzollern possession, and Frederick II was truly able to call himself "king *of* Prussia," a title that his father had earlier begun to use. Unassimilable Polish minorities thenceforth became major problems for Prussia, Russia, and Austria, and "the restoration of Poland," feared by some and promoted by others, a major slogan in international politics.

After some further fighting and negotiations with Turkey, Russia made peace at Kuchuk Kainarja (1774). Russia received a firm footing on the Black Sea, including the port of Azov, moved her southwestern boundary to the Bug River, won the right to navigate Turkish waters, and received with regard to the Orthodox Church in Turkey certain privileges that Catherine's successors were to interpret as the right to protect all Christians there. Thenceforth the advancing might of Russia on the Black Sea and the Balkans—"the Near Eastern Question"—was to share attention with "the Polish Question" as a major international problem.

The Treaty of Kuchuk Kainarja made public the weakness of the sprawling but disunited Moslem state. The Turks' renunciation of sovereignty over Azov and the north coast of the Black Sea at last guaranteed Russia's "window on the south." That the Porte was also obliged to promise better government for certain Christian provinces in Europe and to recognize the tsar as protector of all Orthodox Eastern Christians within the Ottoman Empire made it increasingly simple for Russia to foment discord in the sultan's realm. The rulers of Russia used to great advantage their role as protectors of the Greek Orthodox Christians within the Ottoman dominions. They were thereafter able to interfere easily in the domestic and international affairs of the Turkish state. Less than ten years later, Russia annexed the Crimea; and after a renewal of warfare and a new defeat of Turkey, a treaty in 1792 pushed the Turks to the west bank of the Dniester River, which was now designated as the European boundary between the two empires. This series of agreements between Catherine the Great and the Porte from 1774 on exacerbated the Near Eastern Question—which now became whether the Ottoman Empire should be permitted to survive at all (and if so, under whose domination)—and was to remain an issue of first-rank importance in European diplomacy all during the nineteenth and twentieth centuries.

Portrait of the Emperor Joseph II. The artist, Pompeo Giralamo Batoni (1708–1787), an Italian portraitist, painted a number of Europe's leading sovereigns.

Illustration from an eighteenth-century history of England by Edward
Barnard, showing how rapidly legends arose about the American Declaration of Independence. Independence was not declared "throughout
the different provinces on July 4, 1776," but on that date the Continental Congress in Philadelphia accepted the final draft of the Declaration
of Independence. A Resolution of Independence had been formally
voted on July 2, but the signing of the final draft was not completed
until 1777.

Vûe et Perspective du Château
Dediée

Par son très humble très obéissa

de Versailles, du côté de la Cour.
Au Roy

An unusual aerial view of the Château de Versailles from the courtyards. A symbol of the regal magnificence and the refinement in life of Louis XIV's reign, Versailles, although Paris was the nominal capital of France, remained the center of France's government until October 1789.

Of a series of four satirical paintings by Hogarth entitled *Elections*, this one, *Canvassing for Votes*, was executed in 1757.

"The Bloody Massacre" of Boston, 1770, from a print by Paul Revere. The artist, the well-known hero of the midnight ride to warn the Minutemen that "the British are coming," was a silversmith and engraver. Revere was not present at the massacre, however, and his details are not entirely accurate.

A reproduction of an illustration from an early edition of Goethe's *Sorrows of Young Werther*. It portrays the farewell of the despairing hero and stresses the *sensibilité* of the Sturm und Drang period.

The New Cathedral of Salamanca. The Old Cathedral, dating back to the twelfth century, was by the sixteenth century considered too small and dark. Hence the New Cathedral was built around it, taking from 1513 to 1733 to complete. It reveals features of the Gothic, the baroque, and other styles.

An engraving by the Swedish artist Nils Lafrensen, known in France as Lavreince (1737–1807). Here he depicts the excitement behind the scenes at a ballet performance, presumably in Paris. Note the indifference to decorum.

Windsor Castle, a principal residence of British rulers since the days of William the Conqueror. This eighteenth-century watercolor by Paul Sandby of its Henry VIII gateway illustrates the costumes, vehicles, and crafts of the day.

A view of St. Petersburg done in 1794 by Benjamin Paters. The pontoon bridge in the foreground, known as Isaac Bridge, led to Falconet's equestrian statue of Peter the Great and to the Isaac Church. The bridge, greatly changed, is now called the Palace Bridge.

Sikh noblemen in eighteenth-century India. The Sikh religion combined elements of Buddhism, Hinduism, and Islam. During the eighteenth century the Sikhs were a strictly religious, military people, and the homes of their leaders sometimes displayed striking beauty and comfort.

A Turkish miniature. Taken from a work produced early in the eighteenth century, this picture represents Sultan Ahmed III (1673–1736), the opponent of Peter the Great, at a festival held in the sultan's seraglio Topkapi in Constantinople (Istanbul).

Italian life in the eighteenth century. This scene reflects the vogue of placing everyday events against a background of Roman ruins and highlights the eighteenth-century interest in Classical architecture.

A design for the lid of a comb box drawn by a European craftsman of the eighteenth century. It illustrates the contemporary vogue of Chinese motifs in the West.

EUROPE IN 1789

0 100 200 300 400
MILES

SCOTLAND

DENMARK

IRELAND

ENGLAND

UNITED
NETHERLANDS

TO PR
1791

Paris

AUSTRIAN
NETHERLANDS

FRANCE

SWITZERLAN

SAVOY

MIL
PA

GENOA

CORSICA

PORTUGAL

SPAIN

MAJORCA

SARDIN

A map of Europe on the eve of the French Revolution, including Prussia's subsequent annexations in south Germany in 1791. Emphasis is given to the growth of Austria, Prussia, and Russia at the expense of Poland and the Ottoman Empire, and to the disunity of Italy and the Holy Roman Empire.

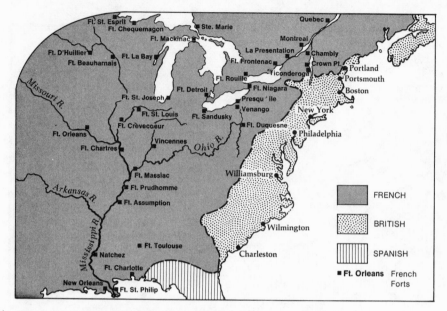

British and French in North America, 1755. The vastness of New France on the eve of the French and Indian War made its comparatively small population all the more sparse. At that time Georgia was limited to the coast, and Maine was a district of Massachusetts.

French and British power in India, 1763. By the Treaty of Paris of 1763 the British acquired full control of Bengal, though they permitted a nawab to rule nominally, and had begun to dominate other provinces in India. The French agreed to maintain their establishments in India as trading posts only, without fortifications or troops.

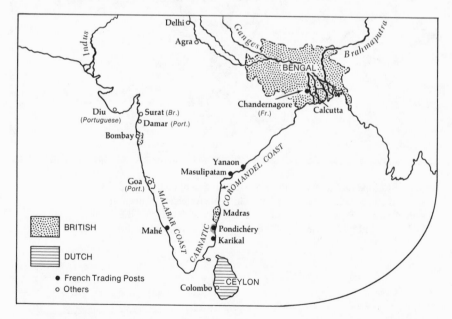

CHAPTER FOUR

Society and Thought
in an Age of Enlightenment
(1700–1775)

The period after the Treaty of Utrecht was one of extraordinary business activity in Europe, due largely to the investment opportunities in the new lands overseas. These areas also provided a great impetus to the curiosity of Europeans that found expression in the literature, art, and manners of their day.

An outstanding feature of the new prosperity was the continued growth of the national banks. Though Amsterdam was to remain Europe's financial center until well into the eighteenth century, Hamburg and London gave it stiff competition. Companies writing marine insurance likewise came into prominent existence during this period. Lloyd's, established at Edward Lloyd's coffeehouse in London, still flourishes as one of the leading insurance companies of our time. This banking and insurance upsurge had the effect of creating large sums of money on deposit ready for remunerative investment. Private stockbroking firms arose and helped the investor find transferable shares to buy in joint-stock companies.

One of the apparently good investments for idle capital was the South Sea Company. Formed in 1711 as a monopoly of the British trade with South America and the islands of the South Seas, it benefited greatly by the award to Britain of the *Asiento* in the Treaty of Utrecht. The company was tied still more closely to the British government in 1719 by an agreement whereby its stocks might be given in payment of government debts. Reflecting a general speculative wave that already had reached a high point in Paris, the demand for South Sea Company stock rose rapidly in London, encouraging new and less reliable firms to engage in feverish imitation and pushing up the market quotations on older stocks. In 1720, when South Sea Company stock was selling at over £1,000, the "bubble" suddenly broke. The discovery of fraud in the company management hastened the collapse. By December the price of South Sea stock fell to 120. Thousands of fortunes were lost in the crash, though the company itself was reorganized and remained in existence until 1853.

In France much of the same kind of boom and crash took place. Its story centers upon the romantic figure of John Law, son of a Scottish goldsmith, who had killed a man in a duel, fled from a London prison, and wound up in Paris. There he gained the confidence of the regent, the Duc d'Orléans. In 1716, in a period of temporary financial depression and of diplomatic tension with Spain, the regent yielded to Law's persuasion and permitted him to set up a general bank. Had Law limited his enterprise to the bank, no speculative fever need have emerged. But he soon (1717) organized the Company of the West (or Mississippi Company) with a monopoly of all trade with Louisiana and of the beaver trade with Canada. The next year he acquired a monopoly of tobacco in France. By 1719 he united all the big French joint-stock overseas companies (such as the Mississippi Company, the French East India Company, the Africa Company, and the China Company) into one huge commercial empire known as "the Company of the Indies." It became difficult for investors to distinguish between Law and the government or between his bank and his Company of the Indies, especially after he used the bank's money to redeem the stock of the company. Holders of government bonds and other debts exchanged their certificates for company stock, and the company began to perform banking and governmental operations, issuing bank notes, collecting taxes, and minting coins. As the company issued more stock, the bank issued more money, and thus, though the increase in the value of each share of stock was more apparent than real, the demand for shares grew until, by the end of 1719, they sold for 10,000 livres each (par 500). Skeptics began to call the whole of Law's scheme "the Mississippi Bubble." When, in January 1720, Law, as comptroller-general, became the chief financial officer of France and the bank and the company were united by the regent's decree, the stock seemed governmentally guaranteed, though its price was at a dizzy height.

Through a series of errors including arbitrary limitations upon the use of specie and a fiat cutting the value of bank notes in half, Law's enterprises lost public confidence. The Mississippi Bubble broke; shares dropped so rapidly that fortunes were lost overnight; and in March 1720 the regent forbade further speculation. Law was almost lynched and fled from France. Three people were trampled to death in the effort to save their investments at the offices of the bank and company. When the government finally announced that it would no longer accept the bank's paper notes, the stock of the company dropped to about a third of its peak value. The French firm of Paris-

Duverney Brothers, financial rivals of Law, finally liquidated it by a process that increased the public debt through an annual payment of 13 million livres to the company's creditors. The Mississippi Bubble experience, fortified by later inflations, has made many Frenchmen even in our own day skeptical of stock certificates, bank paper, and paper money.

All through the eighteenth century new explorations and discoveries continued to fill the imagination of Europeans. The most exciting voyages were to come only later in the century. Captain Louis Antoine de Bougainville sailed around the world for France (1767–1769) and discovered or rediscovered many of the South Pacific islands. Captain James Cook did likewise for Britain (1767–1771), exploring the coasts of New Zealand and Australia. These and even earlier voyages furthered a literary vogue sometimes called "exoticism," reflecting the current interest in the remote and strange places discovered. These far-off lands, especially America, began to appear as a sort of refuge, not only for the poor and persecuted but for the maladjusted in general. The travel literature of the day underlined the popular idealization of America as a haven. The *New Voyages in America* of Baron de Lahontan (c. 1703), a large part of which was the sheerest fiction, gave an account of New France that tended to make its readers think of the American Indian as "a noble savage" and "a natural man," and of the New World as a place where almost every prospect pleased and only European man was vile.

The interest in travel—real and imagined—reached a point at the beginning of the eighteenth century where it colored a number of lasting literary masterpieces. Among these Alain René Lesage's *Gil Blas*, begun in 1715 though not published until 1735, marked a significant stage in the development of the novel. Few enduring French novels had preceded it, with the notable exception of the *Princesse de Cleves* (1678) by Madame de La Fayette. Lesage had already made a reputation as a dramatist. His *Gil Blas* was a picaresque novel, whose hero wandered from place to place through four volumes, mostly in a decadent Spain, encountering many strange people and adventures and becoming a medium of censure of European culture. Lesage's less well-known hero in the *Aventures de Robert, dit le Chevalier de Beauchesne* (1732) better illustrates the contemporary interest in America, since Beauchesne was a freebooter in New France.

The favorite romance of the day was the Abbé Antoine-François Prévost's *Manon Lescaut*. Manon's faithful Des Grieux, a splendid young nobleman, was one of the first of the great lovers created by a novelist; the story of his devotion to Manon, a loving but weak courtesan, has since become the subject of no fewer than three operas. Together the lovers flee their woes in France to seek a new life in Louisiana (which proves, however, to be no less tragic). Prévost's interest in the great travelers who had opened up the world was further revealed in a fifteen-volume collection, *General History of Voyages*, of which seven volumes were translations from the English. Chamblain de Marivaux was one of the few major French novelists of the day whose characters were not travelers in foreign lands. His unfinished *Marianne* was the story of the quest of a calculating young miss for a husband at home in France.

Lesage's novels bore a striking resemblance to those of a leading English contemporary—the prolific Daniel Defoe. Defoe wrote many political tracts and at least two novels (*Moll Flanders* and *Roxana*, both about questionable heroines probably typical of the day) that are generally said to be superior to his series of books on Robinson Crusoe (1719–1720). It is nevertheless by the characters of Crusoe and his Man Friday that Defoe is best remembered. Based upon the actual adventures of living sailors, Crusoe's story enhanced contemporary interest in faraway lands and savage peoples.

Among Defoe's contemporaries in English prose were Steele, Addison, and Swift. Already famous for his *Battle of the Books* (1697) and for his *Tale of a Tub* (1704), Swift also reflected the absorption in remote lands and manners in a set of satirical fantasies commonly known as *Gulliver's Travels* (1726). Simple and interesting enough to have become a children's classic, *Gulliver's Travels* was intended as a burlesque of contemporary social and political behavior—with its Lilliputians, who have ever since lent their name to whatever is diminutive or petty; its Brobdingnagians, who have lent theirs to things gigantic; its visionary and impractical Laputans; its Houyhnhnms, horses that reason; or its Yahoos, men that don't.

Swift's friend, Alexander Pope, though less concerned with fantasies of travel, was no less satirical of certain aspects of contemporary social behavior. His *Rape of the Lock* (1714), in mock heroic verse, poked gentle fun at a contemporary social scandal that occurred when a London nobleman snipped off a ringlet of a lady's hair. His *Dunciad* (1728) employed his skill as a versifier to denounce some contemporary men of letters as literary quacks and pedants, something Swift had already done. Probably Pope's most often quoted poem is his *Essay on Man* (1733), for which the statesman and deist Viscount Bolingbroke is said to have provided the arguments. Pope himself was to become alarmed at how deistic the poem was generally considered. It defined a Deity

> *Who sees with equal eye, as God of all,*
> *A hero perish or a sparrow fall,*
> *Atoms or systems to destruction hurled,*
> *And now a bubble burst, and now a world.*

And it advised man to

> *Know then thyself, presume not God to scan;*
> *The proper study of Mankind is Man.*

This was a reflection of a secular and deistic trend in the current literature. But even deists like Voltaire were to demur when Pope adopted an optimism similar to the philosophy of the German philosopher-mathematician Leibnitz (d. 1716), who held that the sum of good exceeds the sum of evil in "the best of all possible worlds." According to Pope:

> *All are but parts of one stupendous whole,*
> *Whose body Nature is, and God the soul. . . .*
> *All nature is but art, unknown to thee;*
> *All Chance, Direction, which thou canst not see;*
> *All Discord, Harmony not understood;*
> *All partial Evil, universal Good:*
> *And, spite of pride, in erring Reason's spite,*
> *One truth is clear: whatever is, is right.*

The number of outstanding translators of the Classics and original writers who flourished in Britain during the first decades of the eighteenth century has induced some critics to refer to it as "the Augustan Age." A good part of this Augustan literature revealed the intellectual's disgust as Europe's overseas empires expanded and the European middle class grew prosperous and speculative, with the attendant corruption in politics, laxity in manners, and callousness in social responsibility for the miserable and the poor. John Gay's risqué *Beggar's Opera* (1728) reflects the same protest through the medium of the musical play; and William Hogarth used still another medium in his moralistic series of paintings—*The Harlot's Progress* and *The Rake's Progress* (both 1730) and *The Marriage à la Mode* (1745). Engravings were made after these paintings, and all three series had an enormous success.

Across the Channel the Baron de Montesquieu, who was soon to win a reputation as one of the greatest political philosophers of his day, wrote his *Persian Letters* (1721), a satire similar to the works of Swift and his confreres. Montesquieu, also taking advantage of the current vogue of the exotic, invented two Persian nobles who traveled westward, spending most of their time in France and telling of the amazing institutions, cities, and customs that they found there. They contrasted occidental monarchy, Christian beliefs, and the madness of European financial methods (this was shortly after the Mississippi Bubble) with the political and social implications of the Koran and the harem. Though Montesquieu immediately became the leading literary light of the Regency, it was several years before the established authorities would honor him with a membership in the French Academy. Making fun of the king and the church had its hazards in France, where the church still provided the king with political as well as spiritual advisers.

During the first half of the eighteenth century the leading figure in the field of music—at least in the estimation of later generations of critics—was Johann Sebastian Bach (1685–1750). While he received some recognition and honors during his lifetime, much of his work remained unpublished and forgotten until rediscovered in the nineteenth century, when in 1829 Felix Mendelssohn performed his "Passion according to St. Matthew."

Like his famous older French contemporary François Couperin (1668–1733), Bach was both a descendant and an ancestor of a long line of musicians and composers. To Bach, as the composer Robert Schumann in the nineteenth century said, "music owes almost as great a debt as a religion owes to its founder." He wrote numerous preludes and fugues for the organ, besides the forty-eight compositions in his *Well-Tempered Clavier*, much chamber music, several passions and masses (among which the *Passion according to St. Matthew*, the *Passion according to St. John*, and the *Mass in B Minor* are the most famous), and several hundred cantatas. His music combined piety, loftiness, and tenderness with unexcelled contrapuntal skill. As the organist and choirmaster for German princes and churches, he composed music chiefly of a religious and ceremonial nature. Yet, while deeply steeped in the tradition of Lutheran church music, his special genius was in adapting the Italian concerto and the French suite, not without vast improvement upon those earlier models. Frederick the Great invited him to Potsdam toward the end of his life, and his *Musical Offering*, on a theme suggested by Frederick, was dedicated to the king.

The only contemporary composer generally regarded as of nearly comparable stature was George Frederick Handel (1685–1759). A German-born, Italian-inspired, and English-patronized composer, Handel wrote operas that he himself produced when he was well and his theatrical business prospered and resorted to sacred music usually when his health or his business was bad. He wrote forty operas and twenty-five oratorios, the greatest of which, *The Messiah* (1742), blended both his operatic and religious tastes.

Antoine Watteau was the leading French painter of the Regency period, when the elegant profligacy of the nobles set the tone for both social behavior and the arts. His most famous painting, *The Embarkation for Cythera* (Cythera in Greek mythology was a sanctuary of Aphrodite), illustrates a mixture of interest in Classical allusions, contemporary social frivolity, and artistic grace, balance, light, and color. His other paintings show festivities in gardens and groves where handsome and expensively dressed young men and women disport themselves. The contemporary vogue of the Far Eastern cultures led to his introduction of numerous *chinoiseries* (Chinese objects) into his ornamental engravings. Watteau, like Hogarth, painted the society he knew, but Hogarth knew different kinds of society and had a definite didactic purpose in mind—moral uplift. A comparison of their subjects would throw into relief the gaping distance that separated those to the manner born from the proletarians and *nouveaux riches*. So also would a comparison of the gentle satire in Molière's plays (the last written in 1673) and the bitterness in Lesage's *Crispin* and *Turcaret*. *Crispin* (1707) was the tale of a crafty and ambitious valet, and *Turcaret* (1709) that of a coarse, cheating, *nouveau riche* financier. Both were types that were becoming familiar in an age of easy money, and neither was as lovable as Molière's *bourgeois gentilhomme*.

The French Regency came to an end in 1723. But the manners that made the Regency proverbial as a time of loose living and low standards of business morality did not end with the man who gave the period one of its names and in many ways had set its fashions.

After 1723 Louis XV ruled in his own name, if sometimes through
prime ministers. The open spectacle he provided of concubines and
court mistresses following each other in rapid succession furnished
an example that was not readily eschewed by others in high society.
In fact, among the lesser rulers of Europe—and nowhere more than
among the princelings of the Holy Roman Empire, the French model
was studiously copied. Showy palaces went up in imitation of Versailles. Even the sober Frederick II of Prussia did not hesitate to
build the palace named "Sans Souci" at Potsdam and to coddle the
academy at Berlin, both fashioned after the French prototypes. The
new Russian capital of St. Petersburg took on the appearance of a
new Paris as Italian, French, or French-inspired Russian architects
and engineers planned its boulevards and parks and its baroque edi-
fices with their mansard roofs. Close by arose the town of Peterhof in
frank emulation of Versailles.

In these secondary Versailles, grand and petty rulers and their
aristocratic flunkies and mistresses gathered in rococo salons, fitted
with the latest furniture of the Louis Quinze style. They copied the
French fashions, wearing highly colored and elaborate costumes, the
ladies with enormous powdered coiffures and hoops and the men
with great wigs and hats and dainty snuffboxes. They discussed in
French the latest ideas and books from France and submitted to
French rules of court etiquette. Even when the petty rulers acted in
the manner current among the "enlightened despots," they were
likely to cite some French precedent or some French work on political theory as authority.

Enlightened despotism was not to come into its own until the
latter half of the eighteenth century. In the earlier decades governments were less interested in social reform. Low society—the workers and the poor—usually had to seek an escape through other chan-
nels from the evils of poverty and injustice in high places. They
found it partly in emigration to the New World. Germans, Swiss, and
Scotch-Irish began going into the piedmont region of America at the
close of the seventeenth century, and their numbers increased markedly after 1710. British emigration not only continued to the older
colonies but led also to the creation of two new royal colonies—
South Carolina (1719) and Georgia (1733).

The Protestant sect known as "the Moravian Brethren" was one
of the most interesting groups to settle in America. They linked migration and religious devotion together as an answer to the problems
of poverty and immorality. Emphasizing a particularly strict standard

of Christian behavior, the Moravians had managed to survive Protestant persecution in the Austrian possessions following the Thirty Years' War. This survival was largely due to the skillful leadership of their great bishop John Amos Comenius, who, in the seventeenth century, had been deservedly respected as an educator and religious philosopher. But clandestine existence had weakened them to the point that in the next century they chose to leave their homes in Bohemia and to migrate to Saxony, where the Pietist Count von Zinzendorf welcomed them to his estate at Herrnhut (1722). Eventually ordered to leave Herrnhut, the Moravian Brethren—or Herrnhuters, as they were now called—went to America under Zinzendorf. Going first to Georgia, they moved, in 1741, to Bethlehem, Pennsylvania, and from there spread to other communities.

The Moravian Brethren engaged actively in missionary work. Among the immigrants whom they encountered in Georgia was John Wesley. He, with his younger brother Charles and some fellow students at Oxford, had already introduced such a regularity and systematic study into their religion that they were called "Methodists" in derision. After a visit to Herrnhut and further relations with Moravian preachers, John Wesley became convinced of salvation through faith in Jesus and set out to carry his conviction to the world. He traveled about 250,000 miles and preached about 40,000 sermons, speaking at "revivals" in the open air or in barns to townsmen, farmers, and miners. In 1744, Articles of Religion emphasizing the need of repentance and faith for full salvation were drawn up and became the creed of the Methodist churches. John Wesley lived to be nearly ninety years of age (1703–1791) and to see founded the Wesleyan Methodist Church in England and the Methodist Episcopal Church in the United States, though he himself never ceased to be an Anglican cleric.

The churches that looked to Wesley as their founder appealed directly to the lowly and the miserable through their special evangelizing efforts and their emphasis upon direct communion between God and man. From their ranks arose a new emphasis upon the Sunday school and upon humanitarianism. Already in France the word *bienfaisance* (benevolence) had been introduced by the Abbé de St. Pierre to distinguish lay philanthropy from charity undertaken by the church or by the layman as a religious act, and *sociétés de bienfaisance* were being formed to promote the sympathy of the rich for the poor. Wesleyanism, pietistic and evangelical, seeking to alleviate poverty and suffering, worked among the poor and the humble, giv-

ing impetus and focus to social movements that were to lead gradually and ultimately to prison reform, humanitarian penal codes, public hospitals and poorhouses, and the abolition of slavery.

A beginning in this public humanitarianism had been made
when in 1722 the British Parliament provided for the building of
workhouses in which able-bodied paupers could find employment,
and the aged, the sick, and the young could receive care. The last
witchcraft trial and execution on record took place the same year. In
1736, a Public Workhouse and House of Correction was created in
New York City, from which Bellevue Hospital eventually developed.
Still later humanitarianism took nourishment from the sentimentalism and *sensibilité* that the literature of the century was to make
fashionable. The downtrodden serf, the illiterate poor, the virtuous
servant girl, the tortured witness, the mistreated prisoner became the
subject of novels, political tracts, and engravings.

When the disinterested historian attempts to judge whether
belles lettres, publicists' essays, and other forms of literary expression, good, bad, or indifferent, have influenced political action, he
runs the risk of embarking upon a debatable line of thought where
deduction from relevant evidence tends to recede as judgment from
experience, personal or vicarious, looms. To what extent the humanitarianism and other social, political, and economic evolvements of
the eighteenth century were affected by the thousands of relevant
books, essays, poems, encyclopedia articles, dramas, sermons, legal
briefs, street-corner orations, café and salon conversations, and other
media that those decades proliferated will hardly be determined to
the satisfaction of all the experts on the subject even if the most competent of them should ever compute the last available set of relevant
statistics. The safest proposition is that the historian is here concerned with a sort of chicken-and-egg puzzle. There could hardly be
the one without the other, no matter which came first. The writers,
thinkers, and speakers of the eighteenth century (frequently the same
persons) may not have caused the concurrent or subsequent political,
social, and economic measures of their day; one can conceive that
those measures might perhaps have taken place even without the
preliminary written and spoken words. Yet one is also obliged to consider that the media did in fact articulate the current grievances,
help to create a degree of solidarity among the aggrieved and their
sympathizers, direct them toward a program or, more likely, divergent programs of reform that they might otherwise have lacked, and

highlight among the contemporary critics certain names that the disaffected might look to for leadership. Hence, even where the historian might reason that political action would possibly have occurred without antecedent or concurrent intellectual fermentation, nevertheless the intellectuals (meaning, in this case, the literate critics) of the time would have had a significant, even if not a decisive, role in creating it. All the more so if the intellectuals of the time deliberately planned to have a role in creating it. Some of the intellectuals of the eighteenth century had just such a plan.

The worldliness and secularization of the culture that we have been considering in these pages marked an essential characteristic of the intellectual development known by a later generation as "the Enlightenment," the *"siècle des lumières,"* the *"Aufklärung."* Among the outstanding champions of the Enlightenment (and certainly its most self-conscious reformers) were the *philosophes.* The *philosophes* thought of themselves as philosophers (although the name was first applied to them in derision), and in that they strove to understand the world and man and to build up systematic explanations of them, they *were* philosophers. But they were distinguished from the type of writer usually designated under that name by their marked interest in social and political reform and their efforts to reach a wide audience. They not only used the vernacular consistently but they used it limpidly. They wrote not only philosophical tracts, but political pamphlets, plays, operas, poems, critiques of literature and art, satires, *nouvelles à la main,* histories, novels, short stories, scientific treatises, and voluminous letters. The *philosophes* seldom were profound or original, though they borrowed wisely and argued well. They stand forth as political publicists and journalists more conspicuously than as dialecticians and metaphysicians.

Montesquieu's satirical *Persian Letters* is sometimes called the first book in the *philosophe* movement, though the writings of earlier social and political reformers like La Bruyère, Pierre Bayle, Fénelon, and St. Pierre are certainly to be considered forerunners if not directly part of the *philosophe* movement. After selling his post as president of the Bordeaux Parlement, Montesquieu devoted himself to political speculation. His *Considerations on the Causes of the Grandeur and Decadence of the Romans* (1734) was a sober and scholarly history that foreshadowed the theory of historical causation more fully set forth in his masterpiece, *The Spirit of the Laws* (1748).

The Spirit of the Laws was published in the year that the War of the Austrian Succession ended. By that time, Montesquieu was under the influence of at least three separate intellectual currents—sensationalism, or the theory that knowledge is derived exclusively from sensations produced by the reaction of the five bodily senses to the physical environment; its corollary, naturalism, or the belief that human nature and human problems are to be explained in naturalistic and scientific rather than providential or revelationist terms; and libertarianism, or the belief that within the bounds prescribed by law man should be allowed to be free. Montesquieu's indebtedness to England, which he had visited briefly and had studied at length, was obvious. Sensationalism was largely derived—indirectly, at least—from Locke, naturalism largely from the deists and Newton, and libertarianism also largely from Locke and from the English constitution.

English ideas had been widely imported into France, despite the strict censorship, by the circulation of clandestine manuscripts, subterfuges by daring printers and booksellers, conversations in fashionable salons, cafés, and clubs, exchange of travelers and tourists, and similar verbal media. Ideas, it was proved once more, could fairly easily be checked but were hard to kill. This truism was illustrated by a still-young poet-dramatist (about forty years of age), destined to be the leading *philosophe* of the day—François Marie Arouet, better known as "Voltaire." He described his observations in England in a work entitled *Philosophical Letters on the English* (1734). The book was condemned to be burned, and its author, once before jailed and exiled, avoided arrest only by fleeing the country. Nevertheless, the work was widely read. It revealed Voltaire's abiding admiration for Locke, Newton, and English religious and political freedom. Thereafter he wrote a number of other works publicizing Locke's sensationalism, Newtonian science, and English liberal ideas.

The sensationalist psychology appealed to the *philosophes* because they were opposed to formal religion and the dualism (i.e., the belief in the independence of mind and body) that logically resulted from an assumption of innate ideas. A contemporary psychologist, Étienne Bonnot de Condillac, in his *Essay on the Origins of Human Knowledge* (1746), carried forward the war against innate ideas; and in his *Treatise on Sensations* (1754) he argued ingeniously that if a statue were endowed with each of the five senses in turn it might develop a mind. Meanwhile (1748) Julien Offray de La Mettrie had published *Man the Machine*, setting forth a thoroughgoing mechanistic interpretation of human psychology. Other French writers—Denis Diderot, Claude Adrien Helvétius, Baron von Holbach—took up the theme. By the middle of the century it was fully accepted by one school of the French *philosophes* that man's mind was only a result of the impact of the outside world upon his senses—although by that time *A Treatise on Human Nature* (1739) by David Hume, a Scottish skeptic, had raised the question whether from sensations alone it is possible to derive thought or consciousness.

The *philosophes* lived likewise in the midst of a great wave of scientific interest, of which Condillac's and La Mettrie's mechanistic psychology was a reflection. Newtonianism, rendered popular by many editions and vulgarizations, had spread abroad a belief that the world was subject to general and regular laws ascertainable by the human mind. The Deists, though they believed in God as the First Cause, had, by exiling Him to a transcendental heaven, made it possible for others to believe that if God existed at all and was not an anthropomorphic invention, He intended that the world should run itself much as a clockmaker expected his clock to do.

New scientific activities fortified the belief that scientific detachment could help to answer the problems of man. Scientific societies, public and private, multiplied to emulate the academies of England, France, and Austria. Peter the Great founded an Academy of Sciences in St. Petersburg in 1724; Sweden in 1739 and Denmark in 1743 followed suit; and in 1744 Frederick II reorganized the old Berlin Society of Sciences into the Royal Academy of Sciences and Belles Lettres. They all set to work to find out how the clock worked, without much attention to the nature of the Clockmaker.

The natural sciences flourished under such benevolent auspices. A long series of experiments in chemistry from those of Robert Boyle (d. 1691) to those of Georg Ernst Stahl (d. 1734) of the University of Halle led to the propounding of Stahl's so-called phlogiston theory to explain combustion. This theory held that burning releases an otherwise undetectable material known as "phlogiston." Though any schoolboy today knows better, it was an important step in the study of the phenomenon of combustion. Hermann Boerhaave, professor at the University of Leyden, whose lectures Peter the Great had attended, in 1732 published a revised and complete edition of his earlier *Elements of Chemistry*. The new work attempted to apply Newtonian principles to chemistry. Successive improvements in the thermometer by Fahrenheit (1714), Réaumur (1731), and Celsius (1742) led to a mercury thermometer graduated on a centigrade scale, permitting the accurate measurement of temperature. The Swedish botanist Carolus Linnaeus systematized the classification of flora in his *Genera of Plants* (1737) and his *Species of Plants* (1753). Comte de Buffon, director of the Jardin des Plantes in Paris, began in 1749 the first of a series of studies that was eventually (1804) to reach forty-four quarto volumes and, under the title of *The Natural History, General and Particular*, to become a brilliant though uneven encyclopedia of the natural sciences.

To the vogue of scientism reflected by mid-century in these new natural history studies, Montesquieu thought he might add a science of politics. He worked upon a major hypothesis—to wit, that if the true principles of politics could be understood, they would reveal how best to preserve liberty in a country like France. Montesquieu's ideas of liberty arose not alone from his interest in English history and institutions. They were derived as well from his examination of Biblical and Classical writings, his knowledge of the New World, both east and west, and his long study of French law and history. As a jurist and a historian he had been much concerned with the spectacle of growing absolutism in France and was apprehensive about the possible disappearance of liberty even for people of his own class— the nobility. His political philosophy, as expounded in *The Spirit of the Laws*, was based largely upon that apprehension.

In line with a number of earlier writers, Montesquieu held that every nation had a fundamental law. That law was based upon the character of its people, which was in turn derived from its natural environment and its characteristic institutions—that is, from its geography and history. The man-made laws of a country, he argued, ought to be calculated to reinforce the people's natural character. In despotisms, which Montesquieu considered the results of extremes in such natural conditions as size and climate, the fundamental characteristic of the subjects was fear; in monarchies, which were to be found chiefly in temperate climates, honor (in the sense of "distinction"); in aristocratic republics, moderation; and in democracies, which could exist only in small countries, virtue (which he defined as "love of country and of equality"). A country like France—big but not too big, and blessed with a temperate climate—ought to be a monarchy, he argued. It could avoid despotism, however, only by a body strong and distinguished (i.e., "honored") enough to act as an intermediary between king and people. Thus, he contended, a monarchy, to survive, needed a strong nobility to act as a "repository of the laws." Hence his dictum, "No monarchy, no nobility; no nobility, no monarchy." To bolster this argument he appealed not only to the course of French history (to which he devoted most of his attention) but also to the example of England. Analyzing a somewhat idealized English constitution, he declared that it succeeded in guaranteeing liberty because the people through their control of the juries in the courts, the nobility through their control of the House of Lords in the legislature, and the king—the executive—through his control of the police and military force checked and counterbalanced one another.

Montesquieu was not the first to expound this theory of "mixed government" by which social classes or orders cooperate with but restrain each other through a system of checks and balances in the interests of liberty. Classical writers like Aristotle and Renaissance writers like Niccolò Machiavelli had perceived it, and Locke and Bolingbroke, among others, had already discovered it in the English political system. But the emphasis in Montesquieu's thought was on the tripartite division of government into judicial, legislative, and executive branches. The tripartite division of government in the English system became a conscious model of Western libertarians largely through Montesquieu's exposition of it in *The Spirit of the Laws*, which soon won its place as the classic justification for the status of the nobility, at bay between the full-grown absolutism of the king and the rising power of the middle class.

The first stage of the *philosophe* movement was largely embodied in Montesquieu's writings and was therefore largely aristocratic in intention and appeal. Although it was also antiabsolutist, it was not far removed from Jean Bodin and the Huguenot antimonarchists of the sixteenth century. Middle-class and democratic developments were still to come.

In France Louis XV, the once "well-beloved" king, had, since the War of the Austrian Succession, become much despised. His unpopularity brought to France a concomitant distrust of the institution of monarchy. Reflecting this trend of thought, a change of emphasis took place in the political ideals of the *philosophes*, forming a second phase of the *philosophe* movement.

The foremost figure among the *philosophes* after the death of Montesquieu (1755) was Voltaire, now no less famous as a historian and essayist than as a poet and dramatist, but Jean Jacques Rousseau and Denis Diderot were not far behind. These three men were all from the middle class (although some of their circle were of noble birth), and they deliberately appealed to a wider audience than Montesquieu had, writing a simpler prose (Voltaire perhaps wrote the best French prose ever written), deliberately avoiding learned language and philosophical terminology, and using the tract and the pamphlet, frequently pseudonymous or anonymous, to reach audiences that could afford neither the time nor the high prices that lengthy books required.

These *philosophes* were not republicans. It was regarded as an axiom, which all the history of republics up to their day confirmed, that a country as large as France could not be republican without fighting civil wars, splitting up into federal units, and falling prey to its neighbors. But they were not content to find in the geographical environment and the historical tradition of France the lesson that Montesquieu had found there—that France must be an aristocratic monarchy. Rather they thought that the appropriate institutions for France or any other country must be sought in a reasoned examination of man's universal nature, needs, and rights, and in the application of the same rational principles to human problems everywhere.

A turning point in the life of Voltaire came during a lengthy and unhappy visit with Frederick of Prussia in the 1750's. Voltaire in his history of *The Age of Louis XIV* had been optimistic about that recent period, which he considered the greatest in history, because it alone had benefited from the new "natural philosophy." When, however, he came to write about his own generation in his *Age of Louis XV*, he was less optimistic. His *Essay on Manners* (*Mœurs*), together with his volumes on Louis XIV and Louis XV, constituted a sort of universal history including even the oriental world. They showed that he considered the historical process a continuous struggle of the forces of enlightenment against the forces of obscurantism. Although confident that enlightenment would ultimately prevail, he was cynical about his own generation. He came to call the forces of obscurantism, which he identified largely but not exclusively with the Catholic Church, *"l'infâme"* (the infamous thing) and developed among the Voltaireans the slogan *"Écrasez l'infâme"* (Crush the infamous thing).

Though Voltaire had to live much of his life in exile and to deny many of his pamphlets, no voice was more powerful than his. Few neophytes became successful writers without his approval, and when he quarreled with men of established reputation—as with Rousseau —the whole literary set of Voltaireans quarreled on his side. Even great monarchs like Catherine and Frederick were Voltaireans in their way. His plays and poems and novelettes were no less fashionable than his political tracts, and his *Philosophical Dictionary* (1764), alphabetizing his thoughts on many subjects, made him easy to consult. The dictionary rendered plain that, despite many inconsistencies, Voltaire believed that man could easily be led astray by evil rulers and institutions and that a monarch who was both strong and enlightened was the best kind of ruler for people like the French, who (to his regret) were not fit for democracy.

In economic theory, Voltaire was generally sympathetic with that group of *philosophes* who called themselves *Physiocrats*. They were disciples of Dr. François Quesnay, one of the royal physicians, whose *Economic Tableau* (1758) taught that, land being the only true source of wealth, agriculture should be the chief source of revenue. As a consequence of that principle, they advocated a change of the fiscal complexities of France so as to free commerce and industry from many of their burdens, such as the outworn guilds and provincial customs duties, and so as to simplify the multiple and confusing system of taxes by substituting for it a single tax upon land.

Voltaire was also at the front of the fight for toleration. He not only pleaded for it as a principle in his writings but also, at some personal risk, befriended and sought restitution for several actual victims of sectarian intolerance and official injustice. In an age when middle-class ideas of philanthropy took the place of clerical charity and *noblesse oblige,* antiquated prisons, torture to elicit testimony, and ruthless law codes became special objects of criticism. The Italian Marquis di Beccaria's *Treatise on Crime and Punishment* (1764) became famous throughout Europe for its insistence upon making punishment fit the crime, for its arguments against the capital penalty, and for its plea on behalf of more humane treatment of prisoners. In England John Howard conducted investigations of the jails that led in 1774 to Parliament's abolition of the system by which jailers had had to depend upon prisoners' fees and to the establishment of a system of regular salaries instead. Howard published various works on the shocking conditions in the prisons not only of Britain but of other countries as well. He helped to organize the Philadelphia Society for Alleviating the Misery of Public Prisons and the Howard League for Penal Reform, which still exists in London.

The Jesuits steadily campaigned against the *philosophes* by writings as well as by repression but were doomed to defeat. Their defeat was the culmination of a process that had begun with their exclusion from Portugal in 1759. Anti-Jesuit feeling in France fed on the strife over the Jansenists' predestinarianism. They had suffered a severe blow when the papal bull *Unigenitus* (1713), definitely making them heretics, was registered as part of French law in 1730. Nevertheless, Jansenism continued to flourish among the wealthy middle class and found some protection in the parlements, France's highest law courts. When the Parlement of Paris hesitated to register a new bull in the 1750's, a quarrel ensued with Louis XV, resulting in exile and wholesale resignation of the parlementarians and an attempt on the life of the king. The Jesuits, of course, championed the papal bull, and the pro-Jansenist members of Parlement sided against the Jesuits. Parlement won some public support, because it seemed to be championing the cause of toleration against the king and the church, and the *philosophes* joined the attack on the Jesuits.

At first, the king and the Jesuits had their way. In 1761, however, a Jesuit, accused of speculation in a bankruptcy case, appeared before the law courts. That accusation gave Parlement a pretext for a searching investigation of the whole Society of Jesus. Claiming that the Jesuits were a hierarchy of agents loyal to a foreign monarch, Parlement called for the dissolution of the order in France. It was not until 1764 that the king yielded and formally banished the society. Spain, Naples, and Parma did likewise within a few years, and in 1773 Pope Clement XIV suppressed the order entirely. Ironically enough, since non-Catholic countries like Russia and Prussia paid no heed to the pope's expressed wishes, the Jesuits, though bound by a vow of special obedience to the pope, continued to survive there and were finally restored to the Catholic world in 1814.

Louis XV strengthened his position in the struggle with the parlements when the Parlement of Brittany attempted to try one of his officials. In the resulting dispute, Louis abolished the parlements entirely and for the rest of his reign ruled with a set of law courts of his own choosing. The parlements had long been the only body that had dared to claim, though with debatable success, the right to check the king's legislative and judicial authority. Louis' outright suppression of them seemed to mean a more complete victory for royal absolutism than any of his predecessors had been able to achieve.

The *philosophes* had generally been on the side of Parlement; so had some sections of public opinion. When Louis XV died (1774), his successor Louis XVI, anxious to play the role of enlightened monarch, quickly restored the old parlements. But it was not long before he, too, was engaged in a quarrel with them because, more anxious to win power than to correct abuses, they tried to interfere with his program of tax and administrative reform.

It must not be believed that the *philosophes* were a united group. Rousseau eventually quarreled bitterly with Voltaire. This vagabond Swiss, who turned to music and philosophy only late in life, believed in the potential innate goodness of man even more than Voltaire. Voltaire generally avoided meeting squarely the problem of how, in a Lockean-Newtonian universe indifferent to moral values and containing both good and evil, man was able to distinguish between what was right and what was wrong. Voltaire seemed to take it for granted that somehow mankind, especially if enlightened, could and would distinguish morality from immorality without clerical or supernatural guidance.

Rousseau, however, met the problem boldly by a frank dualism. In two early essays, *On the Arts and Sciences* and *On Inequality*, he contended that man had an inherent potentiality both for selfishness and for altruism but that the tendency toward the unnatural and factitious in civilization was likely to develop selfishness and stultify altruism. In later essays he suggested ways of overcoming the adverse effects of civilization while retaining its benefits. In *Émile, or on Education* (1762), he detailed a method of indoctrination that could be adapted step by step to the growing child's capacity to learn, avoiding the corrupting influence of civilization while providing a knowledge of the arts and sciences. In this scheme of education, God (without a priesthood) played a prominent role.

Religion appeared as a tool of the state in Rousseau's political philosophy. In *The Social Contract* (also 1762) he borrowed partly from Hobbes and partly from Locke to present the notion that the true contract was one of the individual with society, but one in which the people were sovereign and the government was merely their servant. Their general will (kept, if necessary, from misguidance by a "legislator") was law, and by their own decisions as to what that will was, they could retain their natural freedom and avoid the chains of oppression that Rousseau found everywhere. A "civic religion," he believed, was necessary for good citizenship in a well-ordered society.

Rousseau's famous novel, *The New Héloïse* (*La nouvelle Héloïse*), contemporaneously the most popular and influential of his works, also upheld the validity of an innate sense of moral values. It was the story of a love triangle in which virtue triumphed over baser emotions. Because Rousseau believed in innate emotions and intuitions as a guiding influence, because he painted the natural environment with remarkable skill and delicacy, and, above all, because, repudiating the bleak sensationalism of other *philosophes*, he preached a personal God, immortality, and a religious conscience as guides to moral behavior, *Émile* and *The New Héloïse* are commonly regarded as early steps in the new Romantic movement. This development was a reaction to the supposed lack of emotionalism in the Age of Reason.

The full break between Voltaire and Rousseau came as a result of minor irritations and some major differences of opinion. In 1755 a horrible earthquake and flood destroyed a large part of Lisbon and its population. Voltaire wrote a bitter ode, *The Lisbon Disaster*, raising doubts about the kindness of a Providence that permitted such abominable things to happen. Rousseau protested this outburst of skepticism; and he later indirectly rebuked Voltaire again by attacking the morality of the contemporary theater. Voltaire's rejoinder, though indirect, was *Candide*, a burlesque of the optimist school of Leibnitz and Pope, with which Rousseau had much in common. Despite a succession of bathetic hardships that ought to have shaken his faith, Candide continued to believe that "all is for the best in the best of all possible worlds" until he finally decided that perhaps it would be better merely to settle down and "cultivate his own garden"—that is, mind his own business.

The two writers were, in fact, not widely apart in their views of religion and morality, but the small difference between them was vital. Voltaire, too, believed in a moral code—he summed it up in an aphorism that is not very different from the Golden Rule—and Rousseau did not believe in an organized church—for which he was persecuted in both Catholic and Protestant countries. But Rousseau's unabashed consciousness of a personal God (to say nothing of his paranoid personality) dug a wide breach between the two men.

Before his split with the Voltaireans, Rousseau (as well as Voltaire and other *philosophes*) wrote articles for Diderot's *Encyclopédie*. The *Encyclopédie* was an ambitious project intended to codify all knowledge and, in so doing, to propagate the political faith of the *philosophes*. So many of the *philosophes* contributed to it that the term *encyclopedists*, as they came to be called, became almost synonymous with *philosophes*. Diderot wrote many of the articles himself —especially the ones on philosophy and technology. The mathematician D'Alembert contributed a famous introduction committing the writers to a Lockean psychology, a Newtonian science, and an empirical philosophy of knowledge.

Diderot used many tricks to avoid complications with the censors; nevertheless, the publication was twice suppressed. Finally in

1765 the last of seventeen volumes of text appeared, to be followed by several volumes of plates and indexes. It was not until 1780, twenty-nine years after the first volume, that the thirty-fifth and last volume appeared, but Diderot had edited only the first twenty-eight of them. Meanwhile, across the Channel, the *Encyclopaedia Britannica* had been published in three modest volumes in 1768–1771.

Diderot's *Encyclopédie* went through seven editions and reached thousands of subscribers—rich subscribers, because the price was high. It differed from the *Britannica* in that it was a sort of literary summary of the *philosophe* movement. It did not preach equality; it did preach the "natural rights" of life, liberty, and property, and the social contract binding rulers as well as the ruled. But it also preached the need for law and order in the well-constituted state. Most of the encyclopedists were reformers, but they were reformers living in a monarchy and having a middle-class point of view (even when they were clergymen or nobles). Reason seemed to them to dictate a strong though restricted and enlightened monarchy in which all the propertied and not the hereditary nobility alone would control political power.

The *philosophes'* program of natural rights was two-edged. They meant not only to alleviate the surviving abuses of economic feudalism but also to destroy the privileges of the nobility. By speeding up the abolition of serfdom, excessive taxation, seignorial payments, *corvées* (or forced labor), nobles' hunting rights, and other generally decried abuses, the *philosophes* hoped to create a more equitable socioeconomic system, but, in so doing, they would also be diminishing the influence of the nobility. By breaking the near-monopoly of the nobles upon the higher offices in the church, the army, and the royal service and by eliminating the nobility's exemptions and preferences in taxation, the *philosophes* hoped to improve those institutions, but, in so doing, they would also be increasing the middle-class influence in them. A more direct appeal for more democratic reform inside of France had to await a third generation of *philosophes*.

The predominance of the nobility was not limited to political and economic matters alone. In art, too, the middle of the eighteenth century was dominated by them. The similarities among the paintings of the period are sometimes striking, largely because of the similar tastes of the patrons. But these similarities are in part explained also by the pertinacious influence of the Italian school. Young English artists—Joshua Reynolds, for example—still went to

Italy to study, and outstanding Italian artists were in demand throughout Europe. The rococo still flourished, particularly in interior decorations, but, as the century moved on, it gave way to the neoclassic.

Giovanni Battista Tiepolo was probably the outstanding representative of the Italian school of painting in the eighteenth century. After a brilliant career in Venice he went to Würzburg in Germany to decorate the archbishop's palace and to Spain to do some frescoes in the royal palace. Tiepolo's subjects, because his temperament and his patrons urged him in that direction, were either religious or mythological and historical, with the luminous colors and delicate fantasy characteristic of the Venetian school. Although he painted in the tradition of the earlier Venetian school, influenced especially by Veronese, his work is distinguished from that of the earlier masters by greater emphasis on the baroque quest for dramatic effect.

In France Watteau found a disciple in François Boucher. Boucher became royal painter and director of the Gobelin tapestry factory through Mme de Pompadour's patronage. Like Watteau, he sometimes painted landscapes in which mythology and the *haut monde* mixed together in pretty pastoral settings, but more often he painted large-scale mythological and allegorical subjects. The influence of "high society" was also exerted on English art. Reynolds, probably Britain's greatest portrait painter, executed somewhere between two and three thousand portraits, practically all of them of rich or distinguished personages or of their children, often with studied attention to the ornateness and expensiveness of their clothes and surroundings. The same was true of Thomas Gainsborough, who, while he rivaled Reynolds as a portrait painter, also distinguished himself as a landscapist.

Italian influence had received an accidental fillip when the sites of ancient Herculaneum (1719) and Pompeii (1748) were discovered. They revealed in almost living detail the life, manners, and art of the Romans seventeen centuries earlier, just as they had been when overwhelmed by the ashes and lava of a Mount Vesuvius eruption. A German historian, Johann Joachim Winckelmann, was intrigued by these discoveries and eventually published a *History of Art in Antiquity* (1764), which not only tended to direct attention once more to Greek models but also was the cornerstone in the development of *Kulturgeschichte* (the history of cultural achievement). The neoclassical tendency in architecture was reinforced by the work of Giambattista Piranesi, whose engravings of Roman buildings and monuments attained an impressive popularity. It was reflected in Jacques-Germain Soufflot's Church of St. Géneviève (now the Pantheon) in Paris (1764) and in Constant d' Ivry's plans for the Church of La Madeleine (completed 1842) to close one vista from the great Square of Louis XV (now the Place de la Concorde).

The rapid development of ceramics in eighteenth-century Europe linked the oriental influence with the neoclassical. In France, under the patronage of Louis XIV, a glossy, yellowish porcelain was developed at St. Cloud. In Germany the chemist Johann Friedrich Böttger was able to perfect white porcelain, using native hard clay, and to develop glazes of several colors. Augustus II, "the Strong" (d. 1733), elector of Saxony and king of Poland, was Böttger's patron but kept him and his assistants virtual prisoners—so jealous was he of their trade secrets. Nevertheless, from their workshop at Meissen the fame of their so-called Dresden china went forth, and their methods were imitated. Workmen, escaping from Meissen, set up shop in Vienna, St. Petersburg, Berlin, and elsewhere.

French ceramics meanwhile improved in an independent development. Under Louis XV's patronage, they centered upon Sèvres, which ultimately became a most important porcelain factory of Europe and still, as the national pottery works, retains its reputation. After 1770 it produced famous vases and figurines in hard clay. From France the ceramic arts spread to Denmark, where the Royal Porcelain Works have ever since produced especially fine blue Copenhagen ware and the brilliant Danish faïence.

Josiah Wedgwood, the foremost English potter of the day, transformed the potter from an artisan into an artist and pottery making from a craft into an industry. Some of his stoneware reflected the neoclassical and the oriental influence at the same time. The two influences are notable in his jasperware vases and the "Wedgwood pattern" common in chinaware today. The straight lines and fluted borders of Wedgwood chinaware still are reminiscent of Greek pottery, while the blue Chinese garden scenes of Thomas Minton's patterns— the famous "willow pattern" ware—recall the debt of the West to the East.

The neoclassical influence was especially marked in British architecture. In the United Kingdom Robert Adam designed many notable groups of buildings including the University of Edinburgh, using what has since come to be called the *Adam Style*. He employed classical columns and classical motifs for interiors as well as exteriors. Adam was the architect of King George III, and his tastes intensified the trend toward neoclassicism in public buildings in England and America (the *Georgian style*) that characterized the reigns of the first four Georges. Under Adam's influence cabinetmakers like Thomas Chippendale, George Hepplewhite, and Thomas Sheraton did for furniture what Wedgwood did for pottery, lifting it to the level of artistry. These designers of furniture succeeded in conveying to chairs, tables, and cupboards some of the features of the Georgian style (such as simplicity of line and classical decorative motifs) but often departed from it—Chippendale especially—to add elements borrowed from the Chinese, the Gothic, and the rococo.

In music this period was not as brilliant as either the previous period, dominated by Bach and Handel, or the one which was to follow, but it did have a special accomplishment of its own. It was the age of Christoph Willibald von Gluck, Niccola Piccinni, and Philippe Rameau.

Gluck, building upon the work of his seventeenth-century predecessors Claudio Monteverdi and Jean Baptiste Lully, was one of the first composers to attempt to dramatize his music to fit the action of the libretto. This development was a musical innovation, for operatic music before that time had been quite independent of the text. The innovation was perhaps related to the contemporary "back to nature" vogue, frequently attributed (perhaps not altogether justifiably) to Rousseau's influence. Gluck's *Orpheus and Eurydice* (1762), *Alceste* (1767), and *Iphigenia in Aulis* (1774) were not well received in Germany. In France they had a greater success, but chiefly because Marie Antoinette, an Austrian (Gluck was her mother's court chapel master), publicly gave him support. When Piccinni, whose more conventional and popular *The Little Hawk* (*La Cecchina*, 1760) had been a European success, was invited to Paris, Gluck was there at the same time, and Piccinni was immediately built up as a rival of Gluck. The theme of Piccinni's opera *Roland* (1777) was deliberately chosen to appeal to a French audience and to compete with Gluck's *Armide* (1777), and both men were induced to compose an *Iphigenia among the Taurians* in competition with each other. Society became divided between Gluckists and Piccinnists, but the queen's prestige and Rousseau's preference for Gluck helped the German to complete his conquest of public approval for his operatic innovations.

Rameau was the most popular of French operatic composers of the day, but he has remained more memorable as one of the world's greatest musical theorists. The preceding century and a half had been an age of important scientific developments, to which even musicians could not continue indifferent. Rameau based his system of harmony on recent discoveries regarding the physical properties of sound.

Altogether, the eighteenth century was a period of remarkable musical innovation. It was the time when opera passed from emphasis upon rococo features such as coloratura arias and irrelevant ballets to an emphasis upon organic unity of text, music, and acting ("reform opera," as Gluck called it). During this century too, the modern piano began to replace the harpsichord, beginning with an instrument designed by Bartolommeo Cristofori in 1709 that permitted tones to modulate from *piano* to *forte* easily and almost instantaneously by lever action. At the spacious auditorium of the enormous palace at Mannheim, the seat of the elector of the Rhine Palatinate from 1719 to 1777, the so-called Mannheim School of music grew up and brought together an outstanding group of conductors, composers, and musicians who laid the foundation of the modern orchestra.

After the War of the Austrian Succession some astonishing achievements took place in the sciences and in technology. The nature of electricity and the principle of the electrical condenser had been partly revealed by the Leyden jar (so called because discovered at the University of Leyden in 1745). In 1752 Benjamin Franklin demonstrated convincingly, by means of a Leyden jar and a kite in a Philadelphia thunderstorm, that lightning was electricity. Franklin's experiment led to the invention of the lightning rod in 1753. In the next decade Dr. Leopold Auenbrugger began the use of percussion in the diagnosis of heart and lung ailments. In 1765 James Watt applied the long-known principle of steam as a source of energy to make a commercially successful steam engine. In 1774 the phlogiston theory of combustion gave way to the correct explanation of oxidation, when oxygen was discovered almost simultaneously by the British scientist Joseph Priestley and the French scientist Antoine-Laurent Lavoisier. Lavoisier was also to classify chemical substances into elements and compounds and to give to chemistry its present scientific nomenclature. The Russian polymath Mikhail Vasilievich Lomonosov (1711–1765), one of the founders of the University of Moscow (1755), which now bears his name, likewise set forth in his *Course on True Physical Chemistry* (1752–1754) principles that seem to have anticipated some of the fundamentals of that science. As early as 1748 he pronounced the conviction that (in words he used in 1760) "all changes occurring in Nature are subject to the condition that if so much is taken away from one substance, just so much is added to another"—thus articulating the general law of the conservation of matter, which several other contemporary scientists, particularly Lavoisier, had also perceived or were soon to perceive.

The increasing knowledge in the disciplines of botany, physiology, chemistry, and physics soon made itself felt in the realm of practical affairs. Jethro Tull in the 1730's had written several essays applying the new scientific theories to agriculture and invented the machine drill for planting. England could now boast a set of "gentlemen farmers" like Lord Townshend, whose enthusiasm over root crops led to his becoming known as "Turnip Townshend," and like George III, who called himself "Farmer George" in articles that he wrote on improved husbandry. These gentlemen farmers applied the latest principles of scientific agriculture to their lands, employing machinery, the rotation of crops, drainage, marl, and fertilization of the soil to use all their land efficiently, whereas previously a third of the soil had been allowed to remain fallow in order to "rest." Among the most famous of these new gentlemen farmers was Thomas Coke of Holkam, who not only applied all of the new methods of agriculture to his land but who, in breeding his sheep, also applied the newest principles of animal husbandry first set forth by "Farmer" Robert Bakewell in 1745. At the same time, Coke earned an enviable reputation for being a kindly and paternalistic landlord. England thus saw the beginning of an "agricultural revolution" that was to help her to cope, though not adequately, with the food problems that were to arise from the so-called Industrial Revolution, which was also beginning to take form in the eighteenth century.

Even though the phrase "Industrial Revolution" has recently been considered a misnomer, no one denies that important industrial changes took place in eighteenth-century Britain. The only question is one of terminology: the word "revolution," conveying an idea of suddenness, does not adequately describe the long and slow evolvement of industry before its more rapid development in the eighteenth and nineteenth centuries. Nevertheless, striking changes did take place in British industry in the 1700's. John Kay's "flying shuttle" (1738) increased both the speed of weaving and the width of the cloth woven. It threw so many hand weavers out of work that there were labor riots, in one of which Kay himself was nearly killed.

When James Hargreaves' spinning jenny made possible the spinning of more than one spindle at once (1770), it became easier for the makers of thread and yarn to supply the increased demand of the weavers. Then Richard Arkwright applied water power to the spinning process with his water frame, improving both the quality of the thread and the speed of its production, and making it possible for spinners to provide even more thread than the weavers could use. Samuel Crompton's spinning mule combined the best features of the jenny and the water frame to make a still-better thread even faster. The weavers were not able to catch up until Edmund Cartwright (about 1787) invented a power loom. By that time steam power was being applied to the textile and other industries.

The result of all these mechanical inventions, and of the utilization of water and steam power in place of human power, was the "factory." A factory was an especially built structure where huge machines were operated at specified hours of the day, requiring the attention of large numbers of workers. Hand craftsmen and artisans were thrown out of work. The small farmer also fared badly; he was placed in competition with scientific farming, which favored the big, unified farm and the enclosure for pasturing prize animals. Oliver Goldsmith as early as 1770, in his poem *The Deserted Village*, lamented the effect of increasing poverty and of emigration upon the rural scene:

> *Amidst thy bowers the tyrant's hand is seen,*
> *The desolation saddens all the green. . . .*
> *And trembling, shrinking from the spoiler's hand,*
> *Far, far away thy children leave the land. . . .*
> *Ill fares the land to hastening ills a prey*
> *Where wealth accumulates and men decay.*

Increasing agricultural and textile production led to a demand for improvements in methods of transportation. The most significant improvement made before the French Revolution was the English system of canals from the mines to Liverpool, Manchester, Birmingham, and other centers of the new factories. The Duke of Bridgewater was largely responsible for planning and financing, and James Brindley for engineering, the first of these canals. With her rivers and canals feeding coal and iron from her mines to her factories, Britain was well on the way by the 1770's to that industrial supremacy that she was to retain for the ensuing century. Only France could rival

her, but France, though now undergoing a similar process of mechanization, was to lose ground as Britain gained it during the French
Revolution.

Although writers had for centuries used fictitious characters and
episodes to tell a story, during this period came the fuller maturing of
the modern novel. From seventeenth-century variants in France, this
literary form had become known throughout Europe, but the new
vogue of the novel depicting credible characters living in a familiar
atmosphere was now still another manifestation of an intellectual climate that had proved conducive to materialism and empiricism in
philosophy and science. In such an atmosphere, not only the realistic
novel but also the naturalistic poem and play found a ready audience, and together they helped to foster that *sensibilité* which, para-
doxically perhaps, flourished at the same time.

Samuel Richardson was one of the first novelists to tell in single
continuous narratives (Richardson's were all lengthy besides) the stories of characters who acted more or less like natural human beings
in usual surroundings. Richardson's novels arose less from any conscious effort to be in tune with the empirical spirit of the times than
from his preoccupation with propriety and morality. His first novel,
Pamela, or Virtue Rewarded (1740), grew out of a projected guide to
proper letter writing, and only after he had begun it did the idea
occur to him of having the letters all center upon a single writer.
Thus Pamela came to tell her parents regularly the details of her
struggles to preserve her purity against her designing master. This
novel's success led (1744–1748) to seven more volumes of correspondence (*Clarissa, or The History of a Young Lady*) in which virtue, far from being rewarded, led only to injustice, grief, and death.
The History of Sir Charles Grandison (1753–1754) embodies Richardson's ideal of a model gentleman, though a later critic (Hippolyte
Taine) thought Grandison was fit only to be stuffed and put in a museum.

Meanwhile other English novelists had appeared. Henry Fielding, whose *Joseph Andrews* (1742) was begun as a burlesque of *Pamela*, in 1748 produced *Tom Jones*, now probably the most esteemed
novel of that day. Fielding abandoned the stylized letter form for
simple narrative. Tobias George Smollett's literary reputation was established with *The Adventures of Roderick Random* (1748), which
was followed at fairly rapid intervals by *The Adventures of Peregrine
Pickle* (1751) and other works. His *Humphry Clinker* (1771) was said

by no less an authority than Thackeray to have been "the most laughable story that has ever been written since the goodly art of novel-writing began." The first volume of Laurence Sterne's *Tristram Shandy* appeared in 1759 and the ninth and last in 1767. It was a running account of its characters' freely associated opinions, rather than a novel. It was followed in 1768 by *A Sentimental Journey through France and Italy*, limited to two volumes by the author's death. That the "sentimental journey" depicted was undertaken during the Seven Years' War, without the traveler from England expecting to encounter difficulties in France, is reflective of the limited warfare of the day. Horace Walpole in 1765 published his *Castle of Otranto*, which, by setting the scene amidst medieval horrors, became a precursor of the "Gothic" novel of the Romantic period and of the modern detective story. In 1766 Oliver Goldsmith produced his short and pathetic tale of the kindly Dr. Primrose in his *Vicar of Wakefield*.

These later novelists, for the most part, abandoned "phony" and histrionic paragons and peopled their novels with figures that were plausible, though sometimes distorted in another direction. Smollett, drawing largely from his own travels and experiences, often made his men and women coarse and bawdy, hard drinking and quarrelsome, with only occasional interest in the arts and the more delicate passions. Sterne's characters were usually more lovable, but their behavior and opinions were seldom less shocking, particularly since their creator was a clergyman. If Goldsmith's vicar was an exceptionally kind man, others in his stories were unbelievable cads. Fielding's characters were usually both more tame and more realistic than those of his contemporaries.

The new emphasis in poetry also mirrored the current stress on naturalism. Studied attention was given to nature as a subject for poems. Gray's *Elegy* and Goldsmith's *Deserted Village* contained often quoted descriptions of rural beauty. James Thomson's *Seasons* (1730), in which heroic couplets gave way to blank verse, rhapsodized the changes wrought by nature.

The contemporary interest in folklore was reflected by a controversy over "Ossian." Ossian was a legendary Gaelic poet and hero of the third century A.D. In *Fragments of Ancient Poetry* (1760) and subsequent collections James Macpherson set forth what he claimed to be literal translations of Ossian's poems, painstakingly collected in the Scottish Highlands. Samuel Johnson and other writers quickly challenged their authenticity, and the literary world was set agog by the ensuing controversy. After Macpherson's death, it was established that only a small part of his work was genuine folklore; he had invented the rest. Macpherson, therefore, is to be remembered more as an original poet than as a collector of folk tales and folk poetry.

Innovations in the drama likewise revealed the current realistic trend. Goldsmith's *She Stoops to Conquer* (1773), Richard Sheridan's *The Rivals* (1775), whose Mrs. Malaprop has ever since lent her name to the ludicrous misuse of words, and his *School for Scandal* (1777) were distinguished by their avoidance of the fantastic, the oratorical, and the bombastic. Even though the characters today might seem overdrawn, they were everyday people, speaking the ordinary vernacular. If they sometimes found themselves in more dramatic and sentimental situations than was usual, they did not behave in an incredibly heroic or villainous manner. When brilliant actors and directors like David Garrick put on these irreverent and realistic dramas before huge audiences at large theaters like Covent Garden and Drury Lane, the theater became a more profitable business than ever before.

Dr. Samuel Johnson (1709–1784), independent in temperament and at the same time conservative, stands out as perhaps the most significant figure in English literature during the third quarter of the eighteenth century. His *Dictionary of the English Language* (two volumes, 1755) was an important contribution in semantic thoroughness and aphoristic sharpness of definition, as well as in choice of illustrative quotations. Already known as a poet and essayist, he contributed to literary periodicals throughout his life. In 1759 he published *The History of Rasselas, Prince of Abyssinia*, which is sometimes compared with Voltaire's *Candide* because Rasselas also wandered far and wide in a futile search for happiness; however, unlike Voltaire's burlesque of optimism, Johnson's story excites pathos rather than ridicule. Johnson became the central figure in the Literary Club which he founded in 1764 and which included celebrities like Goldsmith, Reynolds, and Edmund Burke. In 1765 he produced the best edition of Shakespeare's plays that had yet appeared. During his later years he published *The Lives of the Most Eminent English Poets*, which are still useful biographical and critical accounts of some fifty seventeenth- and eighteenth-century writers. Until his death in 1784 Johnson was a literary dictator in England much as Voltaire, whom he did not always admire, was in France. After his death he became the subject of one of the world's best-known biographies, James Boswell's *Life of Johnson* (1791).

The peopling of English novels and plays with horse-racing, card-playing, and hard-drinking rogues gave England the reputation abroad of being a country whose liberty was matched only by its license. The popularity of English gambling games, racetracks, riding costumes, and landscape gardens nevertheless spread rapidly onto the Continent, reinforcing the vogue of English political ideas. There the English innovations mingled with a continental development called *sensibilité*, which fed on the tribulations of the heroines of English (and other) novels. *Sensibilité* can be inadequately translated by a combination of the two English words *sentimentalism* and *sensitiveness*. It designated the readiness to feel compassion for suffering, particularly in literature, and was fashionable before the French Revolution. Grand dames, who read Richardson's *Pamela* or Rousseau's *The New Héloïse* while their enormous coiffures or intricate costumes were being prepared, earned a reputation for emotional refinement by the ease with which they burst into tears over the hardships that obstructed the path of righteousness. In its more sincere manifestations, *sensibilité* went hand in hand with the new humanitarianism and philanthropy that the century had developed.

Rousseau and other French novelists, among them the encyclopedist Diderot, catered to the fashion of *sensibilité*. *The Nephew of Rameau*, probably Diderot's best novel, was not a sentimental novel, however. It dealt with the problem of ethical standards, in unyieldingly tight arguments, by portraying a sybarite and a moralistic philosopher dialoguing side by side. The novel ended without a decision for either side. Apparently Diderot himself was undecided, and the work, never completely finished, was not published during his lifetime. Neither was his sentimental novel, *The Nun*, portraying an unhappy novice. Diderot's realistic sentimental plays—*The Natural Son* (1757) and *The Head of the Family* (1759)—had a marked contemporary vogue. *Jacques the Fatalist*, like *Tristram Shandy*, presented lengthy arguments about morality and other debatable subjects, was another of Diderot's works that was published posthumously. Diderot's cultivation of the realistic and the bourgeois and his avoidance of classical conventions on the stage inaugurated a type of drama new to the France of the classical tradition of Corneille and Racine. The new emphasis was continued by Beaumarchais. The hero of his *Marriage of Figaro* (1784), the barber Figaro, spent much of his time on stage criticizing the nobility and the middle class. Napoleon Bonaparte is said to have later called this play the beginning of the French Revolution—"the Revolution already in action."

The naturalistic school of dramaturgy moved from Diderot's France to Germany with Lessing's *Minna von Barnhelm* (1767), which, portraying a poor soldier's love for a rich girl, was the first great German comedy. Lessing tried to create a German national art despite the centrifugal provincialism of the Holy Roman Empire. His famous collection of essays on the drama, *Hamburg Dramaturgy* (1768), spoke of a natural and German theater, urging that the Greek dramatists and Shakespeare rather than the French classics be regarded as models. His own dramatic masterpiece was *Nathan the Wise*, in which the Mohammedan Saladin, the Jew Nathan, and a Christian knight plead for toleration while enacting the story of the knight's love for Nathan's daughter.

Lessing's *Nathan* was among the books the Nazis prohibited and burned in the 1930's. Nevertheless, he was one of the founders of the modern German national literature and art and prepared the way for a generation of writers who were to restore Germany to a leading place in the intellectual life of Europe. This generation, which began roughly around 1765, produced the literary period known as the Storm and Stress (Sturm und Drang). Lessing was its leader, but not far behind him came Johann Gottfried von Herder, who was best known as a philosopher of history but who had also written essays on literary criticism, German philology, and folklore.

This generation of German intellectuals also had its forerunners. The earlier French *philosophes* like Montesquieu had their German counterparts in Christian Thomasius, sometimes called the father of the German Enlightenment because of his emphasis upon the validity of common-sense judgments, and Christian von Wolff, who popularized Leibnitz's teachings. Thomasius and Wolff often wrote and lectured in German rather than Latin. They encountered the same sort of opposition and the same sort of success as the *philosophes* in France. Building upon the work of the cameralists and these earlier German philosophers, the generation of Lessing and Herder brought the Enlightenment (*Aufklärung*) to Germany. Wolff was supposed to have been the first person to use the term *"Aufklärung."* The Sturm und Drang was only the literary phase of the *Aufklärung*.

The most brilliant writer of the Sturm und Drang period was Herder's student and friend Johann Wolfgang von Goethe. Goethe's *Götz von Berlichingen* (1773), usually considered the first important work in the Sturm und Drang, followed Lessing's critical principles. Modeled after Shakespearean drama, it was based upon the career of a German patriot hero of the sixteenth-century Peasants' War. Goethe's autobiographical *Sorrows of Young Werther* appeared the next year. It presented a less robust type of hero in a young lover whose hopeless passion led him to suicide. The influence here was strikingly Rousseauean and *sensible*. Goethe in 1775 went to Weimar, at the age of twenty-six, to become a minister of that tiny German state, as well as to continue to cultivate his reputation as the foremost German man of letters. By so doing, he withdrew from the Sturm und Drang to enter another phase of his career that was more directly inspired by the classics. Young Werther meanwhile had many imitators and evoked a sentimental cult that spread Goethe's influence far beyond the confines of the German language and permitted the Sturm und Drang to live on into the French Revolution.

The age that in France was called "the Louis Quinze period" and in England "the Georgian period" was also the Age of Reason, of the Enlightenment or *Aufklärung*. It was likewise the age of the "enlightened despots" (whose work we shall soon examine). It was a time when many felt that the old and traditional ways were not changing fast enough and wished for more sweeping reforms. Reform measures were going to be tried by the enlightened despots, but they were to prove, in several instances, too little and too late.

Louis XV, for all his success with the parlements and for all his military and diplomatic efforts, was engaged only in bolstering up a regime that was bound to collapse. To a certain extent, that was likewise true of other contemporary rulers. The enlightened regimes of George III of the United Kingdom, Frederick II of Prussia, Maria Theresa of Austria, and Catherine II of Russia, fortified the persuasion of *philosophes* that enlightened monarchy was the most acceptable form of government for most of the European countries, but it now seems clear that those triumphs were, in fact, undermining the strength of the monarchs. They encouraged the spirit of innovation, inquiry, and unrest. They gave to many who had no reason to prefer a hereditary king or nobility a personal sense of achievement and dignity and a public prominence that had no relation to their class.

Louis XV is supposed to have said, when told that his credit was running low, that it did not matter; it would last as long as he did and "after me, the deluge." Whether he actually used those exact words is less important than that the prediction came true. The prestige and power of the absolute monarchs was still sufficient to keep them firmly on their thrones. As long as kings were strong, the hereditary nobles, struggle though they might, could be no more powerful than the monarchs would permit them to be. But the middle class, who were a sort of aristocracy of talent and of money, were neither so easily controlled nor so exclusive, especially since they could appeal to the mass of the population. And as the hereditary nobility gave a grudging support to the monarchs, the deluge that Louis XV is supposed to have bidden not to rise in his lifetime was to come from those masses, frequently led by conspicuous members of the upper orders. The program that the popular leaders would demand was being shaped by the political enlightenment, the scientific advances, the literary and artistic realism, the humanitarian *sensibilité*, the religious evangelism, and the other untraditional developments considered above. These developments were gradually fostering both the desire and the ability of more of the governed to be more widely and more directly consulted by those who governed them.

In the Anglo-American colonies the growth of trade and commerce during the eighteenth century increased, in turn, the interchange of ideas and quickened the intellectual life and untraditional tendencies of the colonists. As long as the colonial settlements had remained widely scattered and isolated, ideas had tended to remain static, unaffected by outside impacts, and unable to congeal into a common consciousness and public opinion. But the wandering merchant and sailor, the itinerant peddler and shoemaker, and other tradesmen circulated both their wares and the current views from community to community; and, as roads and transportation facilities improved, the communication of ideas improved with them.

In the early days it had often been virtually impossible to find one's way through the forest even when traveling between the largest colonial centers. The few scattered inns had been unspeakably dirty and unsafe, and it was not uncommon for the landlord to assign a single room to several travelers regardless of congeniality or sex. By the middle of the eighteenth century, however, roads and inns had improved greatly on the main routes. Travel had increased sufficiently by 1732 to warrant the publication in Boston of the first American guidebook, *The Vade Mecum for America, or a Companion for Traders and Travelers*. This book set forth the roads and distances between important points from Boston to Jamestown and included information about local fairs and other attractions. The greater number of coastwise vessels and their increased tonnage and better accommodations also encouraged travel among the colonists, and the seaboard location of the settlements was an inducement to maritime transportation.

Still another factor in the stimulation of colonial thought was the growth in population and importance of the towns. Cities, large and small, tend to be centers of new ideas, new inventions, new associations of people, new styles of dress, new tastes in food, new schemes of politics and economics, new ventures in trade, and new contacts in culture. True enough, during the entire colonial period and for a century to come, the great majority of Americans lived a rural existence. Nevertheless, centers like Boston, New York, and Philadelphia became increasingly important focal points, and in their midst were fashioned the articulate forces of intellectual and political ferment. All were seaports and had access to contemporary European thought.

In this cosmopolitan atmosphere of the cities there sprang up a host of clubs, founded for various purposes and with varying degrees of seriousness, but nearly all intent upon things of the spirit—in every sense of the word. Some of these clubs' names are intriguing. For example, New York could boast of the Hungarian and the Hum Drum clubs. Newport possessed the Philosophical Club (but this might have been a misnomer, for a contemporary tells us that, though the members drank punch and smoked, he "was surprised to find that no matters of philosophy were brought upon the carpet" and "they talked of privateering and the building of vessels"). Philadelphia had among its organizations a Beefsteak Club and a literary-scientific society called "the Junto."

The latter club, founded in 1727 by Benjamin Franklin, was a debating society where young literati read and discussed papers. As an outgrowth of the Junto, Franklin and others founded the American Philosophical Society in 1743. Its secularist purpose was shown by its encouragement of "all philosophical experiments that let light into the nature of things, tend to increase the power of man over matter, and multiply the conveniences and pleasures of life." Included in its membership were some of the outstanding minds in the colonies, together with such eminent European scientists as Lavoisier, Linnaeus, and Buffon and such *philosophes* as Marquis de Condorcet and Marquis de Chastellux (not to mention Marquis de Lafayette). In connection with the Junto, Franklin was instrumental in building up a subscription library that contained scientific works, and that he did not fill its shelves with theological books—as the libraries of the colonial colleges did—was indicative of the new rationalism he did so much to promulgate.

The growth of towns likewise encouraged the rise of a periodical press. The first regular newspaper, the *Boston News-Letter,* appeared in 1704, a small, dull periodical that managed to keep itself alive by printing only innocuous items that would give no offense to the political authorities. Fifteen years later two more papers entered the field, and in 1721 James Franklin, Benjamin's brother, founded the *New England Courant,* resisting the dissuasions of his friends, who assured him that America did not need another newspaper. By 1765 the colonists were reading about forty-three newspapers, three of them in German.

Many of these journals had short lives, and few had real literary merit. They freely copied interesting news items from each other, often weeks or months old, since, in the absence of other means of communication, stale news was still news. They seldom were as large as modern tabloids. They nearly always carried little advertisements or "notices" on every page, and the front page was generally devoted almost entirely to such notices. Benjamin Franklin's paper, the *Pennsylvania Gazette,* was entertaining and influential, while two southern journals, the *South Carolina Gazette* and the *Virginia Gazette,* had literary standards surpassing those of any New England papers.

Despite some censorship the colonial press exerted a considerable influence on its readers, who turned to it for information about events overseas and in neighboring colonies. A victory for American intellectual and legal independence occurred in 1735 when John Peter Zenger, editor of the *New York Weekly Journal,* was acquitted of charges brought by New York's governor in a case involving the reinterpretation of the English law of libel and hence the principle of freedom of the press. The jury's verdict was later termed by Gouverneur Morris, himself a leader in the American Revolution to come, "the morning star of liberty which subsequently revolutionized America."

The first universities established in the New World were founded in Mexico City and Lima in 1551, under the auspices of the Catholic Church. Likewise, the first universities founded in the Anglo-American colonies were launched under religious control—in these instances, Protestant. The oldest is Harvard, authorized in 1636 by a vote of the Massachusetts General Court and endowed by John Harvard, a Charlestown minister, so that young men might in turn become ministers. The second-oldest college is William and Mary, established in 1693 during the reign of the royal pair after whom it was named. The third college to be established was Yale, founded in 1701 as a Puritan institution intended to educate young men "for publick employment both in Church and Civil State." Its endowment came from Elihu Yale, who had amassed a fortune from the East Indian trade. In the middle of the eighteenth century came the great religious outburst known as "the Great Awakening," and it led to the founding of four new colleges—Princeton (1746), which was Presbyterian; Brown (1764), which was Baptist; Rutgers (1766), which was Dutch Reformed; and Dartmouth (1770), which was Congregational. King's College, an Anglican institution, was founded in 1754 and was presently to change its name to "Columbia," in keeping with political innovations.

These institutions were sectarian, and their curricula were traditionally Classical. In America as in Europe, Latin had still been the language of scholarly writing in the seventeenth century, and a knowledge of Greek, though not so essential to learning, had been regarded as desirable. But the eighteenth-century Franklin was self-educated, and his early education had included no Latin, Greek, formal philosophy, or pure science. He conceived of an educational institution whose curriculum would include such utilitarian studies as surveying, navigation, accounting, mechanics, agriculture, physics, chemistry, history, civics, government, trade, commerce, international law, and modern languages as well as the Classics. This was the Academy, and later the College, of Philadelphia. Franklin thereby became the founder of the first institution of higher learning in the Western world to afford training in vocations and trades as well as in the learned professions, in contemporary problems as well as in Classical and theological lore, and in the practical and applied sciences as well as scientific theory. His college became a model for many subsequent American colleges—whether for better or for worse is still a highly debated point. In 1765 a medical school was established in Philadelphia, the earliest of its kind in North America.

In general, colonial institutions of higher learning were marked by rigidity and conservatism of thought and by mediocrity of scholarship. In the general impetus, however, to the advancement of learning that marked the middle decades of the eighteenth century, colonial scholarship seems to have improved appreciably. The intellectual tastes of the colonists were reflected in the books that they read. A farmhouse would probably contain—if the household were literate—a Bible, of course, and a hymn book, and an almanac. Almost every printing house in the colony produced its almanac. The almanac was a small annual magazine, with encyclopedic information—recipes, sermon texts, lists of pills, short stories and poems, interest tables, weather prognostications, distances between taverns, aphorisms, jokes, essays, and astronomical information of sorts. The almanac's accuracy was open to grave doubts, but the average colonist probably seldom entertained them. The best-known was Franklin's *Poor Richard's Almanac*, but it had to compete with a host of rivals.

The townspeople were more catholic than the farmers in their reading, and colonial importers and printers managed to provide an ever-growing number of readers with the latest literature from England and the Continent. Locke and Montesquieu were among the especially popular writers, articulating as they did the colonists' own thoughts on natural law and right. Of course, the Classics also found ready buyers. Franklin, as printer, was able to place before his customers works by Seneca, Ovid, Bacon, Dryden, Locke, Milton, and Swift. Such books soon found their way into private libraries, several of which were worthy of respect.

Meanwhile, those who could not afford to amass book collections of their own had their intellectual appetites at least partly satisfied by the founding of small libraries in the larger cities. Since 1621, when the earliest known library in the Anglo-American colonies was established for Indians, the number of libraries had grown. Here again Franklin's resourcefulness showed itself to advantage, when he instituted the first subscription library in America in connection with the Junto. Together with a small number of mechanics and tradesmen, he started a library by the practical expedient of pooling modest savings. In Franklin's words: "The institution soon manifested its utility, was imitated by other towns, and in other provinces. The libraries were augmented by donations; reading became fashionable; and our people, having no public amusement to divert their attention from study, became better acquainted with books; and in a few years were observed by strangers to be better instructed and more intelligent than people of the same rank generally are in other countries." Franklin was to maintain afterward that the new libraries "perhaps have contributed in some degree to the stand generally made throughout the colonies in defense of their privileges."

Except for Franklin, who consciously modeled his style upon the *Spectator*, no great literary figure appeared in the colonies, North or

South, before 1776. Few outstanding works of art or belles lettres
were produced on the frontier. As the towns grew, literary produc-
tivity grew with them. But writings were generally political and historical tracts rather than novels or poetry or drama. John Woolman,
a New Jersey Quaker, tailor, traveler, and reformer, produced a series of pamphlets in the period around the Treaty of 1763 carrying
such titles as *Some Considerations on the Keeping of Negroes* and *A
Word of Remembrance and Caution to the Rich.* John Wise, Massachusetts pastor, defended the Congregational theory of politics in
The Churches' Quarrel Espoused (1710) and *A Vindication of the
Government of the New-England Churches* (1717), and other pastors
in pamphlets and sermons dealt with the problems of popular government. Samuel Sewall's diary and Mary Rowlandson's story of her
captivity among the Indians were works of interesting personal
record but of little literary merit. The writing of history was seriously
cultivated on the frontier. Cotton Mather's *Magnalia Christi Ameri-
cana* (1702), Cadwallader Colden's *History of the Five Nations of Indians* (Iroquois) (volume I published in 1727), and Thomas Hutchinson's *History of the Province of Massachusetts Bay* (three volumes, of
which the first appeared in 1764) were the most lasting eighteenth-
century efforts. In these American historical accounts, the Indian appeared as a significant figure, even sometimes coloring the author's
prose with a touch of the formal metaphorical style of the Indian ora-
tion and treaty.

Much of the better colonial literature was in the form of sermons. Despite the fact that the importation of Europe's growing rationalism was pushing America's educated classes into a secular and
deistic trend on religious questions, the clergy continued to be the intellectual guides of at least the less educated. Many clerics were anti-
Anglican. A revivalist wave, sometimes called the "Great Awakening," spread through America, beginning in the 1730's, in much the
same way that Quietism, Pietism, Jansenism, and Wesleyanism had
spread through Europe. Jonathan Edwards, a native-born, controversial, unrelenting, strict Calvinist theologian, George Whitefield, visit-
ing from England, and other ministers of various denominations
preached through the country a "new light," a new emotional rap-
port with God, which found expression in the rapid growth of evan-
gelistic sects like the Baptists and the founding of new colleges like
Princeton, Brown, Rutgers, and Dartmouth. Their sermons were frequently printed and widely read.

In other fields of cultural development America also showed the effects of its youth. The great luminary of American science—as of other lines of American cultural achievements—during the colonial period was Franklin. His *Experiments and Observations on Electricity* (1751) set forth, among other things, the daring experiment with a kite that decisively confirmed the identity of lightning and electricity. Other scientists—like David Rittenhouse in astronomy and Benjamin Rush in medicine—were worthy but less outstanding.

Though colonial America had its poets—particularly Philip Freneau and the Hartford group known as the "Connecticut Wits"— and its artists—particularly John Singleton Copley—these men were imitative and of little genius and were to produce most of their best works only in the period following the Declaration of Independence. One eighteenth-century poet, however, deserves special mention. Edward Taylor (1645–1729) privately gave expression to his apparently devout and meditative soul in poems, published only in 1937, that critics now regard as of superior distinction.

Although the New World had as yet produced few great artists, writers, and scientists, the important thing was that, however few, they were beginning to think of themselves as Americans and of their culture as native, no matter how dependent upon European origins and influences. Even in cultural matters America was learning to stand more or less alone.

When in 1763 the British colonies in America finally were relieved of the French menace, they had been in existence for over a century and a half, and about six generations of colonists had built new homes, roads, cities, governments, churches, and other institutions in the wilderness. The span of time between the founding of Jamestown and the Treaty of 1763 was approximately the same as the span between that treaty and the end of the First World War. In other words, it requires only two such spans to cover the history of the Anglo-American people from its beginnings until a fairly recent date.

In the rapidly changing New-World society of the 1760's six generations had brought the development of a sense of solidarity and independence. The failure to form a union at Albany in 1754 and the reluctance to cooperate in the French and Indian War showed that they could not achieve by direct political action what nevertheless was happening by a less perceptible, more impersonal process. What had been sparse and segregated little settlements in the seventeenth century, in several instances had become flourishing cities by 1763.

Where once-timid entrepreneurs had sought military and economic protection in the power of the British army, navy, and law, now vigorous and flourishing business firms felt self-assured and assertive. Where once the British crown had been looked upon as a benign source of paternal guidance, now it was often resented as a malign force for regimentation. Communities that had once dealt with each other chiefly through London now had learned to communicate directly. Social and cultural institutions, at first strikingly similar to England's, had gradually derived from the Dutch, Swedish, German, Indian, Black, and other ethnic fractions of the population at least superficial features that were varied, and even the most firmly ingrained features had been modified by the rigors of the frontier.

Contemporary observers, among them a young French student named Turgot destined to become a great statesman, perceived what was happening. Colonies, he observed, were like children, timid and dependent when they were young, but bound when they grew big and strong to become resentful of restraint and domination. And, indeed, the American colonies had grown big, strong, and self-reliant. "I am not a Virginian," said Patrick Henry as the colonial period drew to a close, "I am an American"; and further: "I am not an Englishman, I am an American." In short, the "one" that was later to be boasted in the motto *E pluribus unum* was gradually being welded, though as yet the welding was far from complete. This oneness was to come not only because thirteen separate parts were being physically joined more closely together but also because they were getting to think of themselves, and to be thought of by others, as having certain interests in common within the British empire. A new nation was being conceived on the North American continent, and if it was not conceived altogether in liberty, as Abraham Lincoln was one day to assert (since some men were slaves and others, though free, were disenfranchised), at least a *greater* liberty was to be found there than almost anywhere else in that day.

CHAPTER FIVE

"A New Nation Conceived in Liberty"

In 1818, several decades after American independence had been firmly established, John Adams wrote: "The Revolution was effected before the war commenced. The Revolution was in the minds and hearts of the people." Although neither the British government in London nor the American colonists at home fully recognized it, a new nation had been in the making ever since the founding of Jamestown in 1607. This new nation was to produce a profound change in the history of Britain, of Europe, and indeed of the world, and on the other hand, the new nation was from the start to be remarkably affected by forces outside the United States of America. America, in short, was born and was to develop in the main currents of European and world history.

We have already examined the way in which the Anglo-American colonies grew from a few straggling settlements into thirteen self-reliant and largely self-sufficient communities. All the great changes of the European past found expression in eighteenth-century America. The religious upheavals of the sixteenth and seventeenth centuries had given it part of its people. The political revolutions of the seventeenth century had affected its institutions. The emphasis upon rationalist philosophy and empirical science since the Renaissance had raised doubts regarding some traditional values in America no less than in Europe. The new commerce and wealth that had ensued from the great discoveries and explorations created problems for Americans as well as Europeans to which old mercantilist theories no longer seemed to provide the correct answers. The same wars with rival powers and stubborn natives that had fostered England's desire for imperial centralization had enhanced the colonies' capacity for local home rule. It was to take only a few disputes with the mother country in the 1760's and 1770's—incidents reflected in repeated disagreements of colonial assemblies with royal authorities and that may well have seemed of minor importance at the time to Britain because in some ways they were less sensational than numerous other disturbances Britain had successfully weathered both before and after—to crystallize these questionings, influences, and aspirations into a concrete program of colonial self-determination.

The resulting clash between British imperialism and American separatism precipitated a revolution in America. In other words, political independence was the end product of a decades-old drift toward economic, social, cultural, and psychological alienation. An American national spirit was being slowly forged by the steady hammering of environment, distance, and historical circumstances. We are now about to explore the events that determined how that national—that is, anticolonial—spirit became manifest, first to the Americans and then to the rest of the world.

Eventually the new American nation was to give itself an enduring constitution. That constitution was not found already inscribed by an American Moses on a Mount Sinai but was to be sweated out in an atmosphere of humidity and contention in Philadelphia. Despite the sometimes earnest debates we shall see that the document finally adopted by the Founding Fathers was a compromise agreement that embodied the political practices as well as the moral, economic, and social predilections of its signers. It was freely admitted to be imperfect at the time by its own creators. It has survived to the present day and has proved flexible enough to continue as the political framework for a nation that has evolved from an agrarian economy of three million people to the foremost industrial and financial power of the modern world. Wherever natural rights and federal government are under consideration, the precedent of the United States Constitution is likely to be cited.

Lest disproportionate emphasis be placed upon economic factors in tracing the origins of the American Revolution, it should be repeated that the New-World spirit had for decades been crystallizing because of doubts concerning a social and political system no longer applicable to conditions in America. Nevertheless, it was around economic and fiscal questions that the differences between opposing camps became polarized, leading to open friction in the 1760's and finally to armed revolt and then to outright revolution in the 1770's.

In 1760, after Wolfe's capture of Quebec, Franklin wrote: "No one can more sincerely rejoice than I do, on the reduction of Canada; and this is not merely as I am a colonist, but as I am a Briton." And when he returned from England in 1763, he felt so warmly toward that country that he could write: "No friend could wish me more in England than I do myself." These were common sentiments during the sixties among colonists and were unashamedly proclaimed in the song, "Virginia Hearts of Oak," which was to be printed and sung with gusto despite the heated controversy already raging:

Though we feast and grow fat on America's soil
Yet we own ourselves subjects of Britain's fair isle;
And who's so absurd to deny us the name
Since true British blood flows in every vein.

In other words, the colonists considered themselves Britons, and many of them maintained this concept of allegiance beyond the very outbreak of hostilities between them and the mother country.

Nevertheless, although the American colonists themselves may not have been fully aware of the process, they had long been permitted to enjoy a marked degree of economic and political self-determination, and their autonomy had for decades been at work bringing about its logical counterpart, a desire for political independence. Full recognition of this process was to come only when the colonists realized that their favored position was imperiled and would remain in peril unless they gained the independent means of safeguarding it.

The economic clash between the mother country and the colonies was rooted in the doctrine of mercantilism. The mercantilists held that the possession of colonies was a blessing. Colonies might furnish raw materials that the mother country herself did not produce and might otherwise have to purchase from a rival state; they might be sources of vital war materials, like naval stores, which it would be wise to keep out of the hands of potential enemies as well as to stockpile for oneself; they were a sure market for the mother country's finished products, stimulating industry and overseas trade for the benefit of the mother country's manufacturers, artisans, shipowners, and merchants; they could sometimes even add directly to the mother country's supply of precious metals; and they would be the homes of new, loyal subjects.

Mercantilism's principal purpose was to further the defense and the prosperity of the realm as a whole, and the colonies were occasionally sacrificed to the welfare of older portions of the realm. As long as the interests of mother country and colonies more or less coincided, all went well and few disturbing questions were likely to be raised by the colonists as to basic premises. But fundamental questions were bound to arise when that condition was reached which the Anglo-American colonies could not avoid and the mercantilist state could not tolerate—when the colonists, becoming capable of self-defense, at the same time became competitors.

The mercantilist doctrine had been enacted into law when Oliver Cromwell controlled England and the most famous of the Navigation Acts was passed (1651). It provided that the carrying trade to and from the colonies would be limited to ships manned mainly by English mariners. The intent of this act was to make this shipping a monopoly of the English and the colonials. In 1660 a new act provided that the goods carried to and from England must be transported in ships that were not only English-manned but also built in England or the colonies. These provisions served to encourage the carrying trade and the shipbuilding industry of both the mother country and the colonies and were therefore looked upon favorably by the latter. But the Act of 1660 also ruled that certain "enumerated" articles—sugar, tobacco, cotton, ginger, indigo, fustic, etc.— which had been grown or manufactured in the colonies could not be shipped to any place except England. As time elapsed, the list of enumerated articles expanded until by 1764 they also included tar, pitch, turpentine, hemp, masts, yards (all naval stores), copper, ore, beaver and other furs, molasses, whale fins, hides, iron, lumber, raw silk, pearlash, coffee, pimento, and coconuts.

The English government sought to prevent the direct importation into the colonies of foreign commodities that would compete with English goods. With the idea of keeping the colonies "in a firmer dependence upon it [England] and rendering them yet more beneficial and advantageous unto it," Parliament required in 1663 that all European goods bound for the colonies must first be shipped to England and then reshipped in English (including colonial) ships to colonial ports. There were a few exceptions, such as salt from Spain for the New England fisheries. Later, because the colonial merchants constantly evaded the Navigation Acts by sending cargoes of enumerated articles directly to European ports, the ire of the English merchants was further aroused. Through their efforts Parliament in 1696 passed an "act for preventing frauds and regulating abuses in the plantation [i.e., colonial] trade." This put teeth into the Navigation Acts, which, as a result, remained fairly effective for several years.

British mercantilists sought to regulate and control not only the colonial carrying trade but also manufacturing in the colonies. To prevent the rise of industries competing with home enterprises, colonial governors were requested to "discourage all manufacturers and to give accurate accounts of any indications of the same." One of the home enterprises of which the English were most jealous was the wool industry. A venerable tradition requires the lord chancellor of England to sit upon a woolsack, as a constant reminder to the noble lords of the importance of wool in England's economy. At the end of the seventeenth century the woolen industry involved over a million people in England and accounted for almost half of that country's exports. All of the northern colonies were by that time, however, manufacturing woolen goods, and Massachusetts was even exporting them to other colonies. In righteous alarm, Parliament passed the Woolens Act in 1699. It provided that no woolen goods could be exported either abroad or from one colony to another, though nothing in the act prevented the manufacture of woolens for consumption within a colony's own borders.

One Englishman's reaction to colonial enterprise is shown in a report at the beginning of the eighteenth century (1705) by the governor of New York:

> I am well informed that upon Long Island and in
> Connecticut, they are setting up a woollen Manufacture,
> and I myself have seen serge made upon Long Island that
> any man may wear. Now if they begin to make serge,
> they will in time make course cloth, and then fine. . . .
> How farr this will be for the service of England, I submit
> to better judgements; but however I hope I may be
> pardoned, if I declare my opinion to be, that all these
> Colloneys, which are but twigs belonging to the main
> Tree [England], ought to be kept entirely dependent
> upon and subservient to England, and that can never be
> if they are suffered to goe on in the notions they have,
> that as they are Englishmen, soe they may set up the
> same Manufactures here, as people may doe in England;
> for the consequences will be that if once they see they
> can cloath themselves not only comfortably but
> handsomely too, without the help of England, they who
> are already not very fond of submitting to Government,
> would soon think of putting in execution designs they had
> long harboured in their breasts. This will not seem
> strange when you consider what sort of people this
> Countrey is inhabited by.

In the eighteenth century new restrictive laws found a way into the British statute books. In 1731, a company of feltmakers caused Parliament to investigate charges that New Yorkers and New Englanders had established an all too flourishing manufacture of beaver hats. The upshot was the passage of the Hat Act of 1732, prohibiting the exportation of colonial hats either to Britain or across colonial boundaries, besides restricting each hatmaker to no more than two apprentices.

Another measure that would have been particularly disastrous to colonial trade if it had been strictly enforced was the Molasses Act of 1733. As we have already seen, a large and prosperous commerce had developed between the West Indies and the northern colonies. The New England merchants shipped fish, forest products, and African slaves to the West Indies and in return brought home rum, sugar, molasses, and money or bills of exchange. Most of this West India trade was carried on with the non-British islands, and especially the French and the Dutch West Indies, for, producing in larger quantities, they were able to undersell the British West Indies planters. This exchange left the British planters with a surplus of sugar beyond that which the mother country, the only remaining customer, was able to consume. As a result they experienced a marked financial depression and eventually asked Parliament to prohibit American trade with the foreign islands. After a strong planter lobby had pressed the struggle in Parliament, the Molasses Act was passed in 1733. In truth the act merely imposed duties upon sugar, rum, and molasses imported from the non-British West Indies and hence restricted but did not prohibit the disapproved practice. Because the customs restrictions were not adequately enforced, the law did little to change actual conditions, and the rich trade, though now illegitimate, went on as briskly as before. The diligent enforcement of the law, however, might have seriously crippled the northern colonies' commerce and industry.

Then, in 1750, the colonial iron industry was restricted. An act was passed permitting the free importation of bar iron into Great Britain but prohibiting the erection in the colonies of slitting or rolling mills, plating forges, or steel furnaces. Here was a pat application of the mercantilist theory: The British ironmasters welcomed the importation of raw materials from the colonies but kept colonial ironmasters from competing in the manufacture of finished articles such as tools and hardware.

Still another source of friction between the mother country and the colonies was the currency problem. Because of the unfavorable balance of trade, metal currency—largely derived from formally unlawful foreign trade—did not remain long in the colonies but found its way to British pockets. Eventually all the colonies resorted to the issuance of paper money. Massachusetts set the pace in 1690 when it issued paper currency without metallic backing to pay its soldiers after they returned from the expedition against Quebec. This issue retained its value because it was accepted in payment of taxes (i.e., as legal tender) at 5 per cent advance over coin. But the very success of the issue caused a veritable flood of paper money in the colonies, most of which quickly depreciated. In 1751, in response to the insistent complaints of British merchants that they were losing money because of the depreciated colonial currency, Parliament passed an act forbidding the governments of New England to issue bills of credit as legal tender.

The disadvantages of the mercantile system were easily recognized by the colonists, who could see without any great effort that their economic interests were usually subordinated to those of the mother country. Much less obvious were the undoubted advantages accruing to the colonists from imperial legislation. For one thing, the mother country gave preferential treatment to many of the products of the colonists. Tobacco was an instance; the customs rates on the colonial product were much lower than those on Spanish tobacco. The same situation obtained regarding iron, lumber, indigo, whale oil, ginger, potash, and pearlash. In addition, substantial bounties were offered on hemp, masts, and certain naval stores—all important to the maintenance of sea supremacy. Again, in the case of many foreign commodities—for example, Dutch linens—brought into the colonies via British ports, the duty was partly or entirely refunded, with the result that the colonists were often able to purchase these products more cheaply than the British. The colonists benefited still further from the military and naval protection that they enjoyed and, in addition, profited from trade privileges with other parts of the empire. There was little or no exaggeration in the observation of Adam Smith that British imperial policy was "less illiberal and oppressive than that of any [other European empire]."

It has sometimes been maintained that the advantages derived from the mercantile system definitely outweighed the disadvantages suffered by the colonists. Certainly prior to 1750, despite the resentment among the colonists against the restrictions imposed upon their business activities, the situation, by and large, was mutually advantageous both to the colonies and to the mother country. This relative satisfaction was to a great extent due to what has been described as the policy of "salutary neglect" that Britain followed during the first half of the eighteenth century. For this policy, Prime Minister Robert Walpole, who took for his motto *Quieta non movere* (freely translated: *Let sleeping dogs lie*), was perhaps principally responsible.

The British government was unwilling to provide the enormous bureaucracy and personnel that would have been required to enforce the mercantilist statutes adequately. Thus, in one way or another, the colonists managed to evade the restrictive laws. It has been estimated that one-half of the trade of Boston in 1700 was in violation of existing regulations. This was notably true, later, of the Molasses Act of 1733. "Salutary neglect" kept that act ineffective until 1763. Laws without enforcement did have the moral effect, however, of making smuggling commonplace. As a result of the mercantilist system, some of New England's leading citizens were mixed up in this contraband trade. John Hancock was conspicuous among them. With John Adams as his lawyer, he was being arraigned by the government as a smuggler about the time that the Battle of Lexington opened the revolutionary war. Trial might have brought half a million dollars' penalty if he had been found guilty.

During the 1750's British statesmen were coming to the conclusion that the colonial system required a thorough revision. For one thing, the belief was growing that the control of lands beyond the Alleghenies needed to be centralized. The situation had become chaotic because the colonies had separate and often conflicting frontier policies. Then again, several of the colonies had shamefully victimized the Indians, so that the British government feared the danger of Indian warfare—a matter of the utmost importance in the struggle still going on with France for continental supremacy. The British government inclined toward limiting the opening up of the West to White settlement, but, on the other hand, immigration into British America was markedly increasing and important groups in the colonies—above all, the numerous land speculators—wanted the western lands populated as quickly as possible.

Involved also in the problem were the colonies themselves. Several, such as Virginia, Massachusetts, the Carolinas, and Georgia, claimed vast trans-Allegheny tracts by virtue of their charter rights. On the other hand, those colonies without claims to western territory feared the added power that the acquisition of new lands would give to their rivals. Obviously, the problem was complex, and although the necessity of an equitable solution had become increasingly apparent to London, the formulation of such a solution proved an awkward stumbling block in the way of the improvement of imperial relations.

British statesmen were also convinced that the time had come for a closer association of the colonies with one another, at least for administrative purposes. They were no longer separated by vast forest tracts, as had been the case a century earlier, but now formed a fairly continuous strip along the entire eastern seaboard. The need of defense against the French suggested a closer alliance among the colonies. The handling of the Indian and western land problems also necessitated greater administrative agreement. In 1754 delegates from New England, New York, Pennsylvania, and Maryland convened at Albany and, arriving at the conclusion that a union of the colonies was "absolutely necessary for their preservation," adopted a plan of union drafted previously by Benjamin Franklin. The plan, as has already been noted, was not accepted even though something like it was generally regarded as desirable. The failure of the colonies to cooperate not only with the mother country but even with each other during the French and Indian War led to questions on both sides of the Atlantic that underlined the gradual parting of their ways.

Just as Americans were beginning to ask more persistently why they should continue to be tied to Britain's apron strings, the demand arose in Britain that the policy of "salutary neglect" in the economic sphere and of loose association in the political sphere should be replaced by one of firmer regulation and association. Any effort to overhaul the colonial system in the direction of greater mercantile restraint and imperial control was thus likely to make relations worse, not better, between Britain and the colonies.

Great Britain came out of the Seven Years' War the richer for substantial additions to her imperial territory, the poorer for equally substantial additions to her national debt. The conflict had cost her over £82 million, and £60 million of this amount had had to be added to a national debt already exceeding £72 million. The necessity of maintaining order in the expanded empire would place new and considerable burdens upon the British taxpayer. In fact, British statesmen sincerely doubted the ability of the British taxpayer to bear the entire weight of the past debt and of increased expenses in the future; government income would therefore have to be augmented by larger revenues from the colonies. They considered such a proposal equitable on the grounds that the new debt had been contracted in waging a war which had saved the colonies from French domination, that the standing army would afford the colonists protection against the Indians, and that the navy would safeguard their ocean commerce.

In 1763 a new prime minister, George Grenville, took office in London. He and his associates at once decided to put an end to the old policy of "salutary neglect." Britain's new imperial stature and her resulting financial insecurity could be adjusted, they thought, by a threefold policy of establishing greater control over the newly won lands in the American West, tightening the existing trade laws, and obliging the colonists to make a greater contribution to the imperial exchequer. Each of these proposals, however, was to encounter bitter opposition in the colonies.

Before 1763, great speculative companies had been formed to exploit the virgin land in the West. One, the Ohio Company, had petitioned the king as far back as 1747 for 500,000 acres on the upper Ohio. Other speculative companies had come into existence since then and were all set to stake out even vaster trans-Allegheny tracts, which they sometimes acquired from Indians who had no proper authority to sell.

Imperial defense had justified trans-Allegheny settlement as a bulwark against the French and the Spaniards before 1763. The victorious conclusion of the Seven Years' War, however, ended that necessity for settlement. Furthermore, with the lucrative Canadian fur trade now in British hands, merchants in London feared that further expansion in the West by colonial competitors would lessen or destroy their profits from that enterprise. Other British investors maintained that the opening of the West would attract settlers from the eastern seaboard, thus populating areas beyond the control of British merchants and depopulating areas where some of them had risked substantial sums. Still another argument put forth in London was that if there was to be any trans-Allegheny development, it should be regulated by the British government, which would thereby gain revenue from the sale of lands, while British land speculators would have access to the profits.

Nor were the Indians indifferent to the problem. They had seen themselves defrauded of lands and furs by unscrupulous speculators and traders and were at last driven to desperate action. In 1763, organized into a mighty confederacy under the Ottawa chief, Pontiac, they took to the warpath. Within a short time they had destroyed every British post west of Niagara with the exception of Detroit, and it was not until the following year that the situation was once more under control. This Indian uprising had the effect of crystallizing action already contemplated in London.

In 1763 the Grenville government issued a notable proclamation forbidding colonial governors to warrant surveys or grant patents "for any lands beyond the heads or sources of any of the rivers which fall into the Atlantic Ocean from the West or Northwest." This Proclamation of 1763 meant that all lands between the crest of the Alleghenies and the Mississippi for a length extending from Florida to 50° north latitude were "for the present" closed to settlers and speculators alike. Indian lands could not be sold except to the crown.

The immediate aim of the proclamation may have been the pacification of the Indians, but it had precisely the opposite effect upon the colonists. The pioneer groups that sincerely desired to trek westward and open up new settlements bitterly resented this shattering of their hopes. Just as enraged, though perhaps for less laudable motives, were the land speculators, north and south, who were thus deprived of an easy means of enlarging their fortunes or paying their London debts. Colonists who, no matter how reluctantly, had helped win this land from the French in the recent war were certainly in no mood to see it slip away from them now. And in 1774, when it appeared possible that Ohio and Kentucky lands would be granted to a British company, Virginians, previously as a general rule loyal to the mother country, began to have misgivings that lands claimed by Virginia would be snatched away by Old-World favorites and speculators. Virginians found ready sympathizers in other colonies.

Grenville had figured that the colonists should justly pay at least half of the cost of their defense, about £150,000 annually. This annual sum could be raised, according to him, through enforcement of the existing mercantile regulations. He proposed that the duties of the old Molasses Act of 1733, which was universally despised and evaded, should be cut precisely in half. The calculating statesman thus liberalized the prohibitive import duty in the hope that American merchants would thereby be encouraged to become more law-observing and pay their duties more regularly. He also raised the duties on refined sugar, placed a tax upon foreign wines, coffee, indigo, and certain textiles, and enlarged the list of the enumerated articles that could be sold only in Britain. In addition, to make sure that the

old as well as the new laws were more effectively enforced, he but-
tressed the ordinary customs authorities by ordering British naval
officers to collect the new customs duties and by giving the British
admiralty courts jurisdiction over smuggling cases. Admiralty courts
were not required to have juries.

There was immediate uproar throughout the colonies. Well
might John Hancock, who himself stood to lose a good income by
Grenville's measures, write that "the times are very bad." The New
England colonies were at once hit by a financial depression, so dependent were they upon the foreign molasses trade. Formal protests
were drafted by mercantile associations. The French and the Dutch
West Indies had hitherto been a major source of hard money—
specie—for the colonies, and the source was now likely to dry up.

To make matters worse, Grenville chose this juncture for further
regulation of colonial paper money. The plight of the colonial merchants was now aggravated by the passage in 1764 of the Colonial
Currency Act. This measure forbade the further issue of unsound
paper money in the colonies and protected the British merchant
against the payment of colonial debts in depreciated currency. Parliament had acted to benefit the British creditor, thereby gaining not
only the support of this group but also the general approval of the
wealthier creditor merchants of the colonial towns. But it alienated
the small debtor farmers and the debtor plantation owners of the
South, who had found inflated paper currency a convenient device
for taking care of their heavy financial obligations. In 1766 Franklin
stated to British leaders that the prohibition of paper currency constituted one of the major reasons for the existence of ill-feeling in
America toward Britain.

Not content with this state of affairs, Grenville proposed another measure designed to produce revenue for defense purposes.
This was the Stamp Act. It subjected the colonists to taxes similar to
those already demanded of Englishmen at home, providing that
stamps, varying in cost from a halfpenny to £10, were to be placed
on almanacs, newspapers, wills, contracts, licenses, and other legal
documents, as well as on playing cards and dice. The Stamp Act, supported by both Whigs and Tories, was passed by Parliament in
March 1765, "with less opposition than a turnpike bill." Even intelligent and well-informed British observers failed to appreciate the significance of that measure or the temper of the Americans. Horace
Walpole, as a member of Parliament, commented casually of those
perilous decisions: "Nothing of note in Parliament, but one slight day

on the American taxes." Nevertheless, Americans, feeling that their economic development had already been seriously hampered by Grenville's restrictive tactics, had come close to the end of their patience.

The colonists' reaction to the Stamp Act was one of universal and unparalleled hostility. The act was an innovation in that it was a direct, internal tax—unlike the import duties previously laid upon the colonists, which were paid at the ports and passed on to the consumer only indirectly. At once there arose protests that the Stamp Act was unconstitutional. Nine colonies sent delegates to a Stamp Act Congress, which met in New York in October 1765, and there a declaration of rights and grievances was issued, maintaining that the American colonists were entitled, among other liberties, to trial by jury (imperiled by Grenville's emphasis upon admiralty courts) and self-taxation (imperiled by his Stamp Act).

British merchants soon were profoundly affected by the colonial defiance. The depressive influence on trade of the new regulations from London was enhanced by an American boycott of British goods. Franklin, summoned before the House of Commons to explain the attitude of the colonists, informed Parliament that only compulsion would force them to submit to the Stamp Act. In fact, violence now made itself felt in no uncertain terms through the actions of newly formed secret societies that called themselves "Sons of Liberty." These organizations were made up generally of mechanics and other elements of the poor and unenfranchised, who showed their dissatisfaction with discriminatory regulations by public demonstrations and riots, burning of officials in effigy, intimidation of stamp collectors, and destruction of property.

On the whole, the situation in the colonies proved highly disagreeable to the authorities and mercantile interests on both sides of the Atlantic, and amid universal rejoicing the Grenville ministry was forced to resign. The Stamp Act was repealed in 1766, and the Sugar Act was revised, the duty on molasses being reduced to one penny per gallon. The British government made clear, however, that in retreating in this instance, it was not surrendering jurisdiction over the colonies. The repeal was accompanied by a Declaratory Act maintaining that Parliament "had, hath, and of a right ought to have full power and authority to make laws and statutes of sufficient force and validity to bind the colonies and people of *America*, subjects of the crown of Great Britain, in all cases whatsoever."

Parliament's claim to this political prerogative was overlooked by the rejoicing colonists, who were apparently more concerned at the time with economic realities than constitutional principles. Bells were rung, cannon were fired, and the king was toasted everywhere with brimming bumpers. Many of the colonial merchants still grumbled that for one reason or another they were not able to make the profits reaped before 1764, but, generally speaking, the colonists were eloquent in their protestations of loyalty to their noble sovereign, George III.

The repeal of the Stamp Act and the reduction of the sugar tax only transferred the burden of raising imperial revenues back to the already heavily loaded shoulders of the British taxpayer—and he did not intend that all of it should remain there. In July 1766 a new coalition ministry came into power, headed by William Pitt, "the Elder" (soon to become Lord Chatham). Pitt was ill during this time, and leadership in the formulation of financial policies fell to his brilliant but mercurial chancellor of the exchequer, Charles Townshend. The chancellor was convinced that the mercantilist philosophy should be enforced strictly and that the existing deficiency in revenue must be overcome. Taxation of the colonies presented a way of achieving both these aims at once and at little expense to the harassed English taxpayer.

Townshend had seen what happened when internal taxes, such as the Stamp Act, were imposed on the Americans, and so he hunted for a form of taxation that might be more agreeable to hypersensitive colonists. In 1767 he had a set of acts passed by Parliament that came to be designated by his name. They called for the imposing of tariff duties on colonial imports of painters' colors, red and white lead, glass, paper, and tea. The taxes were not excessive, but they fell on articles of everyday use and so raised the general cost of living. And the Townshend Acts went further: They provided for the collection of these revenues by British officials appointed by London and paid out of their collections, thus keeping them free of local control and inducing them to be strict in their collections. To assist officers in stamping out smuggling, about the same time Parliament confirmed the legality of writs of assistance, permitting these officers to enter any shop, warehouse, or home in search of illegally imported goods.

The Townshend Acts met with an even more resentful reception than had been accorded the Grenville Acts. Once again the colonial merchants resorted to a commercial boycott—this time less tacit than before—and their nonimportation agreements spread to the

plantation provinces also. Merchants who would not cooperate with
the boycott found themselves bedecked in always undignified, sometimes highly injurious tar and feathers; and other acts of violence
erupted this time more numerous, vigorous, and purposeful than before.

This open defiance of law and order was scarcely to be tolerated
by the British authorities. They decided to station a military force in
Boston. Its arrival from Halifax in October 1768 only inflamed passions the more. Radicals like Samuel Adams, a leader of the Boston
Sons of Liberty, tirelessly fomented unrest, and the redcoats were
pelted with cries of "Lobsters" and "Bloody Backs," together with
more solid missiles such as snowballs and oyster shells.

The situation progressively deteriorated until on March 5, 1770,
an incident occurred that had far-reaching repercussions. On that
day a sentry, snowballed by some youths, called for assistance. A ser-
geant and six men appeared, only to be assaulted with sticks and
stones. When one of the soldiers was knocked down by a club, the
company fired on the crowd, killing five and wounding some others.
This episode became known as the "Boston Massacre," and though
the commanding British officer was defended by John Adams and acquitted, the resentment against the use of military force was exploited by radicals to keep the minds of the people inflamed. According to the royal Governor Thomas Hutchinson: "The Boston people
are run mad."

This all but impossible situation was improved the next April by
the repeal of the greater part of the Townshend Acts. A new prime
minister, Lord North, had taken office. He held the view that the
taxation of British manufactures was "preposterous," and accord-
ingly he arranged for the removal of the tax upon paints, glass, and
paper. But in order to reconfirm the principle that the crown at all
times had the right to tax its colonies, a tax of three pence a pound
on tea was retained. The colonists thus could purchase the beverage
at a lower tax than it could be bought in England, where the import
tax was a shilling a pound.

The repeal of most of the Townshend Acts was highly agreeable
to the colonial merchants, for their uneasiness over mounting disorder grew as their prosperity returned. They had come to worry
about this growing propaganda of home rule spread about by agitators like Samuel Adams. They asked each other: In the event of independence, who would be in control—they or the radicals? In the
event of home rule, who would rule at home? And so some mer-

chants agreed with one of their number that "high points about the supreme authority of Parliament" should best "fall asleep." With the breakdown of the boycott, trade was resumed and imports spurted from a low of £1,604,000 to £4,200,000 in 1771.

Agitation continued, but it was now carried on almost solely by a radical minority, headed by the irrepressible Samuel Adams. A spectacular event took place which aided his efforts. The captain of the revenue schooner the *Gaspée* was detested for the thorough manner in which he searched vessels for contraband. On June 9, 1772, the *Gaspée* ran aground below Providence, Rhode Island, and was attacked by a mob headed by one of Providence's leading citizens. The ship was burned, and the commander wounded. British officialdom, proposing to bring the responsible persons to Britain for trial, could find no one who was willing to accept a reward for naming them.

Sam Adams seized upon the hue and cry to press his cause further. Vehement and eloquent as a pamphleteer and conspicuously talented as a political agitator, he bombarded the public with every possible argument for resistance, asking his countrymen whether they wanted to be "freemen or slaves." To win freedom, Adams constantly reiterated, union and collective action would be needed. In November 1772, he conceived a highly effective organ for propagandizing and solidifying the colonists—the Committee of Correspondence. Rising in the Boston town meeting, he proposed that a committee of twenty-one be appointed "to state the rights of the colonists and of this province in particular, as men, as Christians, and as subjects . . . with the infringements and violations thereof that have been or from time to time may be made." This committee was to be empowered to send emissaries to other towns, and in every way to educate the public against ministerial oppression.

So timely did this innovation prove that almost overnight similar committees of correspondence sprang up everywhere. Massachusetts alone possessed over eighty by January 1773. Two months later, militant members of the Virginia House of Burgesses, including Patrick Henry, Richard Henry Lee, and Thomas Jefferson, succeeded in creating a provincial Committee of Correspondence, designed to communicate with the sister colonies. Within a year, all but one of the colonies had these special committees, whose purpose was to mold public opinion to oppose domination by London.

Despite the growing unrest and solidarity of the Anglo-American colonies and despite the effectiveness of the radical leaders, the more cautious mercantile groups were reluctant to jeopardize their returning prosperity for the sake of greater political autonomy. At this point, however, the government in London unwittingly provided the radicals with powerful ammunition. In 1773 the British East India Company was in dire financial straits, thanks to mismanagement and extravagance. Tremendous quantities of surplus tea were lying in its British warehouses. Bankruptcy of the company would be sure to impoverish a number of British merchants and politicians whose misfortune would have repercussions in other quarters. Parliament decided to avert disaster by advancing the company a huge loan at a low rate of interest, transferring some of its authority in India to the crown in return. Furthermore, in order to facilitate the sale of the surplus tea, Parliament passed the Tea Act of 1773, which permitted the East India Company to ship tea directly to the American colonies in its own vessels and then sell it there through its own agencies. Furthermore, the customary shilling-a-pound tax on tea imported to England was remitted if the tea was subsequently transshipped to the colonies. Parliament's intention, since direct importation to the colonies would eliminate middlemen, was to provide the colonists with tea more cheaply than they had ever before been able to buy it and, at the same time, to insure a certain market in the colonies for the company.

But if Parliament thought that it had pleased everybody, it was soon disillusioned. The act had conferred a virtual tea monopoly upon the East India Company, for it could now afford to pay the three-pence customs tax in the colonies and still reduce the price of tea by 25 per cent. Smugglers and honest shopkeepers would alike be helpless against this monopoly. But the danger was not confined to the tea merchants. What would prevent similar monopolies being granted to other British concerns, with the result that a host of commodities could then be shipped and sold directly to the colonies, thus depriving Americans of the profits of shipping and retailing?

Once again the merchants joined with the radicals, although the means of resistance to be employed still brought disagreement between the two groups. The merchants inclined to the resumption of the technique of economic boycott; the radicals favored more direct action. Popular feeling running high, the radicals won out—and tar and feathers were soon in brisk demand. The first cargoes of tea to arrive in Boston were met with protests that they be shipped back home without payment of duty. The refusal of the obstinate Governor Hutchinson (whose sons were tea consignees of the company) to allow the tea ships to leave port brought a stalemate. Finally, a mass meeting was summoned at which Samuel Adams arose and said: "This meeting can do nothing more to save the country." Although historians will perhaps never know whether these words were meant to be a signal for action, that night a group of men disguised as Indians rushed down to the harbor, boarded the tea ships, and dumped overboard a cargo sometimes estimated to have been worth £15,000.

This "Boston Tea Party" marked the point in the struggle between Anglo-America and Britain at which pacific methods like colonial boycotts and parliamentary concessions became the exception, and violence and coercion the rule. On the one hand, the Tea Party was a signal for militant elements in the other colonies to take strong —and even strong-armed—measures. Rioters came close to physical violence in New York, Portsmouth, Philadelphia, and Charleston; and at Annapolis the *Peggy Stewart* with her cargo of tea was publicly burned. On the other hand, news of the Tea Party brought immediate repercussions among conservative elements both in the colonies and in Britain. They interpreted such action as lawless destruction of private property, which no self-respecting government could overlook. Even a liberal like Franklin labeled the episode "an act of violent injustice" and maintained that the East India Company deserved full compensation.

The reaction in Parliament can be easily imagined. With large majorities, in the spring of 1774, the statesmen at Westminster passed a discontinuous series of four disciplinary measures that have come to be known together as the "Intolerable" and the "Coercive" Acts. First of all, by the Boston Port Bill that hitherto intractable port was closed tightly to all outside commerce until such time as the royal authorities were satisfied that the trade of Great Britain might safely be carried on there and "His Majesty's customs duly collected"; nor was the port to be opened again until the East India Company had been given full compensation for damages suffered. Another disciplinary measure, the Massachusetts Government Act, was aimed at bringing the troublesome colony back to its senses; the old charter of 1691 was virtually abrogated, and town meetings— which in the hands of the stormy Samuel Adams had led to so much of the discontent—were forbidden to assemble without the governor's permission. By the Administration of Justice Act, those British officials charged with murder in the suppression of riots were to be sent to Britain for trial, if the governor or his lieutenant believed that a fair trial in the colonies was out of the question. Finally, the Quartering Act compelled the province of Massachusetts to provide food and lodging for British soldiers.

A fifth measure was also passed, which, while not intended strictly as punitive, helped to intensify ill will. This was the Quebec Act, which extended the boundaries of that province by the annexation of a great tract of land between the Ohio and the Great Lakes, reinstated the French civil law there, and granted religious toleration to the Catholics in Canada. Coming at the time it did, this statute not only incensed the colonies of Virginia, New York, Connecticut, and Massachusetts, whose western territorial pretensions were thereby extinguished, but also infuriated the Puritans of New England. Moreover, it was clear that the generosity of Parliament toward French Canadians was motivated less by a love of toleration than by a desire to separate them from the British colonists and make them look to London for friendliness. The Quebec Act perhaps helped to save French Canada for the British empire and for French culture, but only at the expense of increased suspicion in the English-speaking colonies.

The Intolerable Acts were supplemented by strong administrative measures. General Thomas Gage, commander-in-chief of the armed forces in the colonies, was appointed governor of Massachusetts, and four regiments were ordered to the scene of discontent. Gage believed that the colonists "will be Lyons whilst we are lambs but if we take the resolute part they will undoubtedly prove very meek." Unfortunately for this prognostication, the New Englanders had read too much of Locke and had lived too long as practically self-governing Englishmen to forget that governments rested upon the consent of the governed; and many of them meant to express in no uncertain terms their unwillingness to consent to the Intolerable Acts. Even colonists who had formerly been disturbed by Tea Party vandalism and had been inclined to approve of compensation now were alienated by Parliament's harshness. As Governor John Penn wrote from Philadelphia: "They look upon the chastisement of Boston to be purposely rigorous, and held up by way of intimidation to all America. . . . Their delinquency in destroying the East India Company's tea is lost in the attention given to what is here called the too severe punishment of shutting up the port, altering the Constitution, and making an act, as they term it, screening the officers and soldiers shedding American blood."

Until the Intolerable Acts were passed, the most tangible issue between the British government and the colonists seemed to have been that of taxation, and the slogan "No taxation without representation" had been boldly flaunted by the Americans to justify their opposition to Grenville's and Townshend's acts. Yet it has been questioned whether the Americans would have consented to taxation by the British Parliament even if they had in fact been represented. Since the founding of Jamestown, the colonists had indeed been taxed without representation, but on occasion there had been significant agitation against this generally accepted procedure.

Actually, when the colonists spoke about their political rights as Englishmen, they were interpreting those rights differently from Englishmen. Since the colonies had been founded, English constitutional theories had undergone fundamental changes. The seventeenth century had witnessed the beginning of the victory of parliamentary sovereignty over royal sovereignty. During the eighteenth century, the practice was gradually established that Parliament legislate for the nation as a whole. That practice is still basic in the British constitutional system. A member of Parliament need not be a resident of the constituency he represents, for he is regarded as morally bound to be guided by the national welfare rather than by merely local interests. This representative scheme is known as "virtual representation." In the eighteenth century most Britons believed that it applied to the whole British empire.

But American practice had developed in another direction. At first the colonies had been small, isolated, extremely suspicious of one another, and differentiated by variant and sometimes conflicting rights and privileges set down in their diverse charters. Virginians found it hard to believe that a man from Pennsylvania or Massachusetts could virtually represent them or that a man from London or Glasgow could represent them and Pennsylvanians equally. Furthermore, colonial representatives were generally chosen by a much broader suffrage than in England, and so being elected depended upon winning the suffrage of more than a select few. The greater number of voters also tended to increase the popular interest in issues of a local character. A legislator from a town was expected to represent his town, not some nearby or distant areas; and representatives from tidewater constituents did not expect to win their reelection by scrupulous devotion to the needs of the frontier. Thus, while British practice had developed the concept of virtual representation, colonial practice had brought forth the doctrine of "direct" or "geographical representation," whereby each colony had its own legislative system within which each deputy represented the interests of his own constituents. Americans were prone to believe that the satisfactory resolution of local issues would result automatically in the promotion of the general welfare.

The colonists' champions at first had argued that home-rule privileges had been granted them in colonial charters, which were derived from the crown and antedated the rise of Parliament, and that therefore they were not bound to accept Parliament's pretensions over them. From their point of view, while George III was their ruler, as he was of Great Britain, he ruled over them through a different political system—in other words, the empire was not a unitary but, rather, a pluralistic structure. Since, however, for a century the colonists had accepted the right of Parliament to legislate for them and had rarely questioned its authority, now to deny that authority, basing that denial upon the prerogative of the monarchs who had granted the charters, was somewhat unconvincing.

Eventually the colonial thinkers saw that the justification of their cause would have to be argued on philosophical and rationalistic rather than on traditional and legal grounds. In other words, they would have to switch from historical precedents to logical arguments. The English political philosophers of the seventeenth century offered them the rationalization they were seeking. John Locke's theory of social contract was especially influential. His *Two Treatises on Civil Government* had concluded that

> whensoever . . . the legislative shall . . . either by
> ambition, fear, folly, or corruption, endeavor to grasp
> themselves, or put into the hands of any other, an
> absolute power over the lives, liberties, and estates of the
> people, by this breach of trust they forfeit the power the
> people had put into their hands for quite contrary ends,
> and it devolves to the people, who have a right to resume
> their original liberty, and by the establishment of a new
> legislative (such as they shall think fit), provide for their
> own safety and security, which is the end for which they
> are in society.

The appeal to Locke's *Treatises*, now over three-quarters of a century old, was seldom made directly, but the ideas of "social contract," "fundamental law," "higher justice," and "natural rights" were in the atmosphere of eighteenth-century America. More recent writers on the eternal problem of justice kept these ideas fresh in the minds of the literate. William Blackstone, for example, had maintained in his *Commentaries on the Laws of England* (London, 1765–1769), destined to become the standard law textbook of Englishmen and Americans of that generation, that human laws have no validity if they are contrary to the law of nature or the law of God; and Montesquieu's *Spirit of the Laws,* translated into English, along with other books of the French *philosophes,* confirmed Americans in their belief that a just government was a government of laws and not of men, of enduring principles and not of temporary decisions. The recent conflicts over the stamp, tea, and other taxes had kept such ideas fresh and had made them common property. They were publicly pronounced in town meetings, sermons, rallies of Sons of Liberty, and political pamphlets; and they were proclaimed in private debate at taverns and country stores. These ideas provided the intellectual ingredient in the rising spirit of independence. Here was a set of philosophical principles to justify the colonists' defiance wherever historical precedent might be insufficient. They were much more, however—they provided a program for a "thoroughgoing reform," if the colonists should so decide.

The American colonists were now face to face with the necessity for some bold decision. Previously they had been able to bring pressure against the acts of Parliament to bear upon Parliament itself, and Parliament, favorably disposed, had made timely concessions. But now the Intolerable Acts revealed an unfavorably disposed Parliament intent upon meeting force with force. Would the colonists be made to yield, or would they counter with still more violence?

Massachusetts was the object of the Coercive or Intolerable Acts, and defiance appeared first in her county conventions, but it was Virginia that took the initiative in showing the sympathy of the other colonies. On May 27, 1774, the Virginia House of Burgesses invited the other colonies to send delegates to a Continental Congress that was to meet in Philadelphia in September. The delegates were

> to deliberate and determine upon wise and proper
> measures to be by them recommended to all the colonies,
> for the recovery and establishment of their just rights and
> liberties, civil and religious, and the restoration of union

and harmony between Great Britain and the colonies,
most ardently desired by all good men.

The Congress was attended by outstanding figures from all the colonies except Georgia. John Adams in later years classified the delegates as "one third Whig; another Tory; the rest mongrel." While the
estimate was only a subjective, ex post facto recollection, presumably
the Congress, like the country at large, was about equally divided
into the militant, the cautious, and the undecided.

John Adams, Samuel Adams, and Patrick Henry led the radicals
to victory in the Congress. They persuaded that body to endorse the
"Resolves," adopted a short time before by Suffolk County, Massachusetts. These resolves maintained that the Intolerable Acts were
unconstitutional and should not be obeyed, and urged resistance
through the organizing of a new civil government, the raising of
troops, and the suspension of all commercial intercourse with Britain
and the British West Indies. The radicals were instrumental in defeating a proposal put forward by the conservatives, suggesting that
the colonies form a union and enter into a new constitutional arrangement with the mother country. Then radicals and conservatives
together adopted, on October 14, 1774, a Declaration of American
Rights and Grievances. This declaration, after setting forth the colonists' complaints, asserted that the colonists "are entitled to life, liberty, and property" and "have never ceded to any sovereign power
whatever a right to dispose of either [sic] without their consent." The
declaration went on to state that because the colonists had no voice
in Parliament, they were "entitled to a free and exclusive power of
legislation in their several provincial legislatures, where their right of
representation can alone be preserved, in all cases of taxation and internal policy, subject only to the negative of their sovereign." This
wording was a fairly explicit formulation of the idea that the confed-
erative British crown could veto colonial legislation but that the Parliament of the United Kingdom could not make law governing the
colonies' internal affairs.

To cap this declaration, the radicals pushed through the "Association," pledged to import no goods of any kind from Great Britain
and, should this fail to bring redress of wrongs, to ship no exports except rice to Europe. The Congress was an extralegal body and had no
authority to enforce obedience to the Association. But the radicals
were prepared to cope with this problem. In every city, town, and
county they organized "Committees of Safety and Inspection," made

up of those qualified to vote for members of the colonial legislatures. These committees assumed the responsibility of enforcing the nonimportation agreement, and they sometimes dealt sternly with violators, seizing imported goods and plying tar and feathers. Despite conservatives' qualms regarding the effect of colonial resistance upon trade and the preservation of order, the colonies successively ratified the work of the Congress and approved the Association. How well the Association's boycott was enforced is shown by the drop in English imports from £2,532,919 in 1774 to £82,385 in 1775.

This was by far the most serious decline in business yet experienced by English exporters and induced alarmed mercantile interests in Britain to petition Parliament for repeal of the Intolerable Acts. The cause of repeal was eloquently championed by Edmund Burke, who spoke for conciliation with Americans because they were Englishmen fighting for their traditional rights, and by Lord Chatham, who feared the disruption of the British empire he had done so much to erect. The House of Lords was the setting of Chatham's impressive warning:

> Every motive of justice and of policy, of dignity and of
> prudence, urges you to allay the ferment in America by a
> removal of your troops from Boston, by a repeal of your
> acts of Parliament, and by a display of amicable
> disposition towards your colonies. On the other hand,
> every danger and every hazard impend to deter you from
> perseverance in your present ruinous course—foreign
> war hanging over your heads by a slight and brittle
> thread; France and Spain watching your conduct and
> waiting for the maturity of errors, with a vigilant eye to
> America and the temper of your colonies.

Events were to show that Chatham was right. Certain individuals in France—particularly the minister of foreign affairs, Comte de Vergennes—were waiting for Britain to commit the errors that would split her empire asunder and had sent agents to the British colonies, who let French interest become known. But Chatham's foresight was of no use. Lord North and the Tories had no intention of backing down, either to the radicals in the colonies or to the political opposition at home. North was willing to go only so far as to sponsor, in February 1775, a set of conciliatory resolutions, promising relief from parliamentary taxation for those colonies that assumed their share of imperial defense and made provisions for the support of the crown's local officers. But the apparent pacific import of North's "olive branch," though in fact offered to the colonists, was nullified by his assuring George III that the colonists' rebellious acts would be suppressed and by the Restraining Act of March 30, 1775, whose intention was the destruction of New England's seaborne commerce.

All that was needed in the spring of 1775 was an "incident" to transform the struggle from one of boycotts to one of bullets. The radicals and the more militant colonists had been gathering military supplies and drilling militiamen, to the dismay of the conservative faction and the anger of the British leaders in the provinces. Finally, General Gage, as governor of Massachusetts, decided to seize the military stores that had been collected by the colonists at Concord. A contingent of soldiers was sent off to Concord on April 18, 1775. Early the next morning it encountered at Lexington a small band of American volunteers, or "Minutemen," drawn up on the green. An order by the British officers to disperse resulted in shots destined to be "heard round the world" (as was later said of a shot fired at the bridge at Concord). The Minutemen could not prevent the British from reaching Concord and destroying the stores there. On the way back, however, the British were under continual fire from "the embattled farmers."

Lexington and Concord drove both sides to more uncompromising positions. Lord North's government issued a proclamation against the "rebels," and the military authorities were ordered to deal appropriately with these "traitors." Meanwhile the colonists were marshaling forces against the "butchers" and "massacrers of innocent people," and New England troops in great numbers began to congregate in Cambridge near Boston. "Patriot" forces elsewhere seized British strongholds.

On May 10, 1775, the Second Continental Congress assembled in Philadelphia. It brought together an unprecedented number of able colonial representatives, including Franklin, Washington, Jefferson, Samuel Adams, John Adams, and Hancock. Lord North's "olive branch" was rejected because the Intolerable Acts had not been repealed and because Parliament still maintained its right to tax the colonists. Once more the Congress petitioned George III to redress their grievances, and when this appeal went unheeded, it directed its energies to more belligerent ends. The thousands of volunteers around Boston could not be supplied without aid from the Congress. Congress adopted them as "the Continental Army" and appointed

George Washington its commander-in-chief. Yet, as Jefferson was to write in 1782: "It is well known that in July, 1775, a separation from Great Britain and the establishment of a Republican Government had not yet entered any person's mind."

In the fall of 1775, at least five colonial legislatures of British North America were still on record as opposed to separation from the mother country, and as late as January 1776, the officers' mess presided over by Washington was still toasting the health of His Majesty. But outside the meeting hall of the delegates and the officers' mess, men at country crossroads, parsons in village pulpits, radicals in town taverns, and pamphleteers in city bookstores were expressing ideas and opinions whose general tenor represented a growing demand for national autonomy. Royal governors and officeholders in the colonies recognized the trend, and increasing numbers of them now took passage to England.

The trend became a full-fledged conviction in certain quarters when Thomas Paine published his pamphlet entitled *Common Sense* (January 1776). Paine was a former exciseman who had been turned out of office in England, a social misfit newly arrived in America. With incisive logic and psychological insight, Paine based his appeal on economic reasons. He not only denied that American prosperity depended on union with Britain but went so far as to maintain that any prosperity in America had come in spite of British interference: "America would have flourished as much, and probably much more, had no European power taken any notice of her. The commerce by which she hath enriched herself are the necessaries of life, and will always have a market while eating is the custom of Europe." Then, to tear the colonists away from the sentimental ties that bound them to the mother country in spite of economic disadvantages, Paine dynamited the monarchical principle. With what must have been keen personal relish he exposed the folly and inadequacy of his former royal master in a manner that was convincing to those who were already prepared to believe that kings were an unnecessary evil. Finally, he turned on the sacrosanct British constitution. According to Paine, although the House of Commons was supposed to speak for the common people, it was in reality held in check by the "remains of aristocratical tyranny in the person of the Peers" and the "remains of Monarchical tyranny in the person of the King." There was no other course open, Paine argued, than separation. And so acceptable was his argument that within a short time a hundred thousand copies of it were being read in the homes of New York, the plantations of

the Carolinas, and the already republican-inclined frontier settlements. Thousands of colonists could exclaim with Washington:
"Sound doctrine and unanswerable reasons!"

The cause of independence was now taken up by the provincial
assemblies. It was already quite clear that so long as Europe's monarchs hostile to George III did not interfere, the colonists would
probably not prevail in their quarrel with the British government. It
was equally clear that so long as the quarrel remained one between
the British government and insurgent Englishmen, other European
monarchs would not interfere. Independence, however, might make
a significant difference. Various colonies, such as Massachusetts,
North Carolina, and Virginia, instructed their delegates at Philadelphia to assent with their colleagues to a separation from Britain. On
May 15, the Continental Congress advised the colonies in turn to establish themselves into states with their governments reorganized on
a basis of popular consent. Then, on June 7, Richard Henry Lee of
Virginia moved in Congress that "these United Colonies are, and of
right ought to be, free and independent states; that they are absolved
from all allegiance to the British crown; and that all political connection between them and the state of Great Britain is, and ought to be,
totally dissolved." John Adams of Massachusetts seconded the mo-
tion, and although the conservative delegates were afraid to go along
with his plea for an immediate declaration, a committee was appointed to draft a formal declaration. The committee included Jefferson, Franklin, and John Adams.

Their proposed draft of a declaration of independence was
adopted on July 4, 1776. It was almost entirely the work of Jefferson.
In the introductory and final paragraphs of the declaration he
seemed at times merely to paraphrase the natural-rights philosophy
of John Locke. The Declaration of Independence held that in the relations of peoples with each other just claims were dependent upon a
higher justice than man-made laws, upon the "Laws of Nature and of
Nature's God," explicable in terms of self-evident truths. Among
these truths was the existence of a God-given equality among men.
This natural equality implied an inalienable claim to certain rights,
among which were "life, liberty, and the pursuit of happiness." "To
secure these rights, governments are instituted among men, deriving
their just powers from the consent of the governed." Violation of
such "just powers" by a tyrannical government freed the governed
from their obligation to obey it and enabled them to seek a new government. The treatises which Locke had written in the seventeenth

century to justify revolt against an English king in order to establish the sovereignty of Parliament were, with unpremeditated irony, used by Jefferson and his associates in the eighteenth century to justify revolution against both king and Parliament in order to establish the sovereignty of a new nation. Realizing, in the words of Benjamin Franklin, that if they did not hang together, they would probably hang separately, the signers of the Declaration of Independence, by its final sentence, agreed to "mutually pledge to each other our lives, our fortunes, and our sacred honor."

The portion of the declaration that intervened between the introductory paragraphs and the final pledge was more realistic and concrete. It summarized colonial grievances, twenty-seven in all. George III was made to appear personally responsible for the actions of Parliament. The grievances enumerated were not equally significant or profound; some appear carping, others distorted, and only a few beyond the boundary of peaceful compromise. But the declaration was in part a propaganda document, aimed at crystallizing opinion at home and winning sympathetic support abroad among the enemies of Great Britain. Its influence, derived from the simple epitome of eighteenth-century political rationalism in its opening paragraphs, far outlived the immediate issues that called it into being. It has served as an inspiration in all subsequent struggles for the rights of man.

The adoption of the Declaration of Independence formalized the separation of the colonies from the mother country. It also signified the advent of that critical moment when the colonists had to align themselves in opposite camps, according to their loyalties and convictions. Those who chose to renounce loyalty to the British empire in order to establish a new nation called themselves "Patriots"; those who remained true to the empire called themselves "Loyalists" while the "Patriots" called them "Tories." In their turn the "Loyalists" called the "Patriots" "Traitors." Considered in this light, the American Revolution was not only a war between a nation-in-existence and a nation-in-formation; it was also a bitter civil war. And it rapidly involved Britain's European enemies, thereby becoming an intercontinental struggle.

The adoption of the Declaration of Independence, together with its commitment to armed conflict, had been a victory for the radicals because of their positive program, efficient organization, and skillful propaganda. Nevertheless, as is generally true of the militant factions in significant revolutionary movements, they were only a minority. A good part of the population was either indifferent to the struggle or cautiously noncommittal. Generally speaking, the Patriots were much more powerful in New England and Virginia than in the middle colonies, and in the Deep South they seem to have achieved only parity in strength with the Loyalists.

As might be expected, political affiliations tended to follow social and economic cleavages among the colonial population. Thus, the mechanics, yeoman farmers, and small tradesmen in the commercial North were strong supporters of the Revolution, for in such a victory they saw a chance for a new political, economic, and social order. The well-to-do northern merchants, on the other hand, wanted freedom from mercantilist regulations, but they feared control by the radicals. In Virginia a significant proportion of the most elevated group, the landed proprietors, favored the Revolution—and furnished many of its most important leaders—sometimes because, badly indebted to London merchants or disapproving of the way in which the British government had handled the western lands, they hoped for freer trade and lands in a regime under their own direction. On the frontier the settlers generally favored the Revolution. The frontiersman was often a recent immigrant with small wealth or social prestige. He had little use for either British imperialistic pretensions or the rising economic power of the colonial merchants and planters on the Atlantic seaboard. In the Revolution, he challenged the imperialists of London; later, he was to challenge the domination of his American antagonists.

The Loyalists, looked upon by the Patriots as counterrevolutionaries and traitors, suffered bitterly from the Revolution. Where the Patriots were in power, the Loyalists found themselves disfranchised, deprived of court protection, and denied free speech, if, indeed, they were not banished and their lands confiscated. Since the Declaration of Independence was a repudiation not only of the English crown but, as a consequence, of the Church of England as well—rebellion compounded with heresy—the Loyalists comprised many outstanding conservative colonists. Landowners, lawyers, doctors, college officials, and a large part of the Anglican clergy were to be found among them. In addition the Loyalists had their quota of rich merchants and, of course, the crown officials. While large numbers took ship to England or the West Indies, something like 60,000 Loyalists migrated north to Nova Scotia, Prince Edward Island, Quebec, the upper St. Lawrence, and the lands around Lake Ontario. This migration of the "U.E.L."—United Empire Loyalists, as they are known in Canada—laid the foundation of the English-speaking population of that country. In this respect, the American Revolution was very significant for Canada—and to be a "U.E.L." there is similar to being an "S.A.R." (Son of the American Revolution) in the United States.

In a war against the mightiest imperial power in the world, the obstacles confronting the Patriots were well-nigh insurmountable. Wars cannot be won without heavy expenditures of money—and the Continental Congress had been granted no power by the separate colonies, now self-styled "states," to levy taxes. It had to rely on paper money, requisitions upon thirteen independent and none too cooperative states, and foreign loans. Having virtually nothing to back it up, this Continental currency depreciated so completely that a new expression of contempt passed into English speech: "not worth a Continental!" In the end the situation was so chaotic and ridiculous that Continental bills were used in jest as wallpaper and as material for masquerade costumes. Congress also requisitioned funds and supplies from the states, but without a great deal of success. It was no more successful in its requisitions than Parliament had been in the imperial wars.

If the finances of the colonists were in an almost impossible state, their military preparations were fully as deplorable. Washington never had a sufficient number of soldiers at his command. Throughout the war, he had only a small fraction of the available manpower. In 1776, at its greatest peak, the total force at his disposal numbered not more than 90,000—or approximately one-eighth of the men of fighting age. But in the years 1779–1780, the army had dwindled to half that number—or not more than one-sixteenth of the potential soldiers. Furthermore, the majority of the American forces were militia, and for them the commander-in-chief had little use, complaining that they "come in, you cannot tell how; go, you cannot tell where, consume your provisions, exhaust your stores, and leave you at last at a critical moment."

The suffering of Washington's pitiful army in the winter's encampment at Valley Forge in 1778–1779 and the defeatism of 1779–1780 have become part of the American saga. But sacrifice, treason, and mutiny could have been lessened if the country at large had supported Congress and the army with something of the ardor exhibited in subsequent national wars. The Continental forces lacked clothes, shoes, blankets, tents, and other equipment. The shortcomings of the

medical and hospital facilities beggared description. When the soldiers did get their pay, it was generally in depreciated currency. War
profiteers abounded everywhere, and more than one American
farmer sold his produce to the English for gold, which the Continentals did not have. As early as 1775 Washington had stated bitterly:
"Such a dearth of public spirit and want of virtue, such stock-job-
bing, and fertility in all the low arts to obtain advantages of one kind
or another . . . I never saw before, and pray God I may never be
witness to again. . . . Such a dirty, mercenary spirit pervades the
whole, that I should not be at all surprised at any disaster that may
happen."

Yet, notwithstanding the heartrending conditions, Washington
managed to win out. In large measure this was due to his own leadership and to the quality of his motley but unconquerable followers.
Washington was able to keep something of an army together despite
the necessity of being regularly on the defensive against larger and
better trained forces, to win occasional dashing victories of great importance to morale, and to keep the confidence of most of his generals and Congress through a long period of despair, until finally an alliance with the French helped to turn the tables in his favor.

Another important reason for ultimate American success lay in
the generals and armies opposing Washington. As one of the most
powerful imperial nations in the world, Britain certainly had the
naval and military resources to bring the colonists to their knees, had
those resources been properly utilized. That they were ineptly employed was due in part to the divided attitude in London toward the
prosecution of the war—thus preventing Britain from making the all-
out effort of which she was capable. Some of the British had little
ardor for this civil war, and the redcoat uniforms were sometimes
worn by wretched volunteers and criminals pardoned "on condition
of their enlistment in his Majesty's army." When insufficient numbers were forthcoming, several thousand mercenaries were hired
from German princes. The most inspired soldiers on the British side
were the Loyalist Volunteers, who fought to defend their homes and
principles. One of the most important English generals, Sir William
Howe, was a commander of genuine ability, but his heart was not in
his work. He had opposed the imposition of coercive measures prior
to the outbreak of hostilities; he preferred Boston's social gaiety to a
hard campaign in the field; and he made peaceful overtures to persuade the colonists to give up the struggle, hoping that the war

would terminate without his having to press home the smashing defeats he inflicted on the Americans in New York in 1776. Other British generals, like Sir Henry Clinton and Lord Cornwallis, were mediocre leaders who disputed with each other over strategy.

Geography also presented disadvantages to the British. The world's most powerful fleet was forced to operate three thousand miles away from its base. The results expected from a coastal blockade proved disappointing, especially when the French fleet joined the American privateers. Then, too, the British soldiers were harassed and overcome in the forests of the interior. They captured and held some of the largest ports such as New York, Charleston, and Savannah until the end of the war, but they were unable to capture, or to hold for long, the interior—even in New York, where the Loyalists were strongest and the Indians mostly on the British side.

A large share of the colonists' success was due to the intervention and aid of the French. At the outbreak of war, even before the Declaration of Independence, Congress astutely sent Silas Deane as a secret agent to France, the traditional enemy of Britain, to secure aid. After independence was declared, Deane was joined by Franklin and Arthur Lee. Had the conservative governments of Europe made common cause with the crown of Britain, the American confederation might have eventually had to consider reconciliation. But the French desire for *revanche* and for a share of the trade with the prosperous new states in America proved stronger than the French fear of rebellion. Secret funds were secured by Congress from France even before the French government formally recognized the United States, and afterward from Spain and private Dutch bankers as well. These foreign loans were used to purchase supplies in Europe, and on occasion even to pay interest on domestic bonds. This secret aid from France proved to be one of the war's most decisive factors.

In addition to the desperately needed money advanced to the colonists, a steady stream of supplies and officers, of whom the Marquis de Lafayette was one of the least well trained, left French and French West Indies ports, even while France was still ostensibly neutral. In October 1777, an American victory, won largely with equipment supplied secretly by the French, in the interior of New York at Saratoga (now Schuylerville) proved the turning point of the war. It caused the British to renew efforts at reconciliation and induced the French, out of fear that reconciliation might in fact occur, to make a formal pact of alliance with the United States. Treaties of commerce and alliance were signed in February 1778, whereby France recognized the independence of the United States, correctly expecting Great Britain to declare war in consequence.

Spain and the United Provinces followed France in going to war with Great Britain. Thereupon London had an international conflict, and not merely a colonial revolt, on its hands. In 1780, because the British insisted on searching all vessels for shipments to their enemies, almost all the other large European powers, without declaring formal war, created a League of Armed Neutrality, pledged to defend themselves against British high-handedness on the seas. The League of Armed Neutrality included Russia, Prussia, the United Provinces (before they formally entered the war), the Scandinavian countries, Portugal, and the Kingdom of the Two Sicilies.

Thus Britain paid the penalty of success; almost alone she faced a hostile Europe and America. Her erstwhile ally Prussia gave her no aid, not only because Frederick, rejoicing at the chance to repay Britain for her alleged desertion during the Seven Years' War, now joined the Armed Neutrality, but also because Prussia and Austria simultaneously engaged in another bout of their chronic struggle. They were involved in a war of succession over Bavaria in 1778–1779, which ended after one indecisive campaign with few casualties and only minor territorial changes and without spreading beyond the confines of southern Germany, largely because the potential allies of the two protagonists were otherwise occupied. This War of the Bavarian Succession is sometimes called "the Potato War" because the worst sufferers in it were the farmers' crops.

After the Alliance of 1778 the French fleet and army participated increasingly in the War of American Independence. When the Spanish were induced to join the alliance, the French and the Spanish made a formidable but ultimately unsuccessful effort to invade England. They also laid siege to Gibraltar and continued it until the peace was signed. France sent expeditions to challenge the British in the East and the West Indies, Africa, and South America. Huge loans were made to America and to France's other allies. French ships cooperated with the American Captain John Paul Jones in attacking British commerce, and a French fleet prevented the rescue by sea of Cornwallis' besieged forces at Yorktown. And at Yorktown itself the Patriots' triumph was made possible because 5,745 Continentals and 3,200 militia were strongly reinforced by 7,800 French marines and soldiers. Meanwhile the British government was faced with anti-

Catholic riots at home and threats of rebellion in Ireland. The war continued for over a year after Yorktown because the French were at least as anxious to win control of the West Indies as to free the Americans from Britain and the Spanish were even more anxious to secure Gibraltar. In short, the War of American Independence was much more than the Revolutionary War in America. It was worldwide, fought on all the seas and all the continents—a significant phase of the Anglo-French "Second Hundred Years' War" for colonial and naval superiority.

Early in 1782 the ministry of Lord North fell, and the Whigs came into office. Concerned with fighting France, Spain, and the United Provinces simultaneously and with keeping a wary eye on the Armed Neutrality of the North, the new government took a conciliatory attitude toward the Americans. The Patriots were offered all concessions short of independence, but they refused to accept. When, however, the Americans were finally offered full recognition of independence, Franklin and his colleagues made a separate treaty of peace with the Whig government, although their actions constituted a violation of the alliance treaty of 1778, wherein the Americans had promised not to make peace independently of France. The Americans, not recognizing that French delay in making a general peace was due chiefly to Spanish insistence upon the return of Gibraltar, were motivated by fear of possible secret understandings with regard to North America by Britain, France, and Spain. When the separate "preliminaries" of Anglo-American peace became known, the astute Franklin told the French minister that he hoped the Americans would not lose the friendship of France because of "a single indiscretion."

By final terms of the Treaty of Paris, signed on behalf of Britain, France, and Spain, as well as the United States, on September 3, 1783, the independence of the United States was acknowledged, as were its territorial claims west to the Mississippi, north to Canada, and south to Florida. The Americans were also afforded the right to fish in Newfoundland waters. The United States agreed that there should be no further persecution of the Loyalists, British creditors would not be hindered in collecting debts in courts, and Congress would "earnestly recommend" to the state legislatures that the seized property of Loyalists be restored to them—a recommendation which the state legislatures, incidentally, did not accept, so that relatively few Loyalists ever got their property back, and those few only after a new federal constitution went into operation (1789). All in all, the terms of the treaty were generous to the United States largely because the British had already embarked upon a policy of winning the Americans away from France. Despite vindictiveness on both sides, the habits implanted by generations of interdependence, it proved, were not easily broken even though France also was willing to make generous concessions.

Aside from the loss of the American colonies, the treaties that ended the war were not so disastrous for Britain as might have been supposed, primarily because of British naval successes after the surrender of Cornwallis at Yorktown. At the Battle of the Saints (1782) the English West Indies fleet administered a resounding defeat to the French fleet and once more restored rule of the waves to Britannia. As a result, Britain lost to France only minor colonies—in the West Indies (Tobago) and in Africa (Senegal). To Spain she ceded Minorca in the Mediterranean and the territory in America known as "Florida," which at that time was larger than the present state of Florida. On the other hand, by a separate peace concluded in 1784, she secured from the United Provinces mercantile privileges in the Malayan area and trading stations in India.

Britain emerged from the war still the strongest commercial and imperial power in the world. But it was a chastened Britain that now faced a hostile world. She was isolated, her empire was split, and grave doubts existed whether empires were worth the effort they cost to build up if they were destined to break away when they became strong. If France had not strained her treasury to the cracking point in the effort to break up the British empire, and if Vergennes had not died shortly after the Peace of Versailles, depriving the king of his masterful statesmanship (1787), France, emerging victorious from the War of American Independence, might have put an end to British hegemony in Europe.

If the independence of the United States had meant only that a set of loosely confederated state governments had replaced the British crown in its thirteen former colonies, American independence would merely have been a successful revolt, replacing an old set of "ins" by a new set of "ins." But American independence also brought major social and economic changes at home and made a significant intellectual impact upon Western political thought, and so it may justifiably be called a revolution as well.

For the United States, peace was to bring many challenges. Independence meant a readjustment of American institutions to a new status in relationship not only to the United Kingdom and to the rest of the world but also to each other. Each of the thirteen new states had to provide itself with a constitution immediately after the Declaration of Independence and to decide, from 1777 on, whether to adhere to the union formed by the Articles of Confederation—which all of them did by 1781. Thus those two documents became, to a certain extent, not mere statements of theory but a prescription for the structure of thirteen separate state constitutions. The young republics had to achieve self-reliance, federal cooperation, and international standing, and to endure close inspection as they worked at such problems as modifying aristocratic land-tenure practices, disestablishing churches, and secularizing education. Ideas and ideals, such as the social contract and the rights of man, which had spread far in Europe, were to be tested in actual application and not in theory, and the outcome of the American experiment provoked much speculation and excitement if not deep concern across the Atlantic. The methods that the new confederation was to use in solving the problems that arose from independence were to be keenly observed in Europe, and both the successes that the Americans encountered and the blunders that they made were to be observed just as keenly.

As Europe watched the American efforts to realize a political philosophy that was essentially European, she became increasingly aware of the new nationalism in the United States and of its growing importance in international affairs. European governments saw in the independent American states a chance to acquire new allies and new markets. And for its part the young confederation became increasingly aware that it was in a position to affect the international balance. The United States, however, not only provided an additional potential pawn in the endless game of power politics but also served as a sort of laboratory in political experimentation for Europe and the rest of the world.

For one thing, the victory of the Patriots put an end to Britain's restrictions on the seizure and settlement of trans-Allegheny lands. A process of breaking up large landed estates, which often accompanies successful revolutions, took place also as a result of the American Revolution. All the domains that had previously belonged to the crown now became the property of the states and were eventually to be more accessible than formerly. Furthermore, the old quitrents, which occupants had had to pay to the crown or a proprietor—rang-

ing from a penny an acre to a shilling a hundred acres per annum—
were now abolished. Former unpopular restrictions on land tenure,
such as the reservation of appropriate trees for use by the Royal
Navy, were now ended. As already indicated, many of the Tory estates confiscated or partly confiscated by state legislatures, generally
at the height of the war, were never returned. The largest of the confiscated estates, that of the Penns of Pennsylvania, was worth almost
£1 million sterling, but the Penns were paid $650,000. Lastly the
Revolution dealt a deathblow to certain feudal practices such as entail; on the ground that grants of land did not alienate the royal claim
to it if the direct line of specified heirs failed, entail had prevented
the heir of lands from selling or giving them away as he saw fit. It was
soon abolished by the states. So was primogeniture, the practice by
which all lands were turned over to the eldest son if a father's will
did not otherwise provide. By permitting the breakup of large holdings, the disappearance of entail and primogeniture, more than the
abolition of titles, symbolized the aim of some revolutionary leaders
to discourage the emergence of a hereditary landed aristocracy in the
United States.

Independence also put an end to Britain's regulation of American trade and industry, as well as to her control of finance and coinage. The encouragement of manufacturing enterprises had been recommended to all colonies by the First Continental Congress, and in
1775 the "United Company of Philadelphia for promoting American
Manufactures" was organized to make American woolen, linen, and
cotton cloth on a large scale. The manufacture of munitions and guns
was of prime necessity to the Patriots, and in 1778 a government ar-
mory was founded in Springfield. Gunmaking was carried on in a
number of places, and more than one state offered bounties to encourage production of steel, powder, and so forth. Paper mills increased from thirty-seven in 1776 to over a hundred in 1789. Noninterference and the impetus of the war stimulated the production of
wool in the new states and eventually of cotton in the South. The
Carolinas exported rice, but the indigo industry declined because of
the cessation of British bounties.

The Revolution also wrought far-reaching changes in religious
affairs. Most affected was, of course, the Church of England, which
had been the established church (and therefore tax-supported) in
Virginia, Maryland, New York, the Carolinas, and Georgia. The Revolution stripped the Anglicans of their privileged position, although
separation of church and state did not take place in Virginia until

1786, and in New England the Congregationalists kept their established position until the nineteenth century. The Revolution tended to weaken the popular hold of the churches and, at the same time, strengthen the movement toward greater religious liberty.

The American Revolution, by making American court systems independent of English methods, was partly responsible for the reforming of penal codes in the last decades of the eighteenth century. In keeping with the current humanitarian spirit reflected by the famed European penologists Beccaria and Howard, penalties, prisons, and the treatment of debtors were ameliorated. While the reign of George III saw the list of offenses punishable by death mount in Britain until they exceeded two hundred, the opposite trend was taking place in the American states. Virginia, thanks to Jefferson, and Pennsylvania led the way. The Philadelphia Society for Alleviating the Miseries of Public Prisons was founded in 1787, and in the 1790's Pennsylvania restricted the death penalty to punishment for premeditated murder.

Slowly something was done after independence on behalf of the Black slave in the northern states. Vermont (not yet recognized as a state) declared slavery a violation of natural rights and eventually abolished it in its state constitution, and in 1780 Pennsylvania provided for gradual emancipation. Although John Adams hoped that a proposed Massachusetts emancipation bill would "sleep for a time" since there were already "causes enough of jealousy, discord, and division," the courts of Massachusetts ended slavery in 1781 because its constitutional provision that "all men are born free and equal" made slavery an incongruity. New Hampshire's courts reached the same conclusion. The other states followed these examples at varying rates of speed. The citizens of Danbury, Connecticut, declared that it was "a palpable absurdity to complain of attempts to enslave us while we are actually enslaving others," but it took Connecticut's legislators until 1784 to recognize this anomaly and provide for gradual emancipation in their state. Rhode Island followed suit that year, but New York and New Jersey acted only in 1799 and 1804 respectively.

The Revolution also had a marked effect upon education in the United States. During the Revolutionary War, public, private, and church schools often had to close because of military operations and demands for men and money. The colleges suffered especially, since they were sometimes occupied by armies. For example, the College of William and Mary temporarily served as Cornwallis' headquarters and, after his surrender, was turned into a French military hospital. Reduced enrollments and depreciation of public securities in some cases almost annihilated college revenues.

When the schools opened their doors again, they tended to be less religious and more secular in character. Statesmen like Jefferson, John Adams, and James Madison had previously been concerned about the place of education in the preservation of liberty. During the war Jefferson had drafted "A Bill for the More General Diffusion of Knowledge," suggesting a public school system for Virginia. After the war he revised the curriculum at William and Mary by establishing chairs in modern languages and law to take the place of those in Classics and divinity. Another by-product of the war was the founding at Harvard of a medical faculty. The Revolutionary period also saw a gain in the publication of textbooks. In 1783 Noah Webster's spelling book, which was a sort of Declaration of Independence in the realm of orthography and vocabulary, appeared; over fifty million copies of it were eventually sold. A year later Jedidiah Morse, "the father of American geography," published the first of his textbooks.

Although lacking present-day machinery for turning out war propaganda on a mass scale, the Revolutionary combatants added press and pen to their stock of weapons. As is usually true of propaganda efforts, most of theirs were mediocre and short-lived. Loyalist and Patriot newspapers denounced each other and reviled the opposing side's leaders. Thus the *Pennsylvania Packet* attacked King George as a "second Cain, true likeness of the first," and after the British Major John André's execution as a spy, the New York *Royal Gazette* denounced Washington as a "murderer."

A few Revolutionary poets were worthy of note. John Trumbull, one of the "Connecticut Wits," wrote the humorous epic "M'Fingal," dealing with the opening scenes of the Revolution and burlesquing the Tories. Another of the Connecticut Wits, Joel Barlow, produced a more serious, patriotic epic, "The Columbiad," telling the story of American growth. Philip Freneau, of New Jersey, known in his own day as the "poet of the American Revolution," penned deeply emotional and patriotic poems. He commanded a privateer during the war and on returning from the West Indies was made prisoner by a British vessel. Upon his release in 1780, Freneau wrote "The British Prison Ship." He described his prison as a "slaughterhouse" and cried:

> Americans! A just resentment shew,
> And glut revenge on this detested foe;
> While the warm blood exults the glowing vein
> Still shall resentment in your bosoms reign,
> Can you forget the greedy Briton's ire,
> Your fields in ruin, and your homes on fire,
> No age, no sex from lust and murder free,
> And, black as night, the hell born refugee!

Freneau's indignant outburst was simply an expression of the new spirit of nationalism. However provincial these former colonists might appear when judged by the most advanced European standards, they were now at last their own masters—and they knew it. The new nationalism found expression in the formal annual observance of the adoption of the Declaration of Independence and its highest symbol in the figure of George Washington. His character and appearance, together with his indissoluble association with the victorious outcome of the conflict, enshrined him in the hearts of his countrymen and provided them with a personified emblem of national unity.

Nevertheless, the thirteen former colonies entered the postwar era as loosely united states. As already indicated, back in the fall of 1777, the Continental Congress had hammered out a document known as the Articles of Confederation, which had then been submitted to the individual states for ratification. Not until 1781, when the last state (Maryland) agreed to the proposal, had the Articles gone into effect. So jealous were the states of their prerogatives at this time that the Articles allowed each one to retain "its sovereignty, freedom and independence."

The years during which the nation lived under the Articles of Confederation at one time were called the "Critical Period." The Articles permitted Congress to conduct foreign affairs, declare war, raise an army and navy, borrow money, fix weights and measures, control Indian affairs, provide for the development, sale, and government of the new territories, and exercise authority over certain other matters of common interest to the Confederation. But the all-important right to levy taxes was restricted to the states, as was the regulation of commerce. In addition, certain legislation required the assent of at least nine states; and no amendments could be made to the Articles without the consent of every state. Congress was thus able to raise troops but could not raise taxes to pay them, and its "requisitions" upon the states for money were seldom effective. At the close of their campaigns, the Revolutionary armies faced a return to their homes with their accounts in arrears and little money in their pockets. Discontent reached the point where one band of Pennsylvania troops marched on Philadelphia, frightening the Congress into shifting its quarters to Princeton.

However adequate or inadequate the Articles of Confederation were from the standpoint of effecting and maintaining national unity, they reflected the political philosophy of the period. The Patriots had rebelled against the centralized authority of London, and they were determined not to fall into the same error at home. And as they had overthrown a crowned executive, they made no provision for a one-man executive, lest he become a dictator. The executive function was vested in a committee of thirteen, composed of a representative from each state's delegation to Congress, but its attempts to act when that body was not in session proved disheartening. Nor was any system of national courts provided for in the Articles of Confederation. The absence of a strong executive and a strong judicial branch contributed to the difficulty of enforcing those not inconsiderable powers that the central government had. At every point, a number of political leaders were intent upon having power decentralized and retained by state legislatures. After the weaknesses of the central government became apparent, pressure for a more centralized authority mounted, and the leaders who favored a new, centralized regime were backed by merchants, investors, land speculators, and other groups whose interests were not confined by the limits of their respective states.

The victorious Americans came out of the war hoping to supplement their political freedom with economic prosperity. They were rudely disillusioned from the outset. The republic was gripped by a period of depression and economic stagnation that lasted until 1787. The conflict had diverted men and money from peacetime agriculture and trade to wartime manufacturing and privateering—and cessation of hostilities also brought cessation of the wartime economy. Men were thrown out of work, and only time could effect reconversion. Unfortunately much of the Americans' former prosperity had rested upon the export of raw materials to Great Britain—exports carried largely in American vessels. Not only was the preferential treatment that the British Navigation Acts had given the Americans before the Revolution now ended, but those very Acts automatically placed American commerce in the same category as that of all other foreign nations. John Jay's attempts to secure a reciprocal trade agreement with Britain at this time failed, while new Navigation Acts (1783, 1786, and 1787) sought to keep American vessels out of the British West Indies and to impose heavy tonnage dues upon American ships entering other British ports. Generous concessions made by the French government did not offset these blows, for the Americans preferred British manufactured goods, to which they had long been accustomed. John Adams, sent to London in 1785 as minister, tried to negotiate a commercial treaty, but powerful British mercantile interests killed his proposals, while the British government maintained that the economic advantage of the colonies that had remained loyal should be protected first.

Congress had no powers under the Articles of Confederation to regulate commerce and therefore could take no retaliatory action against the British position. The states refused to grant Congress such powers and finally retaliated individually against British imports. Between 1783 and 1788, ten of the states levied tonnage duties and discriminatory tariffs upon British goods and ships. But these duties differed from place to place and resulted only in the British merchants' seeking out the cheapest port. British goods continued to pour in but could not be counterbalanced by American exports, which continued to be excluded from Britain except on unfavorable terms.

Nor were economic problems confined simply to foreign trade. Each state was jealous of its privileges and powers and suspicious of its neighbors. As a result, bitter economic struggles ensued among them. For example, New York in 1787 levied import duties on the farm products of New Jersey and Connecticut—products required by the markets of New York City. In retaliation New Jersey levied an annual tax of $1,800 on the Sandy Hook lighthouse, which New York had recently acquired. New London businessmen agreed under pledge not to send goods to New York for a year.

The economic life of the new republic suffered grievously also from the plight of its public finances. Now that the war was over and France was having its own financial difficulties, loans were no longer forthcoming from that source. As the Congress under the Articles of Confederation could not raise taxes and thus procure funds to pay interest charges on the national debt, its securities depreciated to a sixth—even at times to a twentieth—of their face value. The holders of these securities, both original subscribers and speculators, had every reason for wanting a firmer government.

The only currency of any real worth was the coinage of foreign origin, but these coins proved insufficient to meet the country's needs, for the unfavorable balance of trade forced their export to help pay for the heavy imports from Europe. The depression of 1785–1786 brought matters to a crisis. Money was scarce, crops were rotting in the fields, and the poor people were in desperate straits. The people of Nantucket, deprived of their British market for whale oil, thought of moving to Halifax and were checked only by a large order from France, wheedled by Lafayette. The demand for more paper money (hence for inflation) spread swiftly. The more conservative elements prevented this demand from succeeding in six states, but the other seven succumbed.

The heated issue of economic reform came to a boil in Massachusetts. In 1786 a tax voted partly to pay off Massachusetts' Revolutionary debts proved hard on the farmers and the debtor class. They demonstrated for relief in vain. Then the farmers of western and central Massachusetts took stronger action. Under the leadership of Daniel Shays, a veteran of Bunker Hill, these farmers, demanding paper money, a reduction of taxes, and the elimination of special property privileges, prevented courts from meeting and eventually set forth to plunder the national arsenal at Springfield. Shays' Rebellion was put down, though with some bloodshed, but this populist movement caused deep alarm among the propertied classes. Although not an alarmist himself, Washington voiced the fears of the conservative groups when he wrote: "I feel . . . infinitely more than I can express to you, for the disorders which have arisen in these States. Good God! who, besides a tory, could have foreseen, or a Briton predicted them! . . . There are combustibles in every State which a spark might set fire to."

For a variety of reasons, a growing number of people were convinced by 1787 that the governmental structure of the young republic must be overhauled. Among them were the mercantile and manufacturing interests, the holders of depreciated national securities, debtors, and small farmers. Some were also disturbed by the impotency of Congress in foreign relations. At this juncture the weakness of Congress was rendered especially conspicuous by its inability to take a strong stand against either Great Britain or Spain for still occupying western territory that had been ceded to the United States by the treaty of 1783. A rising young statesman, Alexander Hamilton, asserted: "We may . . . be said to have reached almost the last stage of national humiliation. There is scarcely anything that can wound the pride, or degrade the character, of an independent people, which we do not experience."

The matter was lifted from the rhetorical level by a dispute arising between Maryland and Virginia over the navigation of the Potomac and the Chesapeake. Delegates from Maryland and Virginia met on Washington's invitation at Mount Vernon in 1785 to examine this controversy. It soon became clear that the general problem of interstate commerce was too great for the two states to decide alone. So an invitation went forth from Virginia, calling for a convention to be held the following year at Annapolis, at which representatives from all the states would "consider how far a uniform system in their commercial regulations may be necessary to their common interests and their permanent harmony." Nine of the states appointed delegates, but those of only five showed up at Annapolis. Hamilton's skill, however, was equal to the occasion, and the delegates adopted his report, which, drawing attention to the critical state of affairs, suggested that another convention be called, to meet in Philadelphia in May 1787.

Hamilton's proposal was forwarded to the state legislatures and to Congress, and Congress issued the call for such a convention, carefully stating that its business would be restricted to the "sole and express purpose of revising the Articles of Confederation." Furthermore, all proposed amendments were to be submitted to the Congress and to the states for approval. To this convention came delegates from every state except Rhode Island, whose farmer government refused to participate in the deliberations.

The fifty-five delegates who attended the convention included some of the recognized leaders and most powerful men in the young republic. First among them was Washington, who, by unanimous choice, was chosen president. The venerable Franklin, young Hamilton, James Wilson, Madison, and many other men of note were also present. Eight of the delegates had signed the Declaration of Independence; seven had been state governors. But some prominent persons were absent. Jefferson was in Paris as minister to France; John Adams was in London as minister to England; and Paine had left that year for Europe. Samuel Adams had not been chosen to represent Massachusetts or any other state, and although Henry had been elected, he "smellt a rat" and would not attend.

Although the Revolution itself had been largely the work of persons who wanted change, and although many of the same men came together at Philadelphia (twenty-one of them had seen military service and thirty-nine had served in the Continental Congress), they now sought to stabilize the gains they had won. They were propertied men who represented a wide range of interests, probably only a few (including Franklin) having risen from humble origins. Some of them held national securities, well over a dozen had invested in lands for speculation, and most of them had investments in mercantile, industrial, financial, or agricultural enterprises. Overwhelmingly these delegates represented towns or groups where wealth was concentrated rather than the small farmers or mechanics. But it would perhaps be anachronistic to insist upon considerations of kinds or degrees of wealth. There were differences of opinion among the delegates, but they centered upon the methods rather than the objectives of federal power. For virtually all agreed that the national government must be strengthened by giving it authority to levy taxes, provide for order and the common defense, regulate commerce, control the issue of currency, establish postal services, and assume the financial obligations of the Confederation.

The delegates had gathered officially to amend the Articles of Confederation, but early in the proceedings they took the stand that the needs of the union demanded a completely new document. A question immediately arose regarding the kind of new government that should be provided. Aware of the example of state legislatures insufficiently checked by other branches of the state governments, the delegates determined that untrammeled legislative supremacy held too many dangers, and so they devised an intricate system of checks and balances. They agreed that governmental authority ought to be divided among legislative, executive, and judiciary branches, each with clearly stipulated checks upon the others. Two major plans for the structure of such a national government were put forward. The Virginia plan, favored by the large states, conceived of a lower house elected by the people, the lower house electing in turn an upper house, and the executive and the judiciary to be chosen by the legislature. Countering this proposal was the New Jersey, or small state, plan, which proposed a plural executive and a unicameral legislature, in which each state, regardless of size, was to have an equal vote. The final draft of the Constitution was a compromise between the two proposals, with a president chosen by electors from the states, and a bicameral legislature, in which the large states were favored in the lower chamber (Representatives) and the small states in the upper chamber (Senate).

The decision to elect the lower chamber on a basis of population, in turn, brought up another problem. The northern states were willing to have the slaves counted as property for tax purposes but not as people for electoral purposes. But the South demanded that slaves be counted in apportioning representation. The result was a compromise, whereby three-fifths of the slaves were to be counted in determining both taxation and representation. In various other ways, also, the Constitution as finally shaped proved to be a set of compromises.

The Articles of Confederation required unanimous consent of the state legislatures before an amendment became effective. The delegates at Philadelphia, realizing the widespread opposition in several states to the proposed constitution, disregarded the existing legal machinery. Instead, they inserted in the proposed constitution a provision that the states should signify their approval through special conventions, and that when nine of these state conventions had ratified it, the document would go into effect. No single state was to be given the chance to prevent the adoption of the Constitution.

A storm broke over the ratification issue and continued from September 1787 to July 1788. Those who favored adoption, known as "the Federalists," included the propertied and the professional groups, together with the army officers. "The Anti-Federalists" were composed largely of small farmers and nonpropertied groups. Thus, the Federalists had on their side prestige, the most articulate voices in the republic, and money.

The tense situation in New York led Hamilton to launch *The Federalist Papers*, afterward assisted by Madison and John Jay. This series of eighty-five well-written and carefully reasoned essays set forth the political philosophy of the so-called Founding Fathers. Published in other states, it played an enormous part in winning general ratification of the Constitution and has since been a major source of constitutional interpretation. Wherever the problem of limiting central authority by federation and a system of checks and balances arises, *The Federalist* is still likely to be quoted. On June 21, 1788, the ninth state, New Hampshire, assented to ratification. New York was the eleventh state to ratify (July 26, 1788). In the end, only two of the states, Rhode Island and North Carolina, refused to accept the Constitution, but when the new government had gone into effect, they were forced by strong pressure to yield.

Whether the people as a whole desired a new constitution is hard to say. A debated percentage of the adult males failed to vote, either because of apathy or because of disfranchisement on account of property, tax, or religious qualifications. It is possible, but far from certain, that if the vote had been heavier, the result might have been different.

Conspicuously, the new Constitution contained no declaration of the rights of man, such as preceded the constitutions of the states. Samuel Adams and other radicals were induced to accept the proposed document only upon condition that a bill of "natural" rights would be added to it. Massachusetts and Pennsylvania as states made similar conditions. And so, at its first session (September 25, 1789), the Congress of the United States adopted a set of amendments that soon, in modified form, was ratified as the American Bill of Rights.

The War of Independence had been a protest against centralization of power in London. The Constitution reintroduced a central legislative body, a strong executive, federal courts reminiscent of royal courts, and a system of taxes and tariffs beyond state jurisdiction. The Revolution, it appeared, had brought about major changes, but leadership had now passed to the men who sought stability, and they called a halt to further revolution.

The young republic thus inaugurated a new and lasting form of government. The Constitution was a compromise document, and its limitations displeased great segments of the American public both in the 1780's and afterward. The text of its amendments is now almost as long as that of the original articles. Many contemporaries, including some of the signers, had grave misgivings about the ability of the constitution to produce good results or even to endure for any length of time. But it gave the country something that had been sorely lacking in the Articles of Confederation—a strong, workable national government, capable of ensuring economic stability and political tranquility at home and of increasing respect abroad.

The American Revolution had followed, in some significant regards, a pattern that historians and sociologists today find fairly characteristic of successful political revolutions. The original discontent had been created by new political, social, and economic developments (such as the growing nationalism of America), and by imposed innovations (such as the Grenville and Townshend acts) that had all been considered abuses by the general population. An active and articulate minority, led by intellectuals (such as Franklin, John

Adams, Jefferson, and Paine), had created a sense of solidarity and a dynamic organization where otherwise there might have been merely apathy or unorganized resistance. These intellectuals, reinforced by dissatisfied or idealistic merchants (like Hancock) and planters (like Washington and Jefferson), had provided leaders for the revolt. They had borrowed from current political theory, as well as from their own experience, a philosophy that both justified their rebellion and set forth a program for bettering their conditions. The failure of the mother country either to make timely concessions or to put up effective counterforce enabled the revolt to become a successful revolution—especially since crowned heads and conservative ministries of other countries failed to perceive that they had more to gain by supporting the status quo against revolutionary upheaval than by humiliating Britain. Seven years of revolutionary war and five years of political instability and change led to a demand for "normal" and firm government, and a sort of political reaction under prudent leaders (such as Washington and Hamilton) followed. The result was a stable regime with a viable constitution, advocated now by an active minority that was able to rally sufficient support from the rest of the population.

This pattern was one that, with many minor and a few major differences, had characterized the English civil wars and would characterize the French Revolution. These revolutions were more than analogous; they were interdependent. Just as the English upheaval could hardly have occurred if it had not been preceded by the Reformation with its doctrine of national, if not personal, determination of religious faith, so the American Revolution might not have occurred if Americans had not learned the doctrines of natural rights, social compact, and "just powers from the consent of the governed" from their background of the English Revolution and its apologists. The American Revolution, in its turn, already had handed or soon was going to hand some of this "revolutionary tradition" over to France, which, however, had also derived much of its revolutionary spirit directly from the Reformation, the English Revolution, and its own *philosophes.*

 CHAPTER SIX

Europe on the Eve
of Revolution

That the crowned heads of Europe would have rallied, in moral sympathy if not in actual military support, to the cause of King George III in suppressing the revolt of his empire across the Atlantic might have been expected. They had not only failed to do so but they actually had aided the insurgents. George III was to have his revenge, however. Louis XVI and Catherine the Great, at least, were to live long enough to regret the Americans' success, as would also the heirs of those other aiders and abettors of rebellion in America who had meanwhile died.

To many Europeans the American Revolution had a twofold spiritual significance. It was, first of all, a violent challenge to the traditional European order, characterized by the authority of kings or nobilities, the mercantilist economic system, the class structure of society, the established church, and the survivals from the old feudal order of Europe. Secondly, it embodied the philosophy of Nature and of Reason (not always synonyms) which had been developed so eloquently by the political philosophers of eighteenth-century Europe. The ringing phrases of Jefferson's Declaration of Independence and the declarations of rights in the new constitutions of the separate states of the United States reechoed some of the most popular themes of European thought. The American Revolution seemed to many European intellectuals to be translating into action the "Laws of Nature and of Nature's God" that they had long been preaching. Sympathy among Europeans for the cause of the rebellious colonies had been widespread, especially after the alliance with France made the success of that rebellion appear likely.

As we have seen, it was not public opinion that sent European forces to the support of the colonies so much as it was the old competition for empire. Anti-British interests had outweighed antirevolutionary sentiments in the governments of France, Spain, and other countries. Britain, in attempting to put down the American revolt, had faced alone a hostile Europe in a war fought on five continents and on all the seas. The major reason for this general European hostility to Britain lay in the latter's predominant colonial and commercial position. To France the War for American Independence had been simply another round in the long colonial match between the two powers—the so-called Second Hundred Years' War. Bested in the Seven Years' War, France had turned to an indirect attack upon the British empire. If she could not have the British colonies for herself, she could at least encourage the colonies to revolt so that Britain would not have them either and could hope thereby to increase her own trade with them at the expense of British commerce. To that end France, as previously mentioned, had secretly supplied the American rebels with officers, money, rifles, artillery, powder, and shoes, even before an open alliance was concluded.

Other nations had opposed Britain for similar reasons of commercial or colonial rivalry. The United Provinces were annoyed at British attempts to exclude Dutch traders from American commerce. The Spanish hoped to regain Gibraltar and Minorca. The League of Armed Neutrality was formed to maintain "the freedom of the seas" in response to the British practice of seizing neutral vessels trading with the "Insurgents" or searching them for contraband of war. Diplomacy during the War for American Independence was, from one point of view, another application of the balance-of-power principle, which came into play whenever one nation grew overly strong and threatened to subordinate the others.

The War for American Independence, as already indicated, was fought all over the world. French and Hessian armies sustained the faltering protagonists in the American colonies. British, French, American, and Dutch forces clashed in the North Sea. Spanish and French forces unsuccessfully attempted to invade England and attacked Gibraltar and the British possessions in the Mediterranean. The French and British navies battled in the Caribbean, the Channel, the Bay of Biscay, and along the North American coast. The British position in India, Africa, and South America was once more challenged by the French. This far-flung attack on Britain was one reason for the ultimate success of the American Revolution. Unwittingly, the monarchies of Europe, by pursuing political and commercial advantages, furthered the movement toward popular government that was soon to threaten their rule at home.

Britain made a speedy recovery from her defeat. The recovery was attributable not only to success in diplomacy but also to her more effective economic system as compared with that of France and other countries. During the eighteenth century nearly all the nations of Europe had experienced an astoundingly rapid increase in the volume of commerce—especially of colonial commerce—and the output of industry. But commercial and industrial growth was greater in Britain than anywhere else. While the Holy Roman Empire was hampered by its hundreds of internal political and tariff boundaries, while France was handicapped by domestic tariffs, its still-powerful guild system, and its strict royal regulation of economic affairs, and while the free flow of European trade was interrupted by numerous invading armies, Britain was comparatively free of these restraints and impediments of trade. Her guild system was all but impotent, supplanted by individual or corporate capitalistic enterprise and relatively free competition. Her navy, still supreme on the seas, had kept her commercial lanes open even in times of war. Her government, in the hands of a commercial-minded oligarchy, pursued tariff and taxation policies intended, despite their mercantilist bias, to help rather than to hinder commerce and industry. And the trend of her economic thinking was already beginning to turn away from mercantilism toward the free-trade policy for which she was to become famous in the next century. In such an atmosphere, the industrial and agricultural revolutions, which were more advanced in Britain than anywhere else in the world before the American revolt, continued uninterrupted despite imperial disruption and military defeat. The decades before the outbreak of the French Revolution were a period of inflation in Europe, when the buyer could expect to pay more, and the seller to receive more for commodities today than yesterday, and more tomorrow than today. The British government, having a strong domestic financial system centering upon the Bank of England, could borrow money freely, but the French treasury, dependent in part upon foreign bankers, found its credit somewhat in doubt.

No great popular revolution had occurred in Europe since the Glorious Revolution of 1688, and that one had been isolated in England. When in 1776 the American people brazenly dissolved "the political bands which have connected them with another" and assumed "among the powers of the earth, the separate and equal station to which the Laws of Nature and of Nature's God" entitled them, it was the first effective display of revolutionary spirit in nearly a century, and it was not isolated. Essentially conservative European governments found themselves entangled in the American disquiet, and some of their less conservative subjects readily accepted the entanglement in a spiritual as well as in a political sense. The American Revolution encouraged a trend already visible in political philosophy because of the impact of recent technological developments—a trend away from the abstract toward the concrete, toward speculation about real people like the Americans rather than about "natural man."

It was not altogether coincidence that Adam Smith's *Wealth of Nations*, the classical British statement of laissez-faire economics, appeared in the same year as the Declaration of Independence, the classical American statement of natural rights. Smith's book was at once an expression of the individualistic, competitive, commercial spirit of the British middle class and a translation into economic theory of the popular idea that human affairs were governed by the same sort of natural order as prevailed in the physical universe. Reversing the old mercantilistic view that a nation's best interest lay in strict government control of production and trade, Smith argued that a nation served its interest best by a policy of free enterprise—freedom of the individual to buy and sell, to lease and to rent, to hire and be hired, without government interference or regulation. If each individual were thus allowed to pursue his own rational self-interest, Smith contended, free competition for land, capital, labor, and commodities would automatically produce a balance between demand for goods and services on the one hand and their supply on the other. In that way, the allocation of limited resources and the production and distribution of the world's supply of goods would be achieved in the best and most efficient way possible. To Smith the old guild system, the fixing of prices, government monopolies and controls, and taxes which restricted the free flow of goods were all impediments to the working of those natural economic laws whereby each man, inspired by self-interest, might contribute to the general welfare. The wealth of nations, which lay not in the amount of bullion a nation possessed, as the old mercantilist theory had it, but in her accumulated and potential goods and services, of which money was merely a measure, would thus be increased by the noninterference of government and the free play of individual tastes.

This policy of "government hands-off" had already come to be called "laissez faire." It held an enormous appeal for the business-minded British middle class. *The Wealth of Nations* was to become in the nineteenth century the cornerstone of British economic policy. Much had been written on economic theory before Smith's time, especially by the French Physiocrats. But whereas the Physiocrats had appealed for freedom from governmental regulation because of their interest in land, Smith was the first to insist in a systematic treatise upon the automatic interplay of land, labor, capital, and risk as factors in the production of wealth. He regarded the landlord's rent, the worker's wages, the moneylender's interest, and the entrepreneur's profit as all necessary incentives to take part in the creation of wealth. His ideas remain an important part of the modern science of economics.

Smith's younger contemporary, Jeremy Bentham, another giant among the English philosophers, published his first work in the same year in which *The Wealth of Nations* appeared. In his *Fragment on Government* (1776) and more systematically in his later *Principles of Morals and Legislation* (1789), Bentham expounded the precept of enlightened self-interest as the criterion by which human institutions ought to be judged. Like Smith and some of the French rationalists, Bentham had derived this philosophy from his concept of the nature of man. Bentham's reasoning was more like Helvétius' and Holbach's than Rousseau's—more materialistic than moralistic. Men naturally seek happiness and avoid pain, he argued, but fortunately one of the measures of the individual's happiness is the number of persons who share in it. Hence, a high correlation between the desires of the individual and the welfare of the public may be expected, and society and its institutions can be so ordered as to enable the greatest number of human beings to enjoy the greatest possible amount of happiness. Rejecting the French rationalists' insistence upon "natural right," he emphasized rather the concept of "public utility." Himself a lawyer, Bentham was most concerned with the reform of British law and judicial institutions. But his influence extended far beyond his immediate work through the efforts of his disciples, known as the "utilitarians"; and his philosophy of "the greatest happiness for the greatest number," borrowed from other eighteenth-century writers, permeated the whole of nineteenth-century thought.

The British rationalists were mainly political theorists and economists like Bentham and Smith. Nevertheless, historians like Edward Gibbon also revealed the rationalist trend of the times. The first volume of Gibbon's monumental *Decline and Fall of the Roman Empire* appeared in the eventful year 1776, the twelfth and last in 1788. Thus, chronologically at least, it fits neatly into the period between the early stages of the American Revolution and the French Revolution. Gibbon's masterpiece attributed the decay of Rome's classical and rational culture in large part to the rise of antirational and mystical Christianity. Thus he belonged to that school of didactic historians like Voltaire whose conception of history was of a "philosophy teaching by example." Those eras of man's past where human reason was allowed the freest scope, they taught, were the eras of greatest cultural creativeness and human happiness, and conversely, those eras where superstition was triumphant were the eras of decline. Gibbon's friend, the Scottish historian William Robertson, though less of a rationalist than Gibbon, in his *History of Scotland* (1759), *History of the Reign of the Emperor Charles the Fifth* (1769), and other lesser works on America and India that appeared after the Declaration of Independence shared the dislike of the Middle Ages as a period of superstition and decline. David Hume's anti-Gothic *History of England* (1754–1762), sometimes said to have been pro-Tory, made him contemporaneously more famous and controversial than did his philosophical dissertations. Gibbon, Robertson, and Hume brought historiography in Britain to a high point of objectivity, naturally not wholly successful. All three men, in addition to avoiding a supernatural interpretation of history, made generous, if sometimes incomplete, use of the best historical sources edited by earlier scholars.

In Germany the philosophers were especially preoccupied with the rational element in human affairs. The Königsberg philosopher Immanuel Kant gave to eighteenth-century rationalism a new orientation. His so-called critical philosophy was a fresh attempt to examine the relations of knowledge and action. More clearly than the French rationalists, he discerned the different modes by which the human mind operates. In his *Critique of Pure Reason* (1781) he sought especially to examine the grounds of knowledge and proceeded to demonstrate that rational arguments cannot be used to construct a satisfactory cosmology (or explanation of the universe), since equally good arguments can be found on either side of such questions as whether space and time are finite or infinite, whether matter is divisible or indivisible, whether the will of man is free or determined, whether God exists or does not exist. These arguments are the famous *antinomies* of Kant. They led him to the conclusion that there are certain realms of thought which cannot be usefully examined by pure reason—among these the problems of freedom of the will, immortality, and the existence of God.

Nevertheless, in his *Critique of Practical Reason* (1788), Kant argued that freedom of the will, immortality, and the existence of God must be assumed as "postulates of Pure Practical Reason" in order to provide a foundation for moral law and moral action. Science and morality therefore became for Kant separate branches of knowledge, each with its own domain. The necessary laws of the sciences applied in the "phenomenal" world, and the prescriptions of morality in the "noumenal" world. Critical philosophy became the method by which to learn both the "metaphysics of nature," which treats the rational principles of physics, and the "metaphysics of morals," which treats the rational principles of morality.

Kant's concept of ethics, admittedly influenced by Rousseau's moralism and probably by his own Pietist background, was largely free from formal theology. He held that morality "leads ineluctably to religion, through which it extends itself to the idea of a powerful moral Lawgiver, outside of mankind." These religious problems he was to treat especially in *Religion within the Limits of Reason Alone* (1793). His ethical argument runs through his several works. Morality has reference, he pointed out, not to objects but to rational creatures; not to the necessity of nature but to the freedom of the will; and it depends, therefore, on prescriptions that should be universal. The fundamental precept of his ethics was his often-quoted *categorical imperative*, which called upon man "to act as if the principle upon which you act is to become by your will a universal law of nature." In other words, "act as you would have others act"—which is a rationalist, depersonalized form of the Golden Rule. Thus he provided room again for the religious concept of *duty* in human behavior.

Kant, like Rousseau, was much concerned with the problem of international peace. His famous essay *On Perpetual Peace* was not to appear until 1795, in the midst of the wars of the French Revolution. Nevertheless, he earlier tried to raise the question of international morality. In *An Idea for a Universal History with Cosmopolitan Intent* (1784) Kant asserted that the ultimate problem for mankind, the solution of which nature forced him to seek, was the achievement of a civil society to administer law universally. He argued that this end could be attained only through arrangements among the states that would preserve the maximum of freedom for the individual and for the various parts of society. But this was a political problem and, as such, was merely "technical" and dependent not upon the "categorical imperative" but upon its own "hypothetical imperative."

Kant thus carefully differentiated between the various applications of reason. In the realm of objects, a scientific necessity obtains, and that realm can be understood by the "theoretical" use of reason; in the realm of morals, freedom of the will forms the basis of action, and that realm can best be ordered by the "practical" use of reason; but political problems are "technical" and depend upon "hypothetical imperatives," and disaster results from confusing them with moral problems involved with the "categorical imperative." The effect of Kant's philosophy was, in his own words, a "Copernican revolution." He abandoned the earlier supposition, held notably by the sensationalists, that our knowledge must conform to its objects, and, placing man at the center of his analyses, he assumed that objects must rather fit within man's ways of knowing. His analyses served to emphasize the place of reason in both the "theoretical" and the "practical" sciences (in his use of those words) and the controlling importance of the "practical" in the whole scheme of knowledge and action.

In the same year that the Franco-American Alliance was formally signed (1778), Voltaire and Rousseau died. The mantle of Voltaire, after resting briefly on the shoulders of Diderot (d. 1784), passed to the Marquis de Condorcet, mathematician and publicist. Condorcet borrowed much from Voltaire and a little from Rousseau. In numerous political tracts, he set forth the theory that the accumulation of knowledge through sensation, reason, and man's inner sense of morality would lead inevitably toward the betterment of man's social institutions and thereby to the improvement of the human race. He was a good representative of what might be called a third generation of *philosophes*, a generation to which the American Revolution gave great encouragement. In several essays, particularly one entitled *On the Influence of the American Revolution on Europe* (1786), he called the attention of his countrymen to the benefits of natural law as applied in America and, with few philosophical abstractions about mankind in general, argued for concrete reforms in France in particular.

Eventually he developed a theory of inescapable progress that received Classical expression in his major work, *Outline of a Historical Presentation of the Progress of the Human Mind*. Written at a time (1793) during the French Revolution when he was proscribed by his political opponents, he argued that nevertheless the Revolution was to lead the world from the eight preceding stages of history through the ninth, which had begun in the seventeenth century with René Descartes's rational philosophy, into a tenth where "the perfectibility of man is . . . henceforth above the control of every power that would impede it."

In a sense Condorcet was the last of the great *philosophes*, for the *philosophe* movement was soon to yield to the French Revolution, with some of the same men as leaders. He had come to the conclusion that man was inescapably destined for continuous improvement of his intellectual and moral faculties—even his biological traits—because his predecessors among the *philosophes* had made it possible for him to start out with the assumption that man is "a being endowed with sensation, capable of reasoning . . . and of acquiring moral ideas." Thus Descartes's rationalism, Locke's sensationalism, and Rousseau's moralism added up at the end of the eighteenth century to the secularistic perfectionism of Condorcet.

Writers like Kant and Condorcet exhibit the influence of a double intellectual trend during their generation. They were largely rationalistic. Yet repelled by other rationalists' attempts to reduce truth to a rational standard, they recoiled from the dreary prospect that men had no inner responsibility or sense of goodness. This rebellion against sheer materialistic naturalism, this insistence that man's salvation lay in the fullest development of the individual through his instincts, intuitions, and emotions no less than his reason, came to be called "romanticism."

Romanticism, stemming largely from Rousseau's and Goethe's reaction to the more naturalistic *philosophes*, was in effect complementary rather than contradictory to the rationalist movement. Playing upon the *sensibilité* current among the reading public, it often depicted in terms of high emotion the plight of the oppressed and the poor. In the Abbé Raynal's *Philosophical and Political History of the Settlement and Commerce of Europeans in the Two Indies* (1770), the natives of the East and the West were described as naturally good men corrupted and exploited by the extension of European civilization. As we have already indicated, Beaumarchais's plays, *The Barber of Seville* (1775) and *The Marriage of Figaro* (1784), made a popular hero out of their leading character, Figaro, a barber-valet, whose lowly birth and dull masters frustrate his ambitions to better himself.

The appearance of the unhappy common man in literature was a relatively new thing, for the literature of the Augustan Age had been usually peopled with kings and court figures, rich bourgeois, or glamorous rogues. Notably in some of the romances of the period like *Pamela* and *The New Héloïse*, the new literary genre was illustrative of the growing wave of humanitarianism, of the new bourgeois idea that the poor and exploited were the responsibility of the wealthy. Romanticism also expressed itself in a sentimental regard for the beauties of nature, in contrast with the stark materialism of the *philosophes'* "natural order."

As was to have been expected, Beaumarchais's satires of aristocratic society encountered royal censorship but eventual box-office success; and Raynal's work, parts of which were written by other *philosophes*, was one of the most popular books of the day. Nor was it accidental that Beaumarchais published the first edition of Voltaire's complete works or that he was one of those adventurers who had engaged in trade with the American insurgents even before France recognized the sovereignty of the United States or that Raynal's *Europeans in the Two Indies* in its successive revisions gave more and more space to America. Philosophy, drama, novels, poetry, Romanticism, humanitarianism, cosmopolitanism, and America were all mixed up in the growing protest against the abuses of the Old Regime.

Perhaps the most notable manifestation of Romanticism was the Sturm und Drang movement in Germany, exemplified by Goethe's *Sorrows of Young Werther*. Its participants were young men, inspired by the Romantic faith in the full expression of individuality, who had declared war against both the tyranny of the *philosophes'* Nature and the conventions and injustices of aristocratic society. Much of their output was mere personal protest. During this period, because of the patronage of the Grand Duke Charles Augustus, Weimar became the "Athens of Germany." Here came not only Goethe and Herder but also other famous men of letters, including in 1787 Johann Christoph Friedrich von Schiller.

Schiller was a young Württemberg army doctor who five years earlier had absented himself without leave from his post to see his first play, *The Robbers*, produced in a nearby town. *The Robbers* soon came to share with Goethe's *Werther* a leading place in the Romantic movement in Germany. It tells the story of a young nobleman named Karl Moor, who is driven by injustice to become an outlaw but in the end is reconciled to law and order. Because of the success of his play and his subsequent imprisonment for absence without leave, Schiller decided to quit the army and medicine for letters. By the time he was invited to make his home in Weimar, he had written some poetry and several new plays, of which *Don Carlos* (1787) was the most significant. *Don Carlos* centered around the legend of the son of King Philip II of Spain, who, perhaps unhistorically, is portrayed as heroically sympathizing with the Dutch in their revolt against his father in the sixteenth century. The parallels of the Dutch with the recent American revolt must have struck the better informed. The theme of heroic revolt was further developed when Schiller, at Weimar, published his *History of the Revolt of the Netherlands* (1788). This work led to his appointment to the chair of history at the University of Jena (1789).

The Sturm und Drang movement at first was characterized by inexperience and youthfulness. German writers, as they grew older, however, tempered their literary allusions with more sober and conservative contemplations of history and philosophy. Out of this transition grew the beginnings of a German national literary surge. Some writers carefully eschewed the French influence so long dominant and turned to their own national past for inspiration. German folk songs and medieval epics were revived, and the Middle Ages, so long mistaken by Rationalists throughout Europe as a long night of unredeemed "Gothic" barbarism, were now idealized as an era of heroic nobles and sturdy peasants. Mozart cried out, "If only we Germans would seriously begin to think in German, to act as Germans, speak German, and even to sing in German!"

The most influential figure in the national revival was Herder. His *Ideas on the Philosophy of the History of Mankind* (1784–1791) supplemented the Rationalists' view of history as a continual war between reason and superstition with a Romantic concept of history as organic growth and change. Under the influence of Montesquieu, Herder conceived of the behavior, thoughts, and institutions of intuitive, emotional, and irrational man as shaped by inexorable historical forces toward a destiny beyond his own making. But the impersonal nature of Montesquieu's philosophy of history was largely offset by the more prominent place given in Herder's work to national folkways and national culture as a molder of man's destiny. While still believing in freedom of the individual, he considered individualism as compatible with adherence to the national group. He thus reflected the intellectual's sympathy with the enlightened systems of government like those of Frederick II of Prussia, Joseph II of Austria, and Charles Augustus of Weimar. In part Herder's emphasis upon national character was a reaction to the undifferentiated cosmopolitanism of the *philosophes,* although he too looked forward to a time when the separate national cultures would cooperate in peace.

Another literary crosscurrent in the decades preceding the French Revolution was the renewed interest in Classicism. Weimar was the center of this movement in the Germanies. Here Goethe, earlier identified with the Sturm und Drang, had been since 1775 not only the leading literary figure but also the principal minister in an enlightened regime, and here he attracted other men of genius. In Weimar Goethe had come under the influence of Winckelmann's *History of the Art of Antiquity* and had written his *Iphigenia in Tauris* (published 1787), telling in Classical form but with modern ideas the story, familiar in drama and sacred literature, of the innocent child sacrificed to a stern god by an overzealous father. A trip to Italy in 1786–1788 enhanced his respect for Classical culture. From it came his *Torquato Tasso* (1790), a drama Classical in form and Renaissance in background but with the Romantic theme of the poet in conflict with the world. Goethe's influence gave to the Neoclassical style and form in literature a temporary lift that somewhat counteracted the contemporary tendency to irregularity and Gothic form.

Strands of both Classicism and Romanticism were to be found in the other arts, too. In sculpture the outstanding figure was Jean-Antoine Houdon, and in architecture Jacques-Germain Soufflot. Francisco José de Goya, even though some of his finest work was yet to come, was already a great artist before the French Revolution. Altogether the generation that flourished on the eve of the French Revolution could not be said (as was said of a later generation) to have courted disaster because of boredom.

Some of the world's greatest composers adorned this period. Franz Josef Haydn (1732–1809), Wolfgang Amadeus Mozart (1756–1791), and Ludwig van Beethoven (1770–1827), the so-called Viennese Classics, inherited the lengthy tradition in musical instrumentation, notation, composition, and performance that had preceded them. Beethoven's major works were to come only after the French Revolution, and so were some of Haydn's, but by that time (not to mention the numerous operas, masses, quartets, and other chamber and church masterpieces that they wrote) Haydn and Mozart had brought the sonata, the symphony, and the concerto to a degree of musical perfection that, by general agreement, has rarely been excelled except perhaps by the later works of Haydn and by Beethoven. On the eve of the French Revolution the stress upon music as a medium of religious expression had diminished, and musical themes, if expressed in words at all, were more likely to be of a secular nature.

While still using the graceful eighteenth-century idiom, Haydn and Mozart introduced elements of naturalism and emotion that carried music from the mathematically precise wizardry of Bach and the rococo delicacy of Rameau further along the way toward a full-bodied Romanticism. Through Haydn's measured music ran the strains of Austrian folk songs; in Mozart's were to be found harmonies that sounded startlingly "modern" to his contemporaries. Both men, as just stated, were among the early exponents of the symphony form, in which so much of the later Romantic music was to be cast; Haydn, who also contributed significantly to the string quartet and the sonata form, is sometimes called "the father of the symphony." Mozart is one of the few musical geniuses who wrote surpassing works of opera as well as great symphonies, sonatas, concertos, and chamber music. Although he died in poverty at the age of thirty-five (1791), more of his music is still regularly played by great performers than perhaps that of any other composer, with the possible exceptions of Bach and Beethoven.

New musical forms reflected a new trend in instrumental music. It was becoming a "platform art" in its own right instead of the mere accompaniment to church service, opera, or the dance. Chamber music, played in courts and aristocratic salons, was of increasing variety, as strings, woodwinds, and brasses were combined to produce new and more full-bodied effects. Thus the modern orchestra developed alongside the modern symphonic form. Technological improvements were also transforming the wooden-framed, brass-stringed harpsichord, whose strings were plucked by quills of different size and texture, into the modern piano with steel frame and strings, producing sounds by percussion and varying their intensity by means of pedals. The piano developed into an instrument of greater tonal depth, variety, volume, and color than could be achieved by the delicate tones of its predecessor.

Similar changes were taking place also in the fine arts, as well as in literature and music. The rococo vogue was superseded by a return to Classicism, severe in form but tempered by a certain naturalism of expression. Simplicity of composition, as well as the affectation of Classical costume and detail, distinguished the painting of Jacques Louis David from that of Watteau and Boucher, but a distinct realism in the delineation of character raised David's work above mere imitation of the Classical. Some of his paintings were on Classical themes—for example, his well-known *Death of Socrates*—but his greatest work was to be the portrayal of episodes and figures of the French Revolution, in which he was to be both by law and by prestige the "art dictator." Likewise, the portrait sculpture of Houdon, best known for his busts of contemporaries like Louis XVI, Lafayette, and Washington and his statue of Voltaire, is imbued with a vitality and freshness which sets it apart from its Classic models. He undertook a journey all the way to Mount Vernon in order to make his study of Washington.

In architecture Neoclassicism resulted largely in imitation of Classical temples and public buildings. Soufflot's domed Church of St. Geneviève in Paris so vividly recalled the Roman Pantheon that by the time it was finished (1790) it was set aside, by a revolutionary generation which thought more of *philosophes* than of saints, as a Pantheon for honored Frenchmen like Voltaire and Rousseau. Meanwhile the Church of the Madeleine was still under construction in Paris, destined not to be completed for decades, but looking meanwhile so much like a Greek temple that the Emperor Napoleon thought of making it his Temple of Glory. In the crafts the Classical ideals of simplicity and proportion replaced rococo ornateness. The restrained elegance of the "Louis Seize" (Louis XVI) style of furniture with its rectangles, arches, and simple lines reflected a reaction to the curves and ornateness of the "Louis Quinze" (Louis XV) period and revealed the revived interest in Classical art forms.

Several artistic geniuses stand apart from the Neoclassic vogue of the period. In 1779, Jean Baptiste Siméon Chardin died. Unlike the contemporaneously more esteemed Jean Honoré Fragonard, he had been no decorative artist depicting scenes of fancy and portraying the pleasures of the nobility. The son of a carpenter, he had been practically self-taught and without powerful friends or patrons. Having no models, he painted still lifes and the everyday episodes about him, becoming a great genre artist, reflecting the lower-middle-class life of his street and his home. His most famous picture is the *Bénédicité*—a little girl saying grace in the midst of a middle-class home. Jean Baptiste Greuze, another contemporary of Chardin and David, likewise set forth everyday scenes, sometimes displaying the *sensibilité* of his day in his pictures of the blind, the sick, and the unhappy, but he also painted portraits of the famous and an occasional scene from Classical history.

In Spain, Goya, like the earlier Hogarth in England, used realis-

tic satire to record the life he saw about him. He first attracted attention as a designer of cartoons—that is, preliminary studies or
sketches—for the tapestries of Santa Barbara. He chose contemporary subjects for his designs, developing a style reminiscent of Hogarth's caricatures. He also painted some pictures on religious subjects, which likewise revealed a vigorous, realistic quality. In 1785 he
became director of the Academy of Arts and, in 1786, a court
painter. His penetrating portraits of the decadent palace life he saw
about him are as broad a social commentary as are his smaller
sketches and watercolors depicting the life of the lower classes. One
wonders why the overdressed royalty, whom he painted with degen-
erate faces against ostentatious backgrounds, continued to employ
him. Caricaturing the Spanish court of the Old Regime proved excellent preparation for Goya's most famous works—his collection of
drawings known as *The Disasters of the War*, bitter and gruesome
protests against the atrocities committed by the French when, under
Napoleon Bonaparte, they invaded his country. As a realistic social
commentator, Goya was to have a wide following among the painters
of the later nineteenth century.

The crosscurrents of Classicism, Romanticism, and rationalism
of the Old Regime give a superficial effect of running off in all di-
rections at the same time. They were nevertheless all expressive of
the new standards of human values. Classicism and rationalism were
two methods of search for order and lasting values in human affairs;
Romanticism reflected the search for the fullest expression of the individual. All these movements were manifestations of the widespread
conviction that human institutions could and should work for the
betterment of mankind. That conviction expressed itself also in a
striking growth of humanitarian sentiment and in numerous reform
movements directed against poverty, ignorance, injustice, and oppression. Reformers, in a day when all was obviously not well with
the world, attacked the imperfections that they detested, sometimes
in the name of "Classical Tradition," which enabled them to hope
again for "the eternal verities"; sometimes in the name of "Reason,"
which taught how things *ought to be;* and sometimes in the name of
the "Romantic Individual," whose full life would necessarily be "the
good life." Theirs was not the first or the last generation to seek salvation through conflicting philosophies.

Regardless of the conflicts among these schools of thought, education played a prominent part in all their schemes to better society.

In the pre-Revolutionary age, the education of underprivileged children attracted the interest of religious and social groups. The first Sunday school was founded in England in 1780 for the benefit of children whose daily employment in the new factories prevented them from going to school during the week. Rousseau's *Emile* influenced the theories of Johann Bernhard Basedow, who founded a sort of learn-through-play school in Dessau called the Philanthropin, and of Johann Heinrich Pestalozzi, a Swiss reformer, who modified Rousseau's somewhat contradictory concepts of guided self-expression and adapted them to group education, laying the foundations of modern "progressive" education. The essence of true education, Pestalozzi thought, was experience rather than rote learning. In experimental schools and in a number of writings, the most famous of which was a novel called *Leonard and Gertrude* (1781), Pestalozzi upheld education rather than political revolution as the best means of social betterment for the working classes. In the nineteenth century, his theories of education were to gain a wide influence through his pupil Friedrich Froebel, founder of the kindergarten.

Another cause inspired by liberal and humanitarian ideals was the movement for the abolition of the slave trade. Led in England by the eloquent philanthropist William Wilberforce, an antislavery league was formed in 1787. The movement was eventually to bear fruit in the abolition of the British slave trade in 1807, although slavery as a whole was not to be abolished in the British empire until 1833. In France a corresponding movement crystallized in the formation of the Society of Friends of the Blacks in 1788, of which Lafayette was the most prominent member. Similar societies grew up in America, where Franklin and Jay became active in the antislavery societies of Philadelphia and New York respectively. French and American abolitionists, except as indicated above, made progress even more slowly than the English.

Humanitarianism, reinforced by the antimercantilist views of the Physiocrats and Adam Smith, also brought a reaction against the restrictive colonial policies left over from an earlier age. "Plenty of good land," wrote Smith, "and liberty to manage their own affairs their own way, seem to be the two great causes of the prosperity of all new colonies." This antimercantilist sentiment had nourished the popularity of the American cause. Now it produced in Britain a movement to reform the government of India and lesser colonies and in France a series of commercial treaties. The Physiocrats and Adam Smith also figured in humanitarian protests against war, adding their calculations of the cost of war to the pleas of the *philosophes*, who counted on reason and enlightenment to persuade humanity of war's futility.

The Enlightenment ideals of religious toleration and the equality of all men fostered a movement for religious emancipation. The Jews in some limited areas of France and Austria were no longer required to live in ghettos and disbarred from civil and legal rights. In some German cities and principalities, in return for protection money (*Schutzgeld*), Jews were granted the status of protected Jews (*Schutzjuden*). Lessing, in his plays *The Jews* and *Nathan the Wise*, made sympathetic figures of his Jewish characters. Among the Jews themselves the writings of the German-Jewish philosopher Moses Mendelssohn, friend of Lessing and sometimes thought to be the prototype of Lessing's *Nathan*, contributed to this movement. Mendelssohn insisted that Judaism and modern Christianity were identical in their essentials—God, immortality, and the law. He translated the Jewish Torah (the Pentateuch) into German and had the translation printed in Hebrew letters so as to acquaint Jews more precisely with German. In this way he performed for German Jews and Yiddish somewhat the same service that Luther had for Christians and German.

The growth of capitalism also aided the movement for emancipation, for the talents attributed to Jews in business and finance were welcomed in some outstanding instances—notably, the so-called court Jews of the German princes. In France in 1787 the Protestants were granted the right to worship in private as they pleased and were regranted some of the civil rights that Louis XIV had taken from them. Lafayette wrote to Washington how pleased he was to introduce to some of Louis XVI's ministers "the first Protestant clergyman who could appear at Versailles since the Revolution of 1685" (by which he meant "since Louis XIV's Revocation of the Edict of Nantes").

The growth of the factory system, the enclosure movement, and the drift to cities from the country—trends that we have already noted as especially marked in England—were increasing at least the visibility if not the actuality of the poverty of the worker and the dispossessed peasant even while the wealth of the middle class was visibly growing. The tendency for prices to inflate was especially marked in the decade before the French Revolution, and wages generally failed to keep pace with the rising cost of living. The peasant, al-

though better able to provide himself with food than the city prole-
tarian and to get higher prices for his produce, nevertheless found
himself, as the value of his seignorial obligations mounted because of
increasing prices, obliged to pay more for the lands he rented. At the
same time he was further frustrated in his land-hunger because the
price of good farmland mounted, causing landlords to insist more vigorously on fuller payments of old seignorial obligations and higher
payments upon new or renewed obligations—a phenomenon sometimes referred to as "the feudal reaction." Such reform measures as
royal philanthropy, work relief, and the dole mitigated rather than
solved the growing problem of poverty, but they were indicative of
at least a favorable attitude regarding the responsibility of society
(rather than the church alone) for the needy.

Because of the crowding in the cities and the patent hardships
of workers, public health received increased attention. The poor, the
sick, the aged, and the insane benefited from the new humanitarian
spirit and the interests of governments and laymen in philanthropy.
In several countries improvements were made in antiquated relief
systems, and more humane treatment was accorded the mentally ill.
In Lyons and Vienna hospitals were erected that were regarded as
models of modern methods; and in Paris the family of Jacques
Necker, founding a hospital that still exists, won an enviable reputation as friends of the sick and the poor. In Britain new hospitals and
clinics ministered to the urban poor, and new maternity hospitals
and improved standards of care reduced infant and maternal mortality rates, which, however, remained pitifully high by modern standards. Improved water, sewer, and street-lighting systems made British and French cities somewhat more healthful, more easily policed,
and less offensive to eye and nose.

Preventive medicine came into being with the new practices of
inoculation, quarantine, and disinfection, reducing the ravages of
smallpox and typhus epidemics. On the Continent prominent families submitted to inoculation. Catherine II introduced it into Russia
by offering herself as the first to receive the new treatment there. Dr.
Edward Jenner in 1775 first noticed that those who had had cowpox
frequently were immune to smallpox, but it was not until 1796 that
he was able to test his theory. He inoculated a boy with matter from
the hand of a milkmaid who had cowpox, introducing the mild disease into the human system so as to build up its immunity to the
more virulent smallpox. Thus he discovered the process now known
as "vaccination."

Disease prevention and sanitation nevertheless lagged. In Paris hospitals a shocked English traveler found patients four in a bed and, in a later generation, the French scientist Georges Cuvier was still able to observe that "the sufferings of hell can hardly surpass those of the poor wretches crowded on each other, crushed, burning with fever, incapable of stirring or breathing, sometimes having one or two dead people between them for hours."

Jenner's observations of cowpox that led eventually to the introduction of vaccination against smallpox was one of the most important scientific improvements of the day. It was the beginning of a development that was to reduce the appalling incidence of a disease that up to that time had killed many, from Louis XV to the humblest peasant, and had disfigured those who survived; and it afforded a solid basis for the study of immunity, or the science of immunology. Other significant improvements were, however, being made in the practical applications of medical science and in industrial technology as well. Scientific theory also moved forward along lines previously marked out.

In chemistry Lavoisier carried forward the work of Priestley. He separated water into its elements, hydrogen and oxygen. He explained the phenomenon of combustion as rapid oxidation, thus discrediting forever the phlogiston theory of combustion. As suggested above, he demonstrated chemically the law of the conservation of matter: that is, that although matter may change form, it can be neither created nor destroyed. To Lavoisier, too, is due our modern nomenclature in chemistry.

In astronomy Sir William Herschel, with highly powerful instruments created by himself, considerably widened the existing knowledge of the solar and other systems. He discovered the planet Uranus and hundreds of new nebulae. He ascertained, among numerous other things, that certain distant stars beyond the solar system circulate around each other according to the same law of gravity as controls the movements of the planets of the solar system around the sun.

The geologist James Hutton studied fossils and rock strata and speculated upon a theory regarding the earth's origin that had already been tentatively advanced by philosophers like Descartes and Leibnitz and scientists like Buffon. In his *Theory of the Earth* (1785), he conceived of the formation of the earth's surface as the gradual operation of cooling processes still at work. According to this conception the creation of the earth was not a comparatively recent event but an evolutionary development thousands of centuries old. This theory gave additional ammunition to deists and *philosophes* by casting further doubt on the story of creation in the Book of Genesis.

The apparent struggle between science and theology was further aggravated by the theories of Pierre Simon Laplace (1749–1827). Appointed professor of mathematics in the famous École Militaire of Paris while still in his teens, he eventually became known as "the Newton of France." A series of memoirs in the 1780's enhanced his reputation as an astronomer and provided astronomical and mathematical data that were to lead ultimately to his books *Explanation of the World's System* (1796) and *Celestial Mechanics* (begun in 1799). The latter work is sometimes said to rank second only to Newton's *Principia* as a monument of mathematical genius applied to celestial movements. In these memoirs and books, Laplace expounded his "nebular hypothesis"—that our solar system evolved from a vast, hot mass of slowly moving, rarefied matter from which smaller masses gradually separated and, upon condensation, became planets, the central mass remaining as the sun. This nebular hypothesis, propounded before Laplace as a philosophical concept by Kant and by the Swedish scientist and mystic Emanuel Swedenborg, provided a scientific foundation for and placed a culminating touch upon eighteenth-century skepticism regarding the literal interpretation of the biblical account of Creation.

More than the developments already suggested in politics, economics, and the arts, these scientific achievements stemmed from the work of earlier specialists in the respective fields and were less reflective of the concurrent social atmosphere. Indeed, even such an upheaval as the French Revolution (if we may look ahead a little) was to have little effect on scientific progress beyond the distraction of some scientists like Lazare Carnot from their theoretical work and the abrupt termination of the career of Lavoisier by the guillotine because he was a tax farmer. During the Revolution Sir William Herschel was to continue his celestial observations and Laplace to write his great books, rounding out the Newtonian system and synthesizing the existing knowledge of science. Luigi Galvani and Alessandro Volta carried on their electrical experimentation, including their dispute over the existence of "animal electricity."

There is discernible, however, a certain change in the emphasis of scientific enterprise, perhaps related to the general climate of opinion. The generation that was to witness the French Revolution was to defy, more generally, openly, and violently than previous generations, accepted institutions and articles of faith in the religious and political spheres. Whereas Newton and his successors had been interested in the mechanical operation of energy, matter, and celestial bodies, scientists in Lavoisier's and Laplace's day raised questions regarding the nature of matter, its origin, and its evolution. This was a reflection of the fuller-blown materialism of the age—the conviction that, as Laplace was to put it one day, all events, whether physical or human, could be predicted if only enough could be known about them. And yet few of them, perhaps because they did not know enough but also because they expected reform from above, predicted the revolution that was to come.

By the 1780's the demand for "rational" human institutions was familiar, and each new scientific theory, casting its modicum of doubt upon ancient beliefs, further weakened the hold of tradition upon the minds of men. The attack on obsolescent customs and institutions, especially those which were thought to impinge on the natural liberties of man and to substitute social privileges for natural equality, had gained momentum since the days of Louis XIV. It even infected the palaces of the leading rulers of Europe.

The American Revolution, it has already been noted, translated theory into action. The English philosopher Dr. Richard Price, friend of Franklin and American independence, in 1784 wrote his *Observations on the Importance of the American Revolution and the Means of Rendering It a Benefit to the World*, and Condorcet made similar observations in France in 1786. The Americans had in fact become a vogue in France. The English traveler Arthur Young found in France "a strong leaven of liberty, increasing every hour since the American Revolution." The Declaration of Independence, the American state constitutions, Benjamin Franklin, and the young General de Lafayette had come just in time to fill a void in the popular clamor for slogans and heroes. Voltaire and Rousseau had recently died; the *Encyclopédie* was coming to an end; the expulsion of the Jesuits, expositors of Confucianism, had diminished the interest in Far Eastern philosophy; the war with Britain had reduced "the English mania." Franklin was one of the foremost among those who filled the niches vacated by these disappearing idols, promoting interest in America both by his reputation and by deliberate intent. He used his talents as writer, printer, and publisher to embark upon a skillful propaganda campaign. Before long the royal press of France was flooding the country with documents of American origin casting doubt upon the validity of royal sovereignty. With the example of the American states to point to in support of a real program of reforms, surviving *philosophes* like Condorcet, Chastellux, Raynal, Abbé de Mably, and Turgot now spoke less of man and the universe and more of Frenchmen and France, less about abstract systems and more about concrete projects for reform. They debated the soundness of American practices and laws with John Adams, Thomas Jefferson, and other Americans in Europe, and the pamphlets in which these debates were set forth were also widely published and read.

The demand for reform was not merely crystallizing as a program; it was also making a more general appeal among the various classes of the population. In Germany a secret society of liberal thinkers known as "the Illuminati" flourished briefly, numbering Herder and Goethe among its members. In France the ideas of the *philosophes* gained currency beyond the salons of the rich and were discussed with fervor in literary clubs, Masonic lodges, and the cafés of Paris and other cities. Such younger Frenchmen as the Comte de Mirabeau, Maximilien Robespierre, Brissot de Warville, and Jean Paul Marat, who might have become known as a younger generation of *philosophes* if events had not conspired to make them leaders of a radical revolution, had already begun to clarify their views, for themselves and their countrymen, in numerous speeches and pamphlets about contemporary political injustices, social inequalities, and economic hardships. Thus, privately and publicly, glittering generalities like the "social contract" and "the rights of man" came to be discussed along with more concrete proposals of reform.

No longer by a gradual process, the revolutionary spirit was reaching an explosive point. All classes of the population—whether clergy, nobility, or commoners—felt aggrieved. A general awareness of this dissatisfaction existed, largely because of the work of the *philosophes;* and even if the nobility tended like Montesquieu to look to the history and older institutions of France for its answers while the middle class preferred with Voltaire the rules of reason and the laws of nature, public opinion was in general favorable to reform. Old writers like Condorcet and young heroes like Lafayette were ready and willing to lead the movement toward change if the opportunity should present itself. Thus the forces in favor of revolution in the 1780's were constantly growing more irresistible.

If revolution did not come until 1789 it was not because the revolutionary forces were weak so much as because the conservative forces were still strong and still wise enough to make the necessary changes and concessions. The government of Louis XVI reflected the enlightenment of his day, and this so-called enlightened monarchy, until its presumptive allies, the nobility and clergy, proved unwilling and too divided themselves to render effective support, was able to stave off revolution for a time.

The leading monarchs of the eighteenth century were proud of their enlightenment. They did not, to be sure, go along with the radical reformers. They had their own philosophy of law, corresponding more closely with that of the political philosophers who visualized a monarch as the father of his people. Still, it was a long step from the divine-right monarch of the seventeenth century to the enlightened despot of the later eighteenth, and it was also a long step from the enlightened despot to the totalitarian dictator of the twentieth century. These "enlightened despots" were, in fact, limited not only in their enlightenment but also in their despotism. While they thought of themselves as the embodiment of their respective states and were generally guided by *raison d'état* (each seeking the advantage of his realm), they were also bound by the dynastic traditions and obligations that they had inherited. They undertook reform more in the hope of increasing their power as hereditary rulers of a prosperous and contented state than out of interest in the people themselves or out of respect for the theories of *philosophes;* and their despotism was tempered by age-old obligations to church, nobility, towns, guilds, and local customs, as well as by other corporate privileges, charters, and treaties. Still, they were generally well-meaning, paternalistic rulers—loosely conforming to the ideal of the *philosophes* if not directly influenced by them.

Probably the most dazzling of the enlightened despots was Frederick the Great of Prussia. The brilliance and the efficiency of his conduct of war and diplomacy were matched by the thoroughness and the energy with which he attacked the internal problems of Prussia. By building canals, reclaiming wastelands, introducing new farming and breeding methods from England, and extending credit to farmers, Frederick enormously increased the output of Prussian agriculture. Similar encouragement to industry through government subsidies, the granting of monopolies, the importation of new industries from other countries, and the improvement of communications turned Prussia from a poor country, especially in times of war, into a prosperous nation producing a remarkable diversity of goods in times of peace. The new territories of Silesia and West Prussia were

welded into the nation by introducing the Prussian system of administration and extensive government-sponsored colonization. Many of
the colonist were non-German, encouraged to settle in Prussia by the
king's liberal policies.

In the last decades of his life Frederick studiously cultivated international peace. The only war he fought after 1763 was the War of
the Bavarian Succession, with its one relatively bloodless campaign
of 1778. By the Treaty of Teschen in 1779 Frederick not only kept
Bavaria out of Austria's control but also acquired Ansbach and Bay-
reuth, as well as a generally recognized leadership among the princes
of Germany.

Frederick also reorganized Prussia's tax system. This change was
made ostensibly to lighten the burdens of the peasantry (which the
reorganization really did little to accomplish) but actually produced
greater revenue for the crown. The seignorial burdens of serfdom
were somewhat lightened by Frederick, but he stopped far short of
abolishing those burdens altogether. Furthermore, his new system of
taxes perpetuated the old aristocratic exemptions. A well-known
story illustrates both Frederick's enlightenment and the sternness of
his tax measures. One day Old Fritz, as he was now popularly called,
encountered a crowd of his subjects craning their necks to look at a
caricature of the king grinding a coffee mill with one hand while
carefully picking up fallen coffee beans with the other—a none too
subtle reference to his grinding and penny-pinching tax methods.
Frederick ordered his groom merely to hang the picture lower "so
they won't have to hurt their necks." The crowd thereupon tore up
the caricature and followed him with cries of "Long live the King!"

Although most of his life committed to *raison d'état*, Frederick
at one time had thought of the king as "only the first servant of the
people." That phrase he had used himself in an early book, *Anti-
Macchiavel*, brought out under the patronage of Voltaire in 1740. It
was written in French, for Frederick preferred that language to his
native German and did little to brighten the German literary lights of
his day like Lessing or Goethe. His famous Berlin Academy of Sciences was crowded with French *philosophes* including, for several
years before they openly quarreled, his friend Voltaire. Although he
was also under the influence of German philosophers like Thomasius
and Wolff, Frederick was somewhat of a *philosophe* himself. In addition to writing books in French on political problems, he reformed
the law code by his *Codex Fridericianus;* and, though it was completed only after his death, his *Allgemeines Landrecht,* or civil code

of Prussia, became an outstanding German code of law, combining
the law of nature with Roman and German ideas of justice. Frederick
also promoted secular education and religious toleration within his
lands.

Yet most of Frederick's reforms had a conservative cast. His agricultural and tax policies favored the great Junker landowners and
tended to promote the system of large estates rather than to provide
any great benefit for the peasantry. His encouragement of industry,
while furnishing a distinct incentive to capitalist development,
hedged in that development with old mercantilist regulations at
every turn. Well-versed though he was in the ideals of the Enlightenment, Frederick was loyal to the tradition of the dynastic, self-sufficient, bureaucratic state that he had inherited from the Prussian
monarchs of the past, particularly his hard-bitten father. The cameralists rather than the *philosophes* were his source of inspiration, and
his aim was an obedient bureaucracy as much as the popular welfare.
No class as such opposed Frederick, nor did he favor one class above
the other. All were required to serve the state obediently and faithfully. In Prussia the three-cornered struggle that went on in France,
for example, between king, nobility, and middle class was not well
defined and was barely discernible. Whatever liberal reform Frederick effected was due only in part to the current political philosophy;
it was also a result of the Hohenzollern concept of rigorous and
efficient monarchy. The *philosophes* admired in Frederick the prototype of the "legal despot" at least as much as he admired in them the
advocates of enlightenment; and it would be hard to prove that they
molded his ideas any more than he molded theirs.

Frederick's rival for German leadership, the Empress Maria
Theresa, pursued a middle course between tradition and reform.
While consistently opposing the more radical measures of her son
and co-ruler Joseph, Maria Theresa, assisted by her able adviser
Kaunitz, met with some success in uniting the diverse elements of
her domains and bettering the condition of her people. In the hope
of regaining Silesia by a victorious war, she instituted the Austrian
movement toward centralization and efficiency after the mortifying
defeat of 1740–1748. Maria Theresa was impressed by Frederick's
successes as a benevolent ruler. Her program was the pragmatic one
of strengthening the unity and resources of her state and establishing
a nice balance among the various elements which made up its soci-

ety, without encouraging any movements for reform from below. Reducing the powers of the local assemblies and instituting a system of royal provincial agents after the French model, she reorganized the Habsburg administration, centralized in Vienna, and made it more efficient. Favorably inclined toward Physiocratic doctrines, she abolished many internal customs barriers and reduced the crown's participation in industry. In order to create a class of peasant proprietors loyal to the crown and able to pay taxes for its support, she took some steps to lower the seignorial obligations of the serf and to make it easier for the peasant to acquire land. She was, however, devoutly Catholic and averse to the religious skepticism of the Enlightenment. She successfully exerted her influence to keep Joseph, on his visits to his sister Marie Antoinette in France, from seeing Voltaire, and Voltaire was apparently more disappointed than Joseph that they never met.

The empress' son Joseph, who became Holy Roman emperor on his father's death in 1765 and inherited the Austrian lands upon his mother's death in 1780, was perhaps the most thoroughgoing example of the enlightened despot. He, too, however, owed more to the royal tradition of paternalism than to the writings of the *philosophes*. He admired the domestic policies of Frederick and Catherine, both of whom he visited personally, more than he did Maria Theresa's. Long impatient over the palliative measures of his mother, Joseph attempted to abolish serfdom completely throughout his realms and launched a program designed to break up large estates and enable more peasants to own land. Following with greater conviction than hers his mother's Physiocratic economic policies, Joseph abolished the craft guilds and reduced to a negligible remnant the crown's controls over industry and commerce, retaining only a protective tariff to encourage native industries. He tried to abolish the existing internal revenue system with its inequalities and exemptions and established in its stead the single land tax so dear to the hearts of the Physiocrats. Even the tithe of the church was sacrificed to his reforming zeal. His tax modifications were short-lived, however, for they aroused so much opposition from vested interests that Joseph was forced to suspend their operation, and upon his death they were revoked by his successor.

Joseph also sought to remake Habsburg law in accordance with equalitarian ideals. In various codes promulgated in the 1780's he set forth the equality of all classes before the law and abolished the death penalty for most offenses. He centralized the judicial system and saw to it that only those were appointed judges who had had intensive training in the principles of "natural law."

The most rigorous of Joseph's reforms was the centralization of government. Eliminating all vestiges of the traditional autonomy in Hungary as a separate kingdom and in other hitherto semiautonomous provinces, he undertook to impose the Austrian administrative system and control on all parts of his realm, even the remote Netherlands and Lombardy. The realm was divided into thirteen districts administered from Vienna, and royal authority replaced local self-government even at the municipal level. This policy met with violent opposition, and the well-meaning emperor's reign was clouded by constant unrest in Hungary and, in its last years, by actual revolt in Belgium.

In part, the revolt in Belgium was due to the thoroughness of Joseph's religious reform, which some Belgians resented because they were devout Catholics and almost all because they opposed Joseph's disregard of their claims to local autonomy. Joseph thoroughly accepted the ideas on the relation of the church to the state promulgated by the German ecclesiastic "Febronius" (pseudonym of Johann Nikolaus von Hontheim). In 1765 Febronius had set forth for Germany a doctrine closely resembling that of Louis XIV's Bishop Bossuet on Gallican Liberties, subordinating papal authority to the national church. Febronius found ready listeners among the German princes. About the very moment, therefore, that the pope felt obliged to suppress his most loyal partisans, the Jesuits, his political power was being challenged in Germany.

Joseph took advantage of this wave of "Febronianism" not merely to assert his adhesion to the theory of Austrian ecclesiastical autonomy but also to diminish the power of the church in his realm. By a series of acts culminating in an Edict of Tolerance in 1781, he confiscated hundreds of monasteries and their properties, releasing thousands of their members from their vows, and reorganized the surviving 27,000 monks and nuns (less than half of the original number) in the remaining 1,324 monasteries. He created state-supported schools on former church properties. He loosened the restrictions upon Protestants and Jews. He attempted to diminish the political bonds of the Austrian clergy with Rome. His characteristic thoroughness in the application of Febronianism gave to his policy the name of "Josephism" and furnished a precedent for the revolutionaries of France, who within a few years were going to attempt to subordinate the church entirely to the state. At home, and especially in the more devout provinces of Belgium, his toleration and anticlericalism encountered resistance.

Before his death Joseph's legal despotism proved, in fact, as much a failure as Frederick's was a success. Most of what he had done was repudiated by his successor because of the opposition that it aroused from all classes. Even the peasants were confused by his reforms and in numerous revolts forced abandonment of his program. A well-meaning emperor, it would seem, cannot force reforms upon an unprepared people, particularly when there is good reason to believe that his purpose is to enhance royal power by overriding local customs. When Joseph died, leaving to his brother the suppression of the revolts in Belgium and the displeasure of the privileged estates elsewhere in his realm as well, he asked that his epitaph should read: "Here lies a prince whose intentions were pure but who had the misfortune to see all his plans miscarry." But when his statue was erected in Vienna it described him as "a performer of great things" and "a planner of greater ones."

Joseph's brother and successor was Leopold II, who had earned an enviable reputation as the enlightened ruler of Tuscany, which he had inherited upon his father's death in 1765. Leopold in Tuscany, like Joseph in Lombardy, had done much to mitigate the evils of feudal survivals and clerical conservatism. He had also improved the laws and the prisons in keeping with the principles laid down by Beccaria, Italy's outstanding criminologist. Improvement of roads, the draining of swamps, and the promotion of agriculture made Tuscany a more prosperous state than it had been since the days of the great Medicis.

Elsewhere in Italy, the petty princes did not play the role of enlightened despot. In Sardinia and Naples the reigning princes proved more despotic than enlightened. The republics of Venice and Genoa continued in their aristocratic lethargy, the latter having been obliged in 1768 to cede Corsica to France in time for Napoleon Bonaparte to be born (1769) a Frenchman. The suppression of the Jesuits in 1773 temporarily eliminated the order's influence in the Papal States, but when Pope Clement XIV dissolved the order, though the Jesuits were especially unpopular in Rome, he acted out of political and not "enlightened" considerations. Little sense of national solidarity arose among the Italians despite their linguistic and religious similarity and their natural pride in the great contemporary figures of

Beccaria, Volta, and Galvani. Such national spirit as did arise found expression chiefly in the lofty poetry of Count Vittorio Alfieri, whose nineteen tragedies, modeled upon the French classics, revealed a profound devotion to liberty. Overshadowed by great foreign reputations in his own time, Alfieri means more to Italy today than he meant to his Italian contemporaries.

Catherine of Russia also paid deference to western theories of enlightenment. Diderot and other *philosophes* visited her, she corresponded regularly with Voltaire and other Encyclopedists, she befriended them when they were in need. She succeeded in establishing many superficial reforms, but she granted to the nobility even greater exemptions from taxes and other burdens of state, without making the least concession of her own autocratic powers. A reorganization of local government resulted chiefly in a cementing of the alliance between the empress and the nobility. The Russian gentry became, like the Prussian Junkers, loyal but unpaid local agents of the crown and received, in return, increased powers over the peasantry. Revision of the tax system, extension of free trade within Russian borders, abolition of state monopolies, and, within limits, greater freedom for private business were likewise achieved. By restricting industrial enterprise to the nobility and at the same time encouraging the middle class in commercial enterprise, she won the support of both groups. An effort to lay the foundation for a program of reform along the lines expounded by Montesquieu's *Esprit des lois* led in 1767–1768 to the convocation of a legislative commission, but it talked much and did little. The peasantry continued to suffer until in 1773–1775 they revolted under the Cossack Yemelyan Ivanovich Pugachev, only to be ruthlessly suppressed. Though Catherine played with the idea of emancipating the serfs, she ended by increasing their obligations to the nobility and implanting still further the institution of serfdom into the Russian social fabric.

Catherine was a genuine patron of arts and letters, however. She brought the French theater and French art to St. Petersburg, notably in the person of Étienne Falconet, who there executed his well-known equestrian statue of Peter the Great; and she began the justly famous art collection at her palace called "the Hermitage." She bought Voltaire's and Diderot's libraries. She also founded the famous Smolny Institute for the education of the daughters of the nobility and other secondary schools in other leading cities, and she encouraged Russians to go abroad for their higher education. Under her, St. Petersburg, which Peter had left an overgrown village, became a capital city of nearly 300,000 with magnificent houses and paved streets. Voltaire called her "the Semiramis of the North," after the legendary queen of Assyria who was believed to have founded Babylon. Moscow showed distinct signs of what has sometimes been called "the French invasion"—the upper classes affecting French manners, French clothes, and the French language. A reaction against French influences was to come with the shock of the French Revolution, all the more marked because of the thoroughness of the earlier "invasion."

In western Europe, home of the Enlightenment, benevolent despots were no more successful than Catherine in rooting out the fundamental inequalities and injustices of the Old Regime. Yet they made some serious efforts in that direction. In Spain the Bourbon King Charles III and a number of enlightened advisers attacked the numerous local privileges in government and law, sought to weaken the power of the great guilds, expelled the Jesuits, rebuilt the Spanish navy, refilled the royal treasury, and tried, by breaking up the vast landed estates, to make it simpler for the peasants to buy land. Agriculture, industry, and commerce experienced a remarkable revival after generations of torpor. Royal funds were expended on schools, hospitals, and orphanages. Spain regained Minorca, Florida, and some of her lost prestige by her participation in the War of American Independence. Altogether, the reign of Charles III was one of the brighter eras in the history of a declining nation.

In Britain George III thought of himself as a "patriot king," along the lines laid down in *The Patriot King* written by the famous Tory Viscount Bolingbroke. If George was more enlightened than despotic, it was because the British crown had long ago lost the independent strength required for despotism. In the early decades of his reign George, however, by his ability to manipulate a parliamentary majority through his control of the patronage was for the most part successful in carrying through his policies. The defenders of the parliamentary principle nevertheless fought against a possible return to royal predominance, and this struggle occupied much of George III's attention before the French Revolution. The success of the American struggle for independence was a defeat for George's policy in the mother country no less than in the colonies. The king's henchmen were driven from power with Lord North in 1782, and George's effort to clench the powers of the crown failed.

But George's reign was not barren of reform, though it was not of his making. It was done, rather, largely under the guiding hand of William Pitt, "the Younger." Pitt came to power after the Peace of 1783 and was to remain prime minister, with one significant gap, until his death in 1806. The tariff was lowered, fiscal reforms balanced the British budget, and certain liberal changes were made in the colonial system.

After the loss of the American colonies the major British imperial holdings were in India. The victory over the French in India during the Seven Years' War helped to stimulate a greater interest on the part of the London government in the administration of those overseas areas. London itself had been aghast at Clive's methods and the exactions he had procured to win his victories. He had used British power to garner large sums of money for the British East India Company and to obtain sovereign rights to huge tracts of land. Subsequently, as governor of Madras and then of Bengal, he succeeded in abolishing some of the corruption of the company and distinguished himself as an able administrator. The problem of India, nevertheless, remained a difficult one for London because of the complicated relations that bound nominally independent and native-ruled states to the semiprivate East India Company.

Official investigation of the company's administration was started in 1768, and the directorate was soon found to be corrupt. A severe famine in Bengal in 1770 made public opinion peculiarly sensitive. Demands for government regulation of the company's activities became overwhelming, particularly after the voyages and discoveries of Captain James Cook opened new Pacific vistas.

Clive, now Baron Clive of Plassey, had returned to England a few years earlier and was chosen a member of Parliament. In 1773 he was himself accused, as we shall see, of having enriched himself in India. Parliament found that he had indeed made a large sum of money at one time but also declared that he "did at the same time render great and meritorious services to his country." Nevertheless, worn out by disease and chagrin, Clive was to take his own life in 1774. He had been one of England's greatest empire builders—ruthless to her enemies, domineering to the natives, energetic in administration, daring in conquest, and occasionally suspected (but never convicted) of corruption.

Meanwhile, India had become a producer of a new source of wealth to Europeans and of pleasure and degeneration to Orientals.

The wealth derived from the opium traffic had grown enormously. In 1773 the British East India Company succeeded in getting an opium monopoly in British India. The British, however, were not the only opium peddlers. The Portuguese, the Dutch, and the French also profited from peddling it. And when the Americans entered the China trade in 1784 they too participated.

In 1772 a Commons committee that had investigated the East India Company made a shocking report of malfeasance and mismanagement. But that did not put an end to the abuses. In the next year the company acquired its monopoly of opium, and Clive was impeached for corruption while in India. Englishmen were outraged. To still the public indignation, the then Prime Minister Lord North, with Clive's support, steered a Regulating Act through Parliament. This was the first of several measures designed to define more precisely the relations of the company to the crown. The Regulating Act laid particular emphasis upon the restriction of the private enterprise of Indian officials and the centralization of Britain's holdings in India. It placed the other governors under the governor of Bengal, who thus became a governor-general. Moreover, it enabled Parliament to nominate the first four men to function as a resident council in the administration of India. The subsequent appointments of governor and councillors were to be made by the company. The Regulating Act was the first step in the direction of an important governmental principle for India—that it should have a centralized administration under controlling direction at home. This measure, however, proved ineffective, and it soon became apparent that a more thoroughgoing reform was required. But at this juncture the thirteen American colonies claimed the British ministry's major attention. Although the British East India Company's tea was involved in the American complications, any new program for India had to be postponed until the growing revolutionary crisis in the American colonies should be resolved.

A decade after Lord North's Regulating Act, Charles James Fox introduced the India Act into Parliament. At its first trial the bill was defeated by Fox's political enemies. The following year, however, Prime Minister William Pitt, "the Younger" successfully guided a similar measure through Parliament. This India Act of 1784 thoroughly reorganized the management of India, placing political affairs in the hands of the home government but leaving the trading interests to the company. The crown was authorized to appoint a Board of Control, whose chief was a cabinet minister, to supervise civil and military administration. The company was still permitted to exploit India economically and to appoint with the crown's approval the highest ranking officials in the government of India except the governor-general. The Board of Control, however, had the power to veto such appointments, to modify the company's instructions, and to communicate directly with officials in India. Minor changes in this administrative system were made from time to time, but the basic system of dual control went unaltered and functioned awkwardly but successfully until 1858.

The British government was considerably less successful in establishing relations with China. Its failure to do so through the diplomatic procedures customary in the Western world strengthened its resolve to resort to extraordinary methods. Furthermore, British merchants in China, as well as many of their backers at home, had become annoyed with the interference of the tradition-bound and apprehensive British East India Company, and their annoyance was not diminished because of the greater freedom enjoyed after American independence by United States traders at Canton. The economic theory now prevalent back home also expounded the virtues of free and unregulated trade. And British factory owners were anxious to have free access to the resources of China and the opportunity to sell the products of British industry in what they fondly hoped would be an almost insatiable market. But not until 1834 was the British government to be forced to abolish the monopoly of the East India Company in the China trade.

Meanwhile, the British government continued its quest for an opportunity to deal directly with the Chinese throne in the effort to open China's doors to British merchants and enterprisers. Conscious of the vast possibilities of the China trade, the British took the lead in what was a general European effort to win recognition, to receive equal treatment, and to be permitted to establish permanent diplomatic relations with China. This effort, however, was destined to be frustrated until China was forced by military action (1839–1842) to agree to open "All under Heaven" to free intercourse and to negotiate with the westerners on something approaching a basis of equality.

In India, however, the problems of the British were not those of suppliants but of sahibs. Their position imposed a double obligation upon them—that of military pacification and that of domestic order. No matter how true it may have been that the British were prompted in India by self-interest, and no matter how justified critics may seem in accusing the British of bleeding India and of ignoring the plight of India's millions, the British thought of themselves also as reformers. They brought a certain degree of national solidarity, a sense of order, and a spirit of equality to India along with the modern political, commercial, and technological methods by which they ruled and exploited it.

Despite the limitations placed in 1784 upon the British East India Company's authority, it continued to grow at the expense of India. Warren Hastings was appointed the first governor-general of India under the Regulating Act of 1773 and still held that office at the time of the India Act of 1784. During that period he laid the real foundations of Britain's empire in India. Following Clive's policy of interfering in Indian affairs in order to reinforce British interests, Hastings used all means at his disposal, whether bordering on the unscrupulous or not, to reap benefits for the company. Displeased with the India Act, he retired from his post in 1784 and was subsequently impeached in Parliament for high crimes and misdemeanors while in India. His trial was made famous by Edmund Burke's accusations and the historical essay later written by Lord Macaulay, but in the end he was acquitted. The impeachments of Clive and Hastings nevertheless tended to indicate that the company's servants in India were accountable to a higher authority.

Hastings was succeeded in India by Lord Cornwallis, the general vanquished at Yorktown. Cornwallis and his successors continued painstakingly the work begun by Clive and Hastings, and they were able through the powers granted to them by the India Act of 1784 to proceed even more vigorously. Cornwallis put the civil servants in India on a better wage basis and then ruthlessly suppressed corruption and graft in the public service. He also reformed the police system and endeavored, by combining native and English codes and judicial procedures, to make legal practices as nearly uniform as possible. Moreover, before Cornwallis left India (1794), the British carried through the so-called Permanent Settlement of Bengal (1793). Inaugurated at the outset of Hastings' regime, this was an effort to straighten out the system of land tenure and to simplify the collection of land taxes.

Although the Permanent Settlement failed to protect the cultivators adequately, it was appreciated in many parts of India as a sincere attempt to improve the conditions of the native population. Under pressure from humanitarian groups in Europe and in the hope that the profits of the East India Company could thereby be increased, the British continued their efforts to suppress native violence, cruel and superstitious traditions, illiteracy, and inefficiency. While British reforms inspired gratitude among some of the Indians, important groups resented foreign domination and continued to wage war against the invaders. Beginning in 1778 three military campaigns had to be fought against the belligerent Mahrattas of southern and central India, but not until 1828 did the diligence of the East India Company's servants bring most of the peninsula under British control. Despite their efforts to better the life of the natives, the British continued to be mainly concerned with their own power, prestige, and profits.

With the extension of British control in India, the attention of scholars, thinkers, and artists shifted away from China to India. In the late eighteenth century, while Europe was embroiled in war over American independence, the spiritual ties with India were drawn even tighter as Britain sought to guard her remaining empire more zealously than ever before. Although the Jesuit fathers in India had learned the vernacular languages of the subcontinent, they had been prohibited by Hindu religious traditions from learning and teaching Sanskrit, the language of the Hindu sacred writings. When Warren Hastings was governor-general, he took the initial steps to secure permission for Sir William Jones and Sir Charles Wilkins to study under Hindu teachers, and they were finally allowed to do so. They were among the first to detect the kinship of the Indo-European languages. It was not until 1790, however, that the first Sanskrit grammar was published in the West. Thereafter the wealth of Hindu thought and tradition could be seriously explored by European scholars.

Meanwhile the British met with striking successes in the Pacific Islands. In 1761 and 1769 the planet Venus crossed the sun's disc, and several learned societies and governments agreed to cooperate in making observations of those otherwise rare phenomena from different points of the earth's surface. As part of the British participation in this international undertaking in 1768, Captain James Cook set sail to Tahiti to observe the anticipated transit of Venus. Instructed also to search for the great "South Land" (probably Tasmania, discovered over a century earlier by the Dutch seaman Abel Janszoon Tasman), Captain Cook circumnavigated New Zealand and landed in 1770 on the eastern coast of Australia at an anchorage he called Botany Bay. After several expeditions northward along the coast, Cook took possession of the land in the name of the British king. Upon returning to England, Cook and his backers successfully stirred up sentiment for colonization of Australia. In 1778 he returned to the Pacific waters and explored the islands that he named in honor of the Earl of Sandwich, the first lord of the admiralty. In the course of these explorations, Cook was killed by the frightened natives of the Sandwich Islands (now known as the "Hawaiian Islands").

British progress in the Pacific, taking place at the same time that British power was growing in India, constituted a serious threat to the Dutch in the East Indies. The British successes were particularly alarming to them because of the now straitened circumstances of the Dutch East India Company. Mismanagement, graft, and reverses during the War of American Independence, coupled with the gradual loss of spice sources and markets, had combined to throw the company hopelessly into debt, and in 1782 it paid its last dividend. (In 1798, while the Dutch were allies of Revolutionary France, its assets and liabilities were taken over by the Dutch government in the public interest. Thereupon the company was permanently disbanded, and its empire became the possession of the Dutch government.)

Colonial and commercial successes and contingencies like these helped Pitt as prime minister to restore much of Britain's lost prestige in international affairs. In 1786 a treaty (named after the British special envoy to Paris, William Eden) permitted a freer exchange, as recommended by the newer trade theories, of British manufactured articles against French agricultural products, particularly wines. This treaty soon appeared to be of greater benefit to the British factory than to the French vineyard. In the 1780's Pitt similarly took advantage of two diplomatic crises that arose over the Netherlands to break the isolation of Britain and to diminish the prestige of France. In 1788 he formed with Prussia and the Dutch stadholder an alliance aimed at the preservation of the status quo, which had been threatened by Joseph II's ambition to make Belgium a great commercial center and by France's support of the antistadholder party in the Netherlands.

Thus, just before the French Revolution, Britain was well on the road toward recovery of her leadership both as a parliamentary government and as an international force. The French Revolution and its bursts of violence were, in fact, to lead to so much fear and unfavorable reaction in Britain as to check the more radical elements. The basic changes for which the reformers of Pitt's day clamored— the abolition of the slave trade, fuller representation in Parliament, and a more liberal franchise—were therefore left for a later age to accomplish.

In France, home of the *philosophes*, who had most vigorously preached the Enlightenment, the accession of Louis XVI in 1774 augured well for the cause of reform. He quickly appointed a group of enlightened ministers and recalled the parlements that Louis XV had exiled. Those who hoped for reform rejoiced. They were soon, however, to learn that they could not count fully upon the good will of their king. Louis XVI, though well-intentioned and by no means stupid, was too easily influenced by his conservative family and court to play the full role of benevolent autocrat or to support consistently a reforming minister.

In Louis' first reform ministry, the comptroller-general was Anne-Robert-Jacques Turgot, the friend of the *philosophes* and Physiocrats. Turgot planned a broad reform program including more equitable taxation, the abolition of the *corvée*, freedom of the grain trade from some of its more onerous restrictions, reduction of court expenditures, and a network of local elective assemblies culminating in an elected national assembly. Within a few years, however, he aroused so much opposition within the royal court that the king reluctantly dismissed him from office. Turgot was admired by Voltaire and many other *philosophes*. Voltaire had long suspected that the parlements were an obstacle rather than a help in the reform movement. Turgot's failure convinced other *philosophes* as well that the restored parlements, which had blocked Turgot's proposals, were more anxious to assert their own prerogatives than to effect true reform. Some historians have subsequently maintained that the last good chance to save the Bourbon monarchy by royal concessions that would have prevented popular revolution vanished with Turgot's departure from office.

After Turgot, various ministers tried various programs. Most of them were directed frankly toward staving off bankruptcy rather than reforming society, for Louis XV's legacy of debt, augmented by enormous French expenditures in the War of the American Revolution, was fast ruining the French government's credit. Palliative measures by a succession of finance ministers failed to restore the credit of the royal treasury. Finally Comptroller-General Charles-

Alexandre de Calonne adopted a radical measure—the convocation of the Assembly of Notables. The notables, designated by the king, had sometimes in the past been called together, in preference to the Estates General, to advise the throne when the opinion of the three estates (clergy, nobility, and commoners) had been sought. Calonne proposed (1787) to convoke an Assembly of Notables and to place the financial crisis before it, though it had been in abeyance for over 160 years. He desired to get from the notables approval of a series of new taxes that the parlements had consistently blocked and, in return, to make some political and social reforms. The proposal was a bold one, since it opened an avenue to public censure through the notables, but Calonne realized that it was necessary to make this concession in order to avoid greater ones.

The notables, however, proved, like the parlements, more concerned with asserting their power than with effecting reform. They made a scapegoat of Calonne, induced the king to exile him, and refused to sanction the major features of his tax program. They did, however, propose toleration for Protestants, which the king now granted, as well as the creation of provincial assemblies where they did not already exist.

Most of these new provincial assemblies, controlled like the parlements and the notables by the nobles, soon joined the general opposition to new taxes. They also voiced the now insistent demand for reviving the Estates General, in the hope of diminishing the royal power and increasing their own through agencies once dominated by the nobility. The king's new minister, Loménie de Brienne, yielded, but without fixing a definite date for the meeting of the Estates General. Brienne could not maintain himself against the steadily growing, sometimes riotous, opposition and finally was obliged to give way to the banker and philanthropist Jacques Necker. Necker had previously, as a government official, shown himself a friend of reform, but the king had hitherto been unwilling to name him a minister because he was a Protestant, a bourgeois, and Swiss-born. Late in 1788, Necker fixed the date of the Estates General's meeting for early in 1789.

Meanwhile the clamor for reform had grown louder. As we have seen, the programs of the *philosophes* had steadily become more radical and more concrete and had reached into the remote corners and among the underprivileged of the realm. They now centered upon the anticipated revival of the ancient representative body, the Estates General. Hundreds of pamphlets, including posthumous works by old *philosophes* like Mably and new appeals by young writers like the Abbé Sieyès argued that the new Estates General must be something different from the old Estates General, last convoked in 1614, and must become rather a more modern body. The old Estates General had been a tricameral, consultative assembly controlled by the nobility, who had made up the upper two estates and dominated the Third Estate. What these writers wanted was a Third Estate that would be as numerous as the other two orders combined, with the Estates General so reorganized that the Third Estate could, if necessary, outvote the other two orders. In a pamphlet published in February 1789, Sieyès, a member of the clergy but a supporter of the Third Estate, asked three questions and gave three answers that have remained famous: "What is the Third Estate? Everything. What has it been hitherto in the political order? Nothing. What does it ask? To become something."

In the early months of 1789 Sieyès's questions and answers were indicative of the general trend of liberal and radical opinion. A prominent part of the articulate public generally held that the Third Estate, which comprised numerically almost the entire nation, ought to be allowed political influence in some proportion to its numbers. This trend of thought broke with tradition, wherein conservative reformers sought to find the proper remedies, and turned toward reason as the source of political truth. The trend was significant in two ways: It aimed at curtailing the time-honored powers of the privileged groups, and it revealed a popular movement to change the Estates General from an assembly controlled by the nobles and merely advisory to the king, as was traditional, into the voice of the sovereign people of France. The Third Estate alone, some openly declared, could and should vote changes in the "fundamental law" of the land, if the privileged orders refused to do so.

The growing demand for popular participation in solving the nation's problems reflected a general apprehension that what enlightened despotism was ready to offer was too little. And, indeed, the weaknesses of the Old Regime could not readily be reformed from above, even when—as was the case for Louis XVI but not for Joseph II —confidence in the ruler was widespread. The privileges and exemptions of the clergy and the nobility, and the preference for nobles in high civil, military, and ecclesiastical office could not be obliterated without great loss to the very groups that monarchs were most inclined to befriend. The confusing varieties of local government, the numerous and often conflicting systems of law and justice, and the inequality of taxes and administration among the provinces were frequently based upon charters and royal grants that kings felt honorbound to respect. The inefficiency, inertia, and corruption of government bred by officeholding through heredity and purchase, and the tensions between the more and the less honored groups within the same ranks of society were due to a quasi-caste system of society that could not well be questioned without calling into question the very principle of kingship. The iniquities arising from ministerial usurpations in the name of an absolute monarch could be remedied only if the problem of ministerial responsibility were squarely faced. The impediments to industry and commerce from guilds and royal controls, and the numerous, unequal, and high customs duties were economic abuses that probably could not be corrected without raising some doubts regarding the extent of the king's economic authority. The antiquated seignorial obligations of the peasantry, and the poverty and degradation of the unorganized and disfranchised city proletariat could hardly be relieved without adding some great burden to already hard-pressed royal treasuries and officials. Few of these evils were likely to be swept away by a reforming monarch, no matter how well-intentioned, so long as he considered (to paraphrase a remark by Joseph II) that "kingship was his business."

Much had indeed been accomplished by the "despots," the nature and extent of the changes varying greatly with the personalities and aims of the rulers and the characters of the institutions they had tried to change. But the enlightened monarchs were dependent upon the privileged classes, especially the upper clergy, who governed their churches, and the military nobility, who ran their armies. They recognized with Montesquieu that monarchies could not survive without an especially honored class. And so, in the end, they failed to provide the answer to the needs of the times, for they were caught on the horns of a dilemma. Reforms aimed at increasing the royal power by centralization and by reduction of privileges would alienate those who had a stake in maintaining the status quo and thus would turn the nobility, the natural defenders of monarchy, against the king. At the same time the spotty reforms that the enlightened monarchs did effect did not go far enough to suit the middle class, the peasants, and the city workers, who could benefit very little without a thorough remodeling of the existing system.

In France the groups favoring change grew in power and numbers while the conservative forces began to betray cleavages between orders as well as within the separate orders. The king hoped to win middle-class support away from the nobility and even the support of the lower clergy away from the upper clergy, and perhaps even that of the liberal nobles like Lafayette away from the more conservative nobles. This maneuvering of the king and the aristocracy for popular support led to a great victory for the Third Estate. Necker, hoping to avoid responsibility for a radical decision, called the Assembly of Notables together again and asked them to consider whether the Third Estate should be double the size of either the clergy or the nobility. The notables, however, insisted on the old forms and traditions, and at the year's close, the minister decided to issue what a grateful nation soon dubbed "Necker's New Year's gift to the people." The Third Estate was granted by royal decree double the number of representatives allowed each of the other two estates, but it was also intimated that only on occasions when the upper two orders consented might the three estates vote as a single body. Thus when they were to vote "by head" and when they were to vote "by body" remained essentially unsettled.

By the time the Estates General met in May 1789, other concessions had been made to the Third Estate. Necker announced a program of reform—conservative enough, since it advocated caution with regard to changes in upper-class privileges, but nevertheless granting the Estates General a voice in taxation and the annual budget. The Third Estate was to be elected by nearly universal male suffrage among the *roturier* (i.e., common) classes, and the lower clergy were to be directly represented in the First Estate. The reform elements might by these concessions to the underprivileged get a clear majority. This favor toward the underprivileged was considerably further than any enlightened despot had yet gone, and had Louis continued in this program, enlightened despotism might still have proved itself capable of solving its problems. In addition, each member of the Estates General was invited to bring from his constituency a *cahier de doléances* (list of grievances). The people of France were thus encouraged to feel that at last the government was going to undertake a thorough reform. Hence the Estates General was to open its meeting in an atmosphere not of rebellion and hatred but of confidence and hope. Yet, because the divided French Establishment lacked the good will to make adequate concessions, the ruthlessness to engage in relentless civil war and repression, or the imagination to invent timely diversions, this promising situation was soon to break into wave upon wave of revolutionary crises, accompanied by bloodshed, tyranny, war, and drastic innovations.

The roll call of the so-called enlightened despots would be incomplete without the names of the contemporary rulers of Portugal, Denmark-Norway, and Sweden. For all three of these realms the major issue was the centralization of government in the royal service by the reduction of the traditional or the newly devised pretensions to authority of the hereditary nobility. Joseph of Portugal (d. 1777) and Christian VII of Denmark-Norway (d. 1808) were themselves ordinary, if not incompetent, but the trend of the times toward benevolent and centralized kingship was carried on by their chief ministers.

The Marquis de Pombal's suppression of the Jesuits in Portugal, coming shortly after the Lisbon earthquake, was an early step in the repression of the clergy as rivals to the royal prerogative. He also repressed both popular riot and nobles' conspiracy by relentlessly meting out capital punishment. As he thus enhanced royal despotism, he at the same time embellished the royal reputation for enlightenment by promoting industry, improving the school system, and patronizing the university. After the death of King Joseph, however, his opponents were able to have him arraigned for abuse of power (1779), and he was exiled from Lisbon in 1780.

Pombal's policy was somewhat parallel to that of Johann Friedrich Struensee. Though born in Halle, Germany, Struensee rose to power as the physician of the mentally unstable King Christian VII of Denmark-Norway and as lover of the queen. He centralized authority in the crown by depriving important nobles of high office, diminishing the semiautonomous regime of Norway, and creating a single judicial hierarchy responsible to the king. At the same time he cultivated the crown's reputation for benevolence by granting a wider freedom of the press, alleviating some of the seignorial dues of the serfs, reforming the municipal government of Copenhagen, and reducing the harsh treatment of unmarried mothers. All of this benevolence, however, was insufficient in the eyes of his enemies to counterbalance the heinousness of adultery with the queen, for which he was beheaded in 1772.

Gustavus III of Sweden (1746–1792) was of a different stripe from Joseph and Christian. Only twenty-five upon his accession to the throne, vigorous and intelligent, he carried out his own program. It was essentially the same, however, as that of other so-called enlightened despots—to domesticate the ancient nobility, to strengthen the royal service, and, in so doing, to win popular support for royal centralization against the probable opposition of the centrifugal interests. Centralization was a particularly difficult problem for Gustavus because of foreign intervention. The Swedish nobility was divided into two opposing camps—the Caps, who looked for support from Catherine of Russia, and the Hats, who considered Louis XVI of France their ally. With the support of France Gustavus was able to crush the Caps and, in a surprisingly successful defensive war against Russia and Denmark (1788–1789), to rally most of the population behind him. After 1772 he ruled Sweden almost unhampered, rarely calling together its noble-dominated Riksdag. Meanwhile he also played the role of the enlightened despot to the hilt, writing works, especially dramas, of distinct literary merit, creating the Swedish Academy, permitting a certain latitude of freedom of the press and of religious toleration, abolishing *torture préalable* (i.e., of witnesses in order to extract evidence), reforming the Poor Laws, the internal tariff duties, the export taxes, and the currency, and greatly improving the navy. The Riksdag, called together in 1786, revealed a marked hostility to Gustavus' reforms, and it was a noble who shot him in the back in 1792, just as he was planning to intervene in the French Revolution on behalf of the humiliated French monarchy.

In some ways the tragic careers of Pombal, Struensee, and Gustavus III illustrate better than those of the more powerful enlightened despots the untimeliness of the policy that sought to prevent revolution by winning broad popular support for royalty against nobility. For on the eve of the French Revolution a large part of the European public was beginning to be convinced that in the three-cornered contest for power (king versus nobility versus people) sovereignty would not rest with the king, whether in alliance with his nobility or in alliance with his people, but with at least the more affluent portion of the people, the governed, with or without alliance with one or the other contestant, the ostensible governors of the people.

CHAPTER SEVEN

Epilogue

In the series of revolutions that rocked the Western world after 1776, the Western Hemisphere, as we have noted time and again, played a considerable role. The first decisive eighteenth-century revolution had occurred in the United States, and it was expected in some quarters of Europe that Americans would favor revolution abroad and be generally sympathetic with revolutionary France, especially since the Franco-American alliance had been so important in winning American independence. Indeed, some in the new republic felt that the destiny of their country was so intimately tied up with the triumph of liberty and equality that they expressed a warm enthusiasm for the French and their revolutionary slogans. But others were no less convinced that America's destiny was to be wrought in America alone, outside of and free from foreign alliances. Part of the young country's early history centered upon the disputes of these two factions—one that today we might call "isolationist" and the other that favored cooperation with friendly powers.

Despite such factional disputes the new nation prospered materially, developed an independent culture, and became the world's foremost champion of republicanism—almost its lone champion after the triumph of Europe's "legitimate" monarchs in 1815. It would perhaps be too bold to claim that because republicanism remained alive in America it ultimately triumphed in most of the modern world, but had it failed in America, as many Europeans hoped it would, probably that ultimate triumph would have been less complete and longer postponed. That the United States not only endured as a republic but grew stronger as a republican federation caused many Europeans to doubt the truth of the proposition, generally considered axiomatic in the eighteenth century, that republics were necessarily weak and that federation among them was likely to be precarious. In fact, it took the American Civil War to determine how strong the American federation really was. But even in earlier events the prosperity and the growing popular base of the American republic became manifest; and its centripetal development though challenged, accumulated that strength which was ultimately to lead to its victory over its challengers.

The beginning of the new constitutional regime in the United States coincided with the first steps in the French Revolution. The Americans were to establish a lasting constitution while the French were to fail. Several reasons account for the Americans' success. Among the more important ones were that the Americans had a long experience with self-government behind them, that their social caste system was not deeply entrenched, that their economic structure was flexible, and that they were three thousand miles removed from the armies and the diplomatic intrigues of Europe. In all these regards they were more fortunate than the French.

Shortly after the American Constitution had been ratified, an election was held for the first Congress of the new federation. The results were overwhelmingly in favor of those who had drafted or supported the Constitution. No other candidate being considered, the Electoral College chose for president the man who had led the revolutionary armies and had later been chairman of the Constitutional Convention, George Washington. On April 30, 1789, he was administered the oath of office on the balcony of Federal Hall in Wall Street, New York, before a wildly cheering crowd. Then he repaired to the Senate chamber, where he delivered a simple but earnest inaugural address. Two days later Louis XVI formally received the representatives of the three estates of the Estates General of 1789, which was eventually to draw up the first of France's many written constitutions.

In the three centuries between the discovery of America and 1789 most of Europe had moved gradually from a medieval to a more modern culture. The rising power of kings had diminished the political power of the nobility; the Reformation had rent the religious unity of western Europe as the dynastic state system increased its political disunity; provincial separatism had appreciably given way to monarchical centralization; the agrarian economy was being modified by the growth of commerce and industry; the monopolistic guild system had declined before the inroads of royal and mercantile enterprise; the rise of the middle class had unsettled the medieval social pattern; science, invention, and natural philosophy were challenging the authoritarianism of medieval scholasticism and politics; the new astronomy, the great voyages of discovery, the rebirth of paganism, and the growth of secularism had turned man's attention from heaven to earth, an earth that was no longer the center of the universe; and dramatic upsets of sacrosanct traditions through wars and revolutions accustomed men to instability and change in human affairs. The cultural pattern of Europe in 1789 probably would look much more familiar to the twentieth-century observer than the pattern of 1492.

And yet in 1789 still-powerful remnants of the medieval past persisted, anachronistic enough even in that day to be recognized as obsolete, yet so firmly entrenched that it was to take a world revolution to root them out. The nobility, still clinging to their honored position as a warrior order and as a political power, not only retained privileges and exemptions deriving from their historic functions but also, though challenged, continued to dominate the social life of their countries. In the face of a rising clamor for representative government, the king maintained his absolute power, at once a culmination and a defiance of the medieval feudal system. The church remained something of a state within the state in an era when absolutist dynasties sought a monolithic unity and centralization of their realms. The guild system and government regimentation of economic activity endured, along with ancient systems of customs duties, local tolls, and royal taxes, to hamper freedom-seeking businessmen. Countless variations in provincial and municipal loyalties, laws, privileges, customs, and administration blocked the achievement of national unity and centralization. Serfdom and slavery lingered on, and men were arbitrarily deprived of freedom and possessions in an age in which it was nevertheless often devoutly stated (sometimes by the slaveholder) that all men were equally endowed with the natural rights of life, liberty, and property.

All these overlapping and contradictory institutions made up the "Old Regime," as the European cultural pattern before 1789 eventually came to be called. They were the result of a profound lag in the adaptation of customs, attitudes, and institutions to the current philosophical and technological challenges. The outspoken victims of this lag were the wealthy, assertive, economically powerful, literate, and self-conscious middle class, whose commerce, industry, and political ambitions were becoming a dominant force in the life of the age. In terms of that class's activities and aspirations, medieval survivals were notably outmoded. The nobility monopolized the political and social positions that the middle class craved. Government regulation of trade and industry interfered with the middle class's business, now reaching an unprecedented scale with the speeding-up of the Industrial Revolution. The social inequalities from which the middle class suffered made it especially receptive to the philosophy of natural rights. Religious intolerance, special privilege, and political and social abuses offended their reason, particularly if they were themselves the sufferers. Absolutism—even a reforming absolutism bent upon wiping out the more patent evils of the Old Regime— stood squarely across the road to the representative government that they desired, at least for themselves. The abuses of the Old Regime were thus painfully apparent to this large and articulate rank of people who suffered from it. Joined by a number of those who benefited from the existing order but had other reasons—sometimes altruistic —for wishing it changed, the middle class helped in 1789 to begin to produce the major changes that we call the French Revolution.

The French Revolution began because the absolute government of Louis XVI proved both unwilling to make enough timely and sufficient concessions, although it made some, to forestall the rising demand for limited government and unable to prevent that demand from growing. Its inadequacy was the consequence of the collapse of effective authority under Louis XVI. That collapse was the culmination of the old three-cornered struggle of king, nobility, and middle class for power. In the past middle-class opinion had generally tended to side with the king against the common enemy, the nobility, but in the eighteenth century that alliance had ceased to be reliable, chiefly because the middle class had grown strong enough to switch sides in a number of public disputes or, with lower-class support, to take a stand against the other two. This three-cornered fight led to a rivalry between the two conservative forces (kings and nobles) for the support of the Third Estate (primarily middle-class notables), and hence to the collapse of the ones favoring the status quo and of the Old Regime.

The pattern of revolutionary causation already indicated becomes visible here, too. The various shortcomings and abuses of the Old Regime have already been described in several contexts. These provocations led at first to an abstract philosophy of reform articulated by the intellectuals of that day, the *philosophes*. That philosophy became a program of direct action, especially after the example of American revolutionary success was provided. Leaders were to arise among not only the discontented and the intellectuals but also the soldiers who had taken part in the American War of Independence. The demand for reform, we have found, at an early stage of the eighteenth century took shape along the lines of Montesquieu's proposals for a powerful nobility to check royal absolutism, but at a later stage Montesquieu's *thèse nobiliaire* was countered by a *thèse royale*, the advocacy of a moderate reform movement through the efforts made by enlightened despots to become reformers themselves, thus postponing the full development of "reform from below." In France this moderate policy was destined to prove too late and too little and to lead to a full-blown revolution.

The programs of the several generations of eighteenth-century *philosophes* had been nurtured upon roots that had spread far and wide in an ancient soil. By the time the Estates General of France met at Versailles in 1789, they had behind them a "revolutionary tradition" (paradoxical though the phrase may seem). They could look back not only to the struggles of the ancient Hebrews and Christians for righteousness and to those of the ancient Greeks and Romans for the good, true, and beautiful, but also to recent centuries of change. Moreover, since the Middle Ages, Europe had experienced extraordinary shifts in its prevalent modes of thought. The Renaissance had tended to secularize, even to paganize, the European's thoughts and work, thus fixing his attention upon the here and now rather than upon a paradise lost and to be regained. The new science had helped turn his speculation to the practical and concrete from the scholastic and ideal. The Age of Discovery had brought him into contact with peoples, cultures, religions, and commodities he had scarcely known before, had challenged his accepted beliefs, and had altered his economic practices. New lands and new technologies had led to a commercial revolution first and then to still-nascent revolutions in industry and agriculture.

The Reformation, despite its bitter disputes over the ways of God with man, had taken another step in the direction of secularizing men's minds. It had secularized even religion. For most Protestants now placed a greater emphasis upon the individual's own responsibility for his eternal salvation; God would help him only if he would help himself. And the deists and *philosophes* doubted divine intervention in human affairs altogether. Meanwhile the religious wars of the sixteenth and seventeenth centuries had taught that although a supposedly divinely inspired ruler might establish a nation's creed by force, its choice might sometimes depend upon the consent of the worshipers. Moreover, quarrels among the rulers made it possible for groups of nonconformists within a state to find allies from without. Religious revolt and political change thus went hand in hand, and were often best articulated or most conspicuously led by those whom the new thought and the new technologies had unsettled or made rich. By 1789 those who accepted the new thought were persuaded that change meant progress, for a benign nature or rational "hidden hand" ordered the universe, and all was, or was someday to become, right with the world.

The revolutionary tradition had within it not only an ancient ideological background but also a long history of sometimes successful resistance to misgovernment and tyranny. The Old Testament's Moses and Pharaoh or Samuel and Saul, the New Testament's Jesus and Pilate, Plutarch's Demosthenes and Philip of Macedon or Brutus and Caesar entered into this history along with William of Orange and Philip of Spain, Cromwell and Charles I, Washington and George III. Not merely outworn beliefs but also stupid or selfish men, the tradition taught, might tyrannize over peoples and interfere with the benignity of nature. Hence man could be set free and kept free only by a benevolent state's discovery and enactment of the laws of nature and of reason or by revolution, and not by ancient creeds and traditional institutions.

Ancient creeds and traditions, however, derive strength from their very antiquity; nor are they devoid of rational grounds for existence. Thus the French Revolution, when it came, was a period of conflict between those who, suspicious of the new, wished to keep the Old Regime with as little modification as was expedient, and those who, despising the old, wished distinct if not thoroughgoing change. Waves of political, economic, and social destruction and construction met with counteracting forces, always at work and sometimes victorious; and violence resulted when one or the other of the opposing forces became dissatisfied with political means alone. A definite revolutionary creed—"the principles of 1789"—grew and crystallized in France and gradually spread by revolt and war to nearby countries. As France herself sought to still her conflicts and stabilize her new institutions, "a man on horseback" emerged in the person of General Napoleon Bonaparte.

This book should end somewhere about 1789, long before events made clear whether Bonaparte would prefer to out-Cromwell Cromwell rather than to follow the examples of William of Orange or Washington. But every schoolboy knows how his efforts to build a great world empire carried the new revolutionary creed not merely to the rest of Europe but to the European overseas empires as well, affecting the East only indirectly but the Americas directly and markedly. And since that creed was in large part the heritage of the eighteenth century, the era of revolution and Napoleon was to a considerable extent a continuation of the Enlightenment, though by other means. Let us consider how far that heritage went.

The year 1799 was a midpoint in the cataclysm that shook the whole of Europe and parts of America, Africa, and Asia between the first upsurge of revolution in France and the achievement of a new European stability in 1815. Yet by 1799 it was already possible to discern the end of an era and the beginnings of many characteristics of life that are more vividly associated with the nineteenth century and are still familiar today. The decade and a half following Bonaparte's rise to power in France were to see startling changes, but the more lasting effects of the Napoleonic era were mere modifications or consolidations of less spectacular changes begun or, at least, speculated upon in the decades preceding the French Revolution.

Revolutions generally destroy before they create. In the revolutionary decade many of the features of medieval life that had survived into the eighteenth century were reshaped into a new pattern. The most obvious of these changes was the replacement of absolute monarchy by representative government. While this had in effect been done in England a whole century earlier, the English product had been almost exclusively for home consumption. The French model, on the other hand, was generously exported. Besides, it contained several features lacking, or as yet merely latent, in the British system. One of these was the idea of government according to the will of the voters, expressed in the extension of the suffrage to the propertied and even, on occasion, to the whole adult male population. By 1799 popular sovereignty had been tried in France and her satellite republics, though temporarily and imperfectly. This temporary victory gave a smart fillip to the antimonarchical and democratic movement that was to provide one of the chief modes of political endeavor thereafter.

Popular government as developed in France during the Revolution also acquired a corollary feature that is characteristic of it today, although writers like Rousseau and statesmen like Washington had decried it—the system of political parties whose opposing platforms were either based upon or intended to appeal to widespread divergencies in public opinion expressed through pressure groups, the press, and other instruments of public opinion. Party politics and popular partisanship sometimes meant also that nationalistic rivalries replaced the humanitarian nationalism of the Rousseaus, the Kants, and the Herders. Without an aura of popular participation the integral nationalisms of succeeding centuries would have been less intense. Some of the enlightened despots of the eighteenth century had already courted popular support at least in theory; yet, through the "nation-in-arms" principle, public and lay education for citizenship, and the distribution, among all classes, individuals, and regions, of responsibility for the national welfare, the popular state assumed greater power over the whole people than kings had ever dared to assert, and the identification of the subject with the state, of the citizen with the nation, became more complete than ever before.

The Revolution also diminished in France and in the French-occupied countries, the surviving privileges of the nobles and the established church, and in their place enthroned the principle, and to a considerable extent the reality, of equality before the law. This concept brought in its wake the principle, though not always the practice, of equality of social classes and of opportunity. In France these changes gave to the businessman greater room to develop his enterprises, to increase his fortune, and lift his political and social prestige, and to the peasant they gave lands that were free from seignorial obligations and that he could manage as he wished. The widespread redistribution of lands confiscated from the royal family, the churches, and the émigrés, even though it did not benefit the peasantry as widely as has sometimes been supposed, did destroy or reduce some of the largest estates. Thus it helped the trend in the direction of small freehold farmers, who until well into the twentieth century were to be generally moderate in politics. The same Revolution that furthered the advance toward moderation of the French peasantry gave to the French proletariat an unfulfilled tradition for which to fight and die on the barricades. It was ironic that just as the French Revolution was making important strides toward the contentment of the peasantry, the so-called Industrial Revolution of the eighteenth century was getting under way, destined to increase the size and influence of the hitherto negligible proletariat.

In still another way the abolition of seignorial privileges produced changes in France not yet paralleled in other European countries. The notion of equality came to have greater meaning in social relationships. The old nobility was sadly discredited, and though titles were to be revived by Napoleon, many of them went to new families and the prestige attached to them diminished. Perhaps the single most egalitarian idea that the French Revolution borrowed from some Enlightenment thinkers, although it was still vague and far from universally acceptable, was that every individual was free to strive to make of himself whatever his inclinations, abilities, and opportunities permitted. Yet, in countries like the Germanies and Russia, where the nobility preserved political and economic power, and even in Britain, where the peerage at no time was summarily wiped out though it gradually shared some of its privileges with classes socially beneath it, great deference of the lower classes toward their "betters" persisted.

Other changes in prevailing attitudes were brought about by the leveling of the special privileges and exalted position of the eighteenth-century church. The Revolution propagated by force of arms the earthly ideals of the rights of man in place of the transcendent duties of man to God. The faith of the eighteenth-century intellectuals in progress and in the perfectibility of mankind broadened its appeal through the missionary spirit of the French Revolution to become the dominant creed of the nineteenth century. The impoverishment of the church by the confiscation of its property—a process that had its precedents even before Josephism was heard of—left the state the principal agent of charity and social services. The secularization of education, which also followed from the disestablishment of the Catholic Church, further contributed to the change in the accepted values and practices. As new state schools were set up to replace the parochial schools, the content of the school curriculum was altered. Republicans, firm believers in education for citizenship, were slow in establishing elementary schools, to be sure, but they achieved more at higher levels and by their philosophy did much to promote the ideal of secular, universal, and public education. If illiteracy did not disappear rapidly under their ministrations, it at least came to bear the civil stigma with which it is marked today. The church, however, was not ready to give up the struggle for the souls and minds of men, and the fight was continually renewed.

The centralization of government achieved by the various revolutionary regimes put an end to several territorial medievalisms in France, the Germanies, Italy, and Switzerland. This centralizing tendency was less a departure from the ways of the absolute monarchs than were some of the other revolutionary changes. Louis XIV, the enlightened despots, and other kings both before and after them had sought to create unified states. Revolution completed the process by sweeping out the old systems of local government or unviable principalities and, generally disregarding provincial traditions, by drawing new boundaries. Similarly, royal arbitrariness in collecting taxes was diminished and the special provincial and town privileges in taxation were widely abolished, providing an opportunity for a new, unified, and more equitable system of national budgeting. With the centralization of new governmental responsibility and the election of local officials in France and in some of the neighboring lands that temporarily fell under French control, the old practices of hereditary officeholding and the buying and selling of government positions disappeared.

The businessman profited in a multitude of special ways from the Revolution. The reorganization of the tax system was a particular stimulus to French enterprise. Goods could move more freely throughout France in the absence of conflicting and onerous provincial customs and privileges. The metric system, now standard throughout the country, and eventually throughout the Continent, enormously simplified computations, since a kilogram of grain, for instance, was now the same amount everywhere and could be sent to other places in the expectation of a standard price for a standard quantity. The abolition of the eighteenth-century guild system and of workers' protective groups such as the *compagnonnages* gave the employer a free hand in recruiting workers. The industrialist benefited from some of the government controls that still remained, such as the high protective tariff, designed to keep out British goods, and from government encouragement of invention and research. Perhaps most important of all, the new revolutionary psychology favored the businessman; it was a middle-class revolution, tending to level the ranks above but sanctifying private property, prohibiting workingmen's associations, and not enfranchising the poor.

The Revolution also was extremely profitable in cash for some businessmen. The inflation that moved from France to other countries provided ample opportunity for the accumulation of fortunes by speculation, while the sale of confiscated estates wherever French armies of occupation saw fit to dispossess "tyrants," "aristocrats," and clergy, made it possible for entrepreneurs to obtain land on highly favorable terms. The war proved remunerative, as usual, for industrialists who held war contracts. To be sure, the mechanization of industry, which had been almost as advanced in France as in Britain on the eve of the French Revolution, was retarded by the unsettled conditions that followed, and France was not to renew its industrialization on a big scale until the 1830's. Yet the vast and immediate needs of the Revolutionary armies provided opportunities for profitable investment in gun foundries, horse raising, powder works, and the manufacture of uniforms and shoes. Many new fortunes were thus created in the French Revolution, and the newly enriched were not to be found among the counterrevolutionary forces. From the newly enriched Napoleon Bonaparte was soon to choose some of his imperial nobility.

In a somewhat different way, some of the same things were concurrently happening in Great Britain. No political upheaval produced equally spectacular opportunities for making easy money. In fact, the wholesale damage inflicted on British merchants by French privateers in the wars of the French Revolution caused great economic stress. The hardships of war, particularly the enormous export of specie for subsidies to Britain's allies, obliged the Bank of England to go off the gold standard for the first time in 1797 and stay off until 1819. Nevertheless, the war provided a powerful incentive for industrial development. And the very absence of upheaval, inflation, and fighting on Britain's own soil made possible a steadier and stabler development than that which took place in France. In addition, the British continued their eighteenth-century control of the seas, which meant that they could exploit worldwide overseas markets with little competition; and although France and French-controlled territories were sealed against them, they had European allies to supply with war materials, in addition to their usual markets. Moreover, the damage done by the war to the French, Spanish, and Dutch empires allowed Britain to profit still further from her maritime superiority by obliging their overseas possessions frequently to yield to British naval or commercial domination. Already well advanced in an industrial revolution, Great Britain in the 1790's considerably increased her advantage over her nearest rival, France, and left other countries far behind in the contest sometimes designated as "the Second Hundred Years' War."

The war also brought to Europe a phenomenon characteristic of wars today but relatively uncommon in practice, if not in theory, in the eighteenth century—universal military service. Gone were the feudal days when the defense of the realm was in the hands of a separate and privileged warrior caste. Henceforth, it was the duty of every able-bodied male to defend the country which, as a member of the sovereign people, he helped to rule. This was a concept that, once its military effectiveness was demonstrated by the amazing success of French arms, was in the Napoleonic period to spread from

France to other countries. It was to outlive the Revolutionary and Napoleonic wars in the form of universal peacetime military training —an institution relatively unknown in the United States and Britain until recently but familiar in Continental Europe.

The "nation-in-arms," while primarily a military weapon, was also evidence of a new attitude. Out of the creed of the eighteenth-century *philosophes* the French revolutionaries had fashioned the slogan of "Liberty, Equality, and Fraternity," which, with a sort of religious fervor, they defended and propagated in revolution and war. But with their missionary effort, the spirit of nationalism advanced toward a new stage. The spirit of 1789, born of the peculiarly cosmopolitan and humanitarian culture that eighteenth-century Europe had enjoyed, ended by largely obliterating cosmopolitanism. Now that the French people ruled instead of the Bourbon dynasty, and the whole population fought wars against "tyrants" and professional armies, patriotism and popular enthusiasm nourished a most intense French nationalist spirit to which other nations reacted in kind. In the countries annexed by France, the inhabitants, however much some of them may have wanted annexation in the beginning, learned a lesson that was to become more vivid under the Napoleonic sway—that "liberty and equality" simply meant the French way of doing things. It was not long before they were to adapt the French slogans to their own national aspirations, and to conceive of "liberty" as freedom from French domination and of "fraternity" not as the brotherhood of all mankind but as national solidarity against the French, who were as a band of brothers joined against them. In the Napoleonic era that followed, this reinterpretation of the ideals of 1789 in terms of national consciousness, this intensification of national antipathies, was to grow more pronounced, and the new integral nationalism, as modified from the humanitarian nationalism of the *philosophes,* was to prove perhaps the most potent of our inheritances for both good and evil from the French Revolution.

Viewed broadly and in twentieth-century perspective, the French Revolution affected the rest of Europe as much as it did France. The forces of liberalism and nationalism which crystallized in France in those turbulent years were later to change such nations as Germany and Italy far more radically than they did France. The tradition of resistance to oppression and the ideals of liberty and equality were to grow everywhere into radical movements aimed at deeper alterations of the social order than the revolutionary movement of France had achieved. Democracy, stemming from such disparate roots as Biblical and Classical teachings, English experience, the French *philosophes*, and the American Declaration of Independence, found clear-cut expression in the "principles of 1789," Jacobinism, and the ill-fated Constitution of 1793. Socialism and communism, harking back to the Spartans, Plato's *Republic*, early Christianity, More's *Utopia*, and Rousseau's *Social Contract*, became political movements with the abortive protosocialist programs of the Hébertists, Robespierre's Republic of Virtue, and Babeuf's Society of Equals. Republicanism, tried on a small scale by the city-states of Greece, Rome, and Germany, the cantons of Switzerland, the provinces of Holland, and the states of the United States, reached an impressive form in the French Republic of 1792–1799, marred though it was by Terror, Thermidorian Reaction, and Directory *coups d'état*. National self-determination, struggling through the local patriotisms and the feudal, religious, and dynastic loyalties of earlier centuries, reached a high development with the "nation-in-arms" of the Terror and the militarism of the Directory.

Contemporary social and political thought, building upon foundations laid earlier, was thus largely molded in and exported from France in the last decade of the eighteenth century. Some countries, like Russia, Turkey, and Spain, were able with more or less success to resist the Enlightenment and the French Revolution. They were thus destined to spend a large part of the next century relatively free from conflicts over Liberty, Equality, and Fraternity. But they were to find in the twentieth century that a flood may be all the more disastrous for having been dammed up if ever the dam is broken. In the eighteenth century, despite advocates of the "agrarian law" and of "virtue," revolution was essentially a struggle between the privileged orders and the middle class for political power. With the nineteenth-century Industrial Revolution, it was to broaden its base until in the twentieth century it became a struggle not of classes but of masses and involved not merely a seizure of political power but the establishment of totalitarian dictatorship.

In 1799 Schiller finished his *Wallenstein*, and one would fain believe that thereby he meant to presage the appearance of the new military hero who was to dominate the first fifteen years of the nineteenth century. Like the soldierly roustabout of the Thirty Years' War, General Napoleon Bonaparte by his spectacular military and diplomatic success had captured the imagination of the Continent. Unlike Wallenstein, however, Bonaparte was not merely an adventurer and a man of war. Although he had plundered Italy in 1797 and seemed to have conquered Egypt in 1799, Bonaparte's popularity at home had been derived as much from his skill in diplomacy as from his military genius.

After a decade of turmoil, the French people, eager for order and peace, awaited a patriot-hero who would perpetuate the gains of the Enlightenment and the Revolution and at the same time quell factional strife and lull the antagonisms resulting from it. But his task would not be easy. Hostile coalitions, general confusion in domestic administration, civil war in royalist areas, and the paralysis of industry and commerce were among the heritages of the new ruler from the defunct Directory.

The times now seemed to demand an interlude of general peace and reconstruction, but Napoleon Bonaparte was to give France reconstruction without peace. His career would demonstrate once more that continuity and change go on side by side in the course of human affairs. As he built up a new society and political regime in France, he was required by his sense for expedient administration and his quest for wide popular approval to wed the old with the new, to select precedents from both eighteenth-century monarchical institutions and revolutionary innovations in order to make fresh institutions that promised stability.

Faced with the task of winning peace and building an empire, Bonaparte was to develop a program of reform based upon centralized authority, strikingly resembling that of the eighteenth-century enlightened despots. Since the Revolution had swept away many of the institutions and practices of the past, his task was at first to be somewhat easier than that undertaken by the enlightened despots, for they had had to struggle against the established order without benefit of the purgative effects of revolution. For Bonaparte the painful and costly job of destruction was already done. Feudal survivals, the nobility, the church, and the administrative structure in both local and national affairs had all undergone radical change, and many other entrenched interests had been largely eliminated. Bonaparte's initial tasks therefore were to reconstruct order out of disorder and to lay firmly the foundations of future stability. This concept of reform from above was quite in harmony with the *philosophe* tradition. Bonaparte represented the culmination of one line of eighteenth-century political thought, while the "democratic" experiment of the

Revolution constituted another. Until he was distracted by the imperialist urge, he was to resemble the Physiocrats' legal despot.

Bonaparte's brand of despotism was to be a gradual growth, modified by a high degree of practical political wisdom and a respect for
the gains of the Revolution. The Revolution had to be preserved but
disciplined. Institutions from the Old Regime could not be revived
without consideration for dissimilar or contravening institutions established by the Revolution. Rhetoric on civil liberty, widespread desire for equality of opportunity, and extension of France's frontiers
were achievements of earlier decades that could not easily be discarded. Even the grossest acts of despotism therefore would have at
times to be cloaked by Bonaparte in Enlightenment or revolutionary
language, and the most obvious political coups would be submitted
to the population for formal ratification. The general will was to
function through a well-beloved despot rather than through representative assemblies or a Rousseauean servant-prince of a sovereign
people. Eventually, by his second marriage, Bonaparte was to become related to Louis XVI and Marie Antoinette, to the ancient li-
neage of the Bourbons and the Habsburgs, but he was always careful
to show an outward deference also to a written constitution and the
popular will.

It still rouses admiration that Bonaparte succeeded as often as
he did in wedding the Old Regime to the Revolution. But the success
was made possible only by his being in a position to disregard those
who felt he was yielding too much to one side or the other, only by
his being able to make of himself more and more the arbiter of
France's and Europe's destiny. At home Bonaparte was to become
increasingly "totalitarian," and abroad an insatiable conqueror, constantly seeking new fields of conquest. In his conquests abroad he
was at first still the liberator. But in the liberated countries, when he
failed to give power to the native-born and made ever-growing demands for men and money, he roused an intense national resentment.
And in the countries that fought off his "liberation," defiance was
sometimes made possible by a similarly intense nationalistic counter-
effort at reform and defense.

Thus reform and nationalism went hand in hand in Napoleonic
Europe. In some countries reform was to come through the direct
efforts of Bonaparte and in others by reaction against him. In some
countries the national spirit likewise would grow stronger through his
direct efforts (e.g., France, Poland, Croatia, Italy), in others by reaction against him led by the ancient rulers (e.g., Britain, Prussia, Rus-

sia, and Austria), and in still others by reaction against him through popular resentment (e.g., Spain, the Spanish-American colonies, and Haiti). Since reform and nationalism sometimes arrived without revolution, it was not clear, on Napoleon's downfall in 1815, that revolution was a necessary third companion to the other two. Hence Europe was left undecided not only how much reform and how much nationalism were still to be achieved but whether they should be achieved from the top down or from the bottom up.

Once established firmly in power, Bonaparte proceeded to round out the reforms earlier initiated by the enlightened despots or the revolutionary assemblies and to inaugurate a series of new measures designed to increase the efficiency of France's governmental machinery. The adjustment of local administrative and judicial units to the new national structure became one of his immediate objectives. He replaced elected local officials by his own appointees, aiming at a higher degree of centralization than had generally existed in the revolutionary years. He retained the system of departments and its subdivisions devised during the Revolution, placing each department in the charge of a prefect reporting directly to his minister of the interior. Each official of the new regime was responsible for almost every detail to the official immediately above him in the hierarchy. Virtually nothing was left to the discretion of local authorities. The centralized bureaucracy developed in the Old Regime was thus in principle restored but conspicuously modified by a revolutionary reorganization, and so reconstructed, it has since remained a striking feature of French government.

Reorganization of the local administrative and judicial structure was designed also to aid in the suppression of internal disorders. Royalist civil wars had been almost continuous since 1793. Aided by the British, the insurgents were able to prevent the revolutionary governments from exercising anything more than nominal control over the western departments. Pacification was accomplished in part by easing the restrictions on religion, proclaiming an amnesty, and providing an opportunity for peaceful surrender to the new government. Those who refused to take advantage of Bonaparte's clemency were ruthlessly hunted out.

Bonaparte's strengthening of the country's finances and economy was essential to the smooth functioning of the new government. Ever since the days of Louis XIV, France's financial plight had become increasingly serious. The revolutionary governments had been particularly baffled by monetary and fiscal problems, accentuated by the indiscriminate issue of paper currency, and businessmen and bankers hesitated to advance money to Bonaparte's government, whose tenure might be as short as that of the ones which had preceded it. By careful judgment and the expenditure of much effort France's economy was gradually centralized under national control and began to revive. The first important measure in this direction was the establishment in 1800 of the Bank of France, which, though it initially derived its capital from private sources, became an agent of the government. Regulation of accounts through national agents largely eliminated the corruption that had before been common in local finances. With a greater degree of central control, the government was better able to estimate receipts and expenditures and hence could more accurately prepare its annual budgets. By 1801–1802 the budget appeared to balance, a rare feat in government finance, rendered possible by the close supervision of the fiscal system, the indemnities and tributes derived from military conquest, and economy measures practiced in every department of government. The Bank of France, until it was "democratized" in 1936, dominated the financial structure of the nation, and its stockholders became known (somewhat inaccurately) as the "two hundred families" that were said to control French society.

The place of religion in society was another of the problems that had occupied the best minds of the Enlightenment and that Bonaparte had inherited from the revolutionary era. Every hamlet in the land had suffered from the schisms and the "de-christianizing" movements produced by the Revolution. Appreciating fully the importance of religion to the people, Bonaparte determined to effect a religious settlement, although, since he was a child of the Enlightenment and the Revolution, religion had had but a slight influence on himself. In a spirit of political expediency, in 1801 he finally concluded a concordat with the papacy that was to govern France's relations with the church until 1905 and has left them complicated ever since.

At no time did Bonaparte intend to reestablish the largely autonomous prerevolutionary church of the eighteenth century. In this regard he was more Febronian than Emperor Joseph II had been. Repeatedly he expressed some such sentiment as that "the people needs a religion, and its religion must be in government hands." To negotiate a satisfactory agreement with Rome, he felt, would provide an easy solution to an ancient and highly complex problem. At every turn in the discussions, however, he insisted upon both the Gallican Rights that Louis XIV and his successors had failed to secure and the church's voluntary abandonment of its claim to the properties confiscated and sold during the Revolution. When the papal emissaries hesitated, he brought the papacy under direct pressure from his troops stationed in Italy, and a reluctant papal representative was finally obliged to sign the concordat. By the new agreement Catholicism was recognized as the religion of most Frenchmen, and bishops were to be consecrated by the pope upon nomination by the state. Since the Revolutionary land settlement was recognized by the church, and the tithe was not restored, the government had to assume the financial support of the French clergy, for it was left without other sources of revenue.

In the wake of the settlement with the Catholic Church, arrangements followed for religious minorities. Calvinists and Lutherans were granted freedom to practice their faith in France and were given some government support. Even the Jews, though still subject to restrictions, when it met with Bonaparte's aims, were granted special privileges and organized on a national religious basis. To Bonaparte, the main function of all religions was to aid in the maintenance of law and order, and in so doing to act as a semiofficial agency of the state. "I do not see in religion," he admitted, "the mystery of the incarnation but the mystery of the social order. It attaches to heaven an idea of equality which prevents the rich man from being massacred by the poor."

France's system of education also underwent a thorough overhauling under Bonaparte's direction. Traditionally under the supervision of the clergy, educational institutions had been without adequate personnel or leadership for almost a decade. Although the *philosophes*, especially after the expulsion of the Jesuits, and certain Revolutionary leaders had worked out on paper a national system of education, practical problems postponed the realization of their ambitious program. In 1799 elementary schooling was particularly deplorable, but at all levels essentials were lacking. Little had been done to maintain or replace the school buildings of the Old Regime. Adequately trained lay teachers were few. Rapid changes of government had also played havoc with educational funds and administration. For a time education had been left almost completely in the hands of local government, but the Terror government had sketched a program of centralization that Bonaparte filled in.

After Bonaparte concluded the Concordat of 1801, he was able to develop a comprehensive educational program, for he solved the problem of teacher shortages by using the talent of the restored clergy. He was determined, however, that, like the church, the school should be subject to the dictates of the government. He also endeavored to maintain lay supremacy in the educational system at whatever points he could—a difficult task because of the clergy's superior training, experience, and willingness to serve. Bonaparte realized that the priests would almost inevitably dominate elementary education. His reforms were designed, therefore, to provide the secondary and higher schools with lay teachers who should, as time went on, become increasingly prominent at all levels. In 1808, after he became emperor, he organized the University of France as a central clearing house and control agency for higher education—a sort of national board of education, which strictly centralized the university system. As with his religious organization, Bonaparte dedicated his educational enterprises to the task of helping the state maintain law and order and, ultimately, to the duty of teaching citizens to be loyal to his dynasty.

The democratic spirit of Pestalozzi and other eighteenth-century educational theorists made but a slight impression upon the administrators of France's new elementary school system. Free instruction for all was not provided. On the contrary, tuition fees beyond the primary level were high, and clerical and lay masters ran private educational establishments. By the end of the era, state supervision of education was much more conspicuous in theory than in the classroom. Furthermore, Bonaparte's boasts of educational uniformity were either calculated or unwittingly incorrect. His regime provided neither democratic nor uniform education. The centralizing machinery interfered with rather than helped local initiative. The educational practices of the Old Regime with its emphasis on the Classics and its clerical preferences retained a vitality and appeal in France that Bonaparte, who favored vocational and technical training, would never have admitted willingly.

One of the most remarkable features, in fact, of Bonaparte's educational system was the emphasis upon the natural sciences. In a Europe where humanistic education was still dominant, the French program of studies signified a decided departure. At the lower levels the curriculum was conservative and more nearly in conformance with the Classical tradition in education. In the universities and the professional schools, such as the newly established École Polytechnique with its most extraordinary faculty of great scientists, emphasis was on technical and scientific training. The ideal of free inquiry,

so often proclaimed by the *philosophes*, particularly on social and political problems, was definitely not encouraged. The Revolution had
reorganized the old academies into a National Institute, but when
Bonaparte refashioned the Institute, he suppressed the Section of
Moral and Political Sciences as subversive. Training for military, industrial, and state service was for him the main aim of education.
Like Hitler and other autocrats, Bonaparte endeavored to coordinate
education and to direct thought to political and utilitarian purposes.

After the exhortations of the *philosophes* in favor of equality before the law and the legal changes attempted by codifications during
the Revolutionary era, the need for a uniform law code became more
pressing than ever. In 1800 Bonaparte inaugurated discussion of a
new civil code by appointing a committee of experts to draw up a
tentative draft. Some ideals of the Revolution were too persistent to
be ignored. The committee's proposed code reflected the humanitarianism of the Enlightenment. It assumed the equality of all citizens in
the courts; it acknowledged the right of every person to choose his
own career and to advance in it according to his merit; it stated ex-
plicitly the superiority of state over church and provided for universal recognition of the freedom of individual conscience. It also protected the interests of the new propertied classes created during the
Revolution, and thus permanently insured France against a revival of
the ancient privileges of the upper orders of society, substituting an
easily ascertainable system of mortgages, leases, contracts, and torts
for seignorial dues and local customs. Although an astoundingly complete and thorough work, it was designed primarily for an agrarian
society and neglected, perhaps understandably, to provide comprehensive regulations for the industrial era that was in process of development. Discussions of the Civil Code and its implications were carried on for four years before it was finally promulgated. It became
known as the "Code Napoleon." A Code of Civil Procedure, a Commercial Code, a Criminal Code, a Code of Criminal Procedure, and a
Penal Code completed the series associated with the Code Napoleon.
As with Bonaparte's other reforms, the main objective of the
codes was to make government easier and more efficient. Although
civil liberties were ostensibly guaranteed to all, the codes were essentially authoritarian in spirit. Workers were subjected to their em-
ployers, wives to their husbands, children to their fathers. Preservation of individual rights and liberties was considered important only
so long as they did not interfere with the aims and interests of the
government. Some punishments that today we should consider cruel

and unusual—such as cutting off the thumb of a parricide—were still retained. Nevertheless, the codes of Bonaparte were recognized as the most humanitarian and modern system of law of their day, despite some of their reactionary features. They were to be exported beyond the confines of France to the areas that he conquered or that chose voluntarily to model their systems on his. The Code Napoleon is still the national code of France, Belgium, and Holland, and has exercised a discernible influence upon the codes of Louisiana, Quebec, Italy, West Germany, Japan, and other countries that in the nineteenth century faced the problems of building a new system of law.

Bonaparte was particularly conscious of the power of the press as an instrument for molding public opinion. Uniformity of law, religion, education, and loyalty required, in his philosophy, a controlled press. In 1800 the government decreed that the number of newspapers published in the city of Paris should be limited to thirteen. The *Gazette national ou le Moniteur universel*, founded in 1789, became the official organ of the government. Strict censorship was also instituted. Bonaparte sometimes personally insisted that a particular newspaper should be penalized for violating the censorship and hence endangering the nation's security. Minor as well as grave offenses might be punished severely and swiftly. Besides, Bonaparte allowed no free expression of opinion in books. When Mme de Staël, one of the famous novelists and literary critics of her day, too openly showed political opposition, she was exiled, and her literary coterie was silenced. The extent of influence exerted by the press, however, was doubtful. Circulation of books and newspapers was still limited by the high price of paper and printing and the inability of many persons to read for themselves.

Bonaparte recognized the desirability of winning support as well as discouraging opposition. He studiously distributed praise and honors wherever words, titles, and decorations would suffice to make friends. He created the Legion of Honor to reward those who had served the nation faithfully, whether in a military, civil, or other capacity. At first, the distinction was something more than an empty decoration; it carried with it a stipend, and until some of the old nobles were ready to return and new ones were created when Napoleon became emperor, the members of the Legion were the only "nobles" of France. Some of the toughest republican-minded soldiers who now were made knights and officers in the "republican nobility" found it easier to accept the Bonapartist regime.

Coordination of all aspects of life under the Bonapartist dicta-

torship was reminiscent of the governing system of the Bourbons and
foreshadowed the passion for uniformity in twentieth-century totalitarian governments. Above everything else, however, Bonaparte
placed the security of his personal regime. Consequently, he made
showy concessions to the demand for liberty, equality, and fraternity
released in Europe by the Enlightenment and the French Revolution. Conspicuous among them was his studied courting of general
approval by plebiscites. Although these plebiscites were far from free
and unfettered elections or scientific samplings of public opinion, Bonaparte and his several constitutions were truly acceptable to the
French people.

When Napoleon was defeated at Waterloo in 1815 and the Congress of Vienna tried to restore as much as it could of the "legitimate" system that had prevailed before the Revolution, "legitimacy"
appeared to have won the victory. But the forces of republicanism,
anticlericalism, constitutionalism, Bonapartism, and other creeds
born of or matured during the Enlightenment and the Revolutionary
and Napoleonic unrest had not died. They remained alive and fresh
in the hearts of many devotees. The people of western Europe and of
their colonies overseas now were less likely than ever to be appeased
by reforms handed down by a monarch, no matter how enlightened.
The memory of popular constitutions and of patriotic fervor became
vivid hallmarks of a widespread political conviction. Bonaparte had
been defeated in the final analysis by aroused nationalities even if
they sometimes rallied around their ancient dynasties. No matter
how brutally he had trampled upon "liberty, equality, and fraternity," and no matter how great had been the fall of the once idolized
hero, the Revolutionary slogan still was to rouse loyalty not only in
Frenchmen but in "liberals" everywhere. "Liberty and equality" was
to become the "liberalism" of the nineteenth century; "fraternity"
was to become its "nationalism."

"Legitimacy," on the other hand, was the basic principle which
guided the Congress of Vienna. It was the slogan of those souls who
had had enough of war and revolution and hoped for continued international peace and domestic concord. It won the scorn and con-
demnation of liberals because it served as a pretext for disowning the
new democracy and the new nationalism in Germany, Italy, Belgium, Poland, and elsewhere.

Still at many points "legitimacy" had been ignored in deference
to the welter of agreements and bargains concluded before and dur-

ing the negotiations. It had proved impossible at Vienna to reconstruct the old order in its entirety. After the profound changes effected by the Revolutionary and Napoleonic epochs, restoration of the Old Regime was accomplished only in part. Compromises everywhere had to be made with the Enlightenment and the Revolution. Serfdom could not be reestablished in most countries. The Catholic Church in France could not have its lands restored; and the *émigrés* were to hope in vain for full compensation for their confiscated properties. The French Bourbons could return in the person of Louis XVIII but not as absolute monarchs; the Holy Roman Empire could not be reconstructed; and the counterfeudal effects of the Code Napoleon could not be eradicated. In drawing up the new "legitimate" order, Europe's statesmen, even though afraid, had occasionally been forced to concede the ideas and principles of popular government propagated by the French Revolutionary armies, who commonly thought of themselves as the carriers of the Enlightenment.

These concessions explain in part why the "legitimate" order created in Europe at Vienna underwent no major changes and few minor ones for more than forty years. But the success of the Congress of Vienna was due also to the fact that its arrangements were carried into force by the collective action and the police power of the "Concert of Europe." Despite its injustices and reactionary spirit, the Treaty of Vienna did in fact provide a "legitimate" foundation for the international order which the Saint Pierres, the Rousseaus, and the Kants had preached in the eighteenth century and which the great powers under British leadership saw fit to enforce most of the time. The "Pax Britannica" endured, broken by a few local wars but no general conflagration, until 1914. And the local wars were to come in several instances because the travail of the Enlightenment, of the French Revolution, and of the Napoleonic period had not clearly established whether reform comes best from those in power or from the general will of the people.

Selected Readings

GENERAL BIBLIOGRAPHY
The "Selected Readings" below have been chosen because they are good interpretations in English of the eighteenth century or some aspect thereof. The reader who may desire a fuller bibliography should consult Curt A. Zimansky, ed., *The Eighteenth Century: A Current Bibliography for 1970* (Iowa City: University of Iowa, 1971), which is vol. 50, no. 3 (July 1971) of the *Philological Quarterly* and to which regular annual sequels are promised. This initial issue occasionally reaches as far back as 1968 and as far forward as 1971 for bibliographical items. It is intended to be the successor to (but is more interdisciplinary than) the serial numbers of *A Bibliography of Modern Studies*, of which vol. 4 was G. J. Kolb and C. A. Zimansky, eds., *English Literature 1660–1800* (for the years 1957–1960) (Princeton: Princeton University Press, 1962). For still earlier titles consult *The International Bibliography of Historical Sciences*, of which vol. 25 (for 1966) was edited by Michel François and Nicolas Tolu (Paris: Armand Colin, 1969), as well as Mary-Margaret H. Barr, *Quarante années d'études voltairiennes. Bibliographie analytique des livres et articles sur Voltaire, 1926–1965* (Paris: Armand Colin, 1968). The standard bibliography for the history of art is Mary W. Chamberlin, *Guide to Art Reference Books* (Chicago: American Library Association, 1959).

Titles that have asterisks either are paperback editions or are available in paperback editions. Although several titles would fit under more than one chapter heading, no title has been repeated.

GENERAL WORKS

M. S. Anderson. *Europe in the Eighteenth Century, 1713–1783.* New York: Holt, Rinehart & Winston, 1961.

Stuart Andrews. *Eighteenth Century Europe: The 1680's to 1815.* New York: David Mckay Co., Inc., 1965.

C. B. A. Behrens. *Ancien Régime.* New York: Harcourt Brace Jovanovich, 1967.°

G. N. Clark *et al.,* eds. *The New Cambridge Modern History,* vol. 7. J. O. Lindsay, ed. *The Old Regime, 1713–1763,* vol. 8. A. Goodman, ed. *The American and French Revolutions, 1763–1793.* Cambridge, U. K.: University Press, 1957 and 1965.

Alfred Cobban. *History of Modern France.* Vol. 1, *Old Regime and Revolution, 1715–1799.* 3rd ed. New York: George Braziller, Inc., 1965.°

Louis Gottschalk, L. C. Mac Kinney, and E. H. Pritchard. *The Foundations of the Modern World, 1300–1775.* Vol. 4 of "The UNESCO History of Mankind." New York: Harper and Row, Inc., 1969.

David Ogg. *Europe of the Ancient Regime, 1715–1783.* New York: Harper and Row, Inc., 1965.°

R. J. White. *Europe in the Eighteenth Century.* New York: St. Martin's Press, 1965.

Basil Willey. *Eighteenth Century Background.* Boston: Beacon Press, 1961.

Ernest Neville Williams. *The Ancien Régime in Europe: Government and Society in the Major States, 1648–1789.* London: The Bodley Head Limited, 1970.

CHAPTER ONE: *The Turn of a Century: Europe and the East*

Elinor G. Barber. *The Bourgeoisie in 18th-Century France.* Princeton: Princeton University Press, 1955.°

C. R. Boxer. *The Dutch Seaborne Empire: 1600–1800.* New York: Alfred A. Knopf, Inc., 1965.

Walter H. Bruford. *Germany in the Eighteenth Century: The Social Background of the Literary Revival.* New York: Cambridge University Press, 1935.°

Basil Davidson. *Old Africa Rediscovered.* London: Gollanz, 1959.

Franklin L. Ford. *Robe and Sword: The Regrouping of the French Aristocracy after Louis XIV.* Cambridge, Mass.: Harvard University Press, 1953.°

Hajo Holborn. *A History of Modern Germany.* Vol. 2, *1648–1840.* New York: Alfred A. Knopf, Inc., 1963.

Bernard Lewis. *The Arabs in History.* 4th ed. London: Hutchinson University Library, 1966.°

John Lough. *An Introduction to Eighteenth-Century France.* New York: David McKay Co., 1960.°

K. M. Panikkar. *A Survey of Indian History.* 4th ed. New York: Asia Publishing House, 1964.°

J. H. Parry. *Trade and Dominion. The European Overseas Empires in the Eighteenth Century.* London: Weidenfeld & Nicolson, 1971.

John H. Plumb. *England in the Eighteenth Century: 1714–1815.* Hammersmith, Middlesex: Penguin Books, 1950.°

Marc Raeff. *Imperial Russia, 1682–1825: The Coming of Age of Modern Russia.* New York: Alfred A. Knopf, Inc., 1970.°

Abram L. Sachar. *A History of the Jews.* 5th ed. New York: Alfred A. Knopf, Inc., 1965.°

George Bailey Sansom. *A History of Japan.* Vol. 3, *1615–1867.* Stanford: Stanford University Press, 1963.°

Percival Spear. *India: A Modern History.* Ann Arbor: University of Michigan Press, 1961.

CHAPTER TWO: *The Turn of a Century: The Americas*

Charles M. Andrews. *Colonial Period of American History.* With a new foreword by Leonard W. Labaree. Vol. 4, *England's Commercial and Colonial Policy.* New Haven: Yale University Press, 1964.°

Carl Becker. *Beginnings of the American People*. Ithaca, N.Y.: Cornell University Press, 1966.°

Daniel J. Boorstin. *The Americans*. Vol. 1, *The Colonial Experience*. New York: Random House, Inc., 1958.°

C. R. Boxer. *Four Centuries of Portuguese Expansion, 1415–1825: A Succinct Survey*. Berkeley: University of California Press, 1961.°

Carl Bridenbaugh. *Mitre and Sceptre: Transatlantic Faiths, Ideas, Personalities, and Politics, 1689–1775*. New York: Oxford University Press, 1962.°

Charles Gibson. *Spain in America*. New York: Harper and Row, Inc., 1966.°

John C. Miller. *Origins of the American Revolution*. Stanford: Stanford University Press, 1959.°

Roland Oliver and J. D. Fage. *Short History of Africa*. Baltimore: Penguin Books, Inc., 1966.°

Mariano Picón-Salas. *A Cultural History of Spanish America: From Conquest to Independence*. Translated by J. A. Leonard. Berkeley: University of California Press, 1962.°

Richard H. Shryock. *Medicine and Society in America: 1660–1860*. Ithaca, N.Y.: Cornell University Press, 1962.°

Louis B. Wright. *Atlantic Frontier: Colonial American Civilization, 1607–1763*. Ithaca, N.Y.: Cornell University Press, 1964.°

Silvio Zavala. *The Colonial Period in the History of the New World*. Abridged in English by Max Savelle. Mexico City: Instituto Panamericano de Geografía e Historia, 1962.

CHAPTER THREE: *The Struggle for Empire (1714–1763)*

Basil Davidson. *African Slave Trade: Precolonial History, 1450–1850*. Boston: Little, Brown & Co., 1961.°

Walter L. Dorn. *Competition for Empire, 1740–1763*. William L. Langer, ed. "Rise of Modern Europe." New York: Harper and Row, Inc., 1940.

J. F. Fuller. *Military History of the Western World*. Vol. 2, *From the Defeat of the Spanish Armada, 1588, to the Battle of Waterloo, 1815*. New York: Funk and Wagnalls, 1955.

Alfred T. Mahan. *Influence of Sea Power upon History*. New York: Hill and Wang, Inc., 1957.°

Milton W. Meyer. *Brief History of Southeast Asia*. Totowa, N.J.: Littlefield, Adams & Co., 1965.°

G. P. Murdock. *Africa: Its People and Their Culture History*. New York: McGraw-Hill Book Company, 1959.

Howard H. Peckham. *The Colonial Wars, 1689–1782*. Chicago: University of Chicago Press, 1964.°

Tamara Talbot Rice. *Elizabeth, Empress of Russia*. New York: Praeger Publishers, Inc., 1970.

Penfield Roberts. *The Quest for Security: 1715–1740.* William L. Langer, ed. "Rise of Modern Europe." New York: Harper and Row, Inc., 1947.°

Hans Rosenberg. *Bureaucracy, Aristocracy and Autocracy: The Prussian Experience, 1660–1815.* Cambridge, Mass.: Harvard University Press, 1958.

Vincent A. Smith. *Oxford History of India.* 3rd ed. by Percival Spear. London: Oxford University Press, 1958.°

Albert Sorel. *Europe under the Old Regime.* Translated by Francis Herrick. New York: Harper and Row, Inc., 1964.°

George F. Stanley. *New France: The Last Phase, 1744–1760.* London: Oxford University Press, 1968.

R. J. White. *Age of George III.* New York: Walker & Co., 1968.°

CHAPTER FOUR: *Society and Thought in an Age of Enlightenment (1700–1775)*

Robert Anchor. *The Enlightenment Tradition.* New York: Harper and Row, Inc., 1967.°

Theodore Besterman. *Voltaire.* New York: Harcourt Brace Jovanovich, 1969.

Émile Bréhier. *The History of Philosophy.* Vol. 5, *The Eighteenth Century.* Translated by Wade Baskin. Chicago: University of Chicago Press, 1967.°

Ernst Cassirer. *The Philosophy of the Enlightenment.* Translated by C. A. Koelln and James P. Pettigrove. 2nd printing. Boston: Beacon Press, 1960.°

James L. Clifford and Donald J. Greene. *Samual Johnson: A Survey and Bibliography of Critical Studies.* Minneapolis: University of Minnesota Press, 1970.

Lester G. Crocker. *An Age of Crisis: Man and the World in Eighteenth-Century France.* Baltimore: Johns Hopkins Press, 1959.

———*Nature and Culture: Ethical Thought in the French Enlightenment.* Baltimore: Johns Hopkins Press, 1963.

———*Jean-Jacques Rousseau.* Vol. 1. New York: The Macmillan Co., 1968.

Peter Gay. *The Enlightenment: An Interpretation.* Vol. 1, *The Rise of Modern Paganism.* Vol. 2, *The Science of Freedom.* New York: Alfred A. Knopf, Inc., 1966 and 1969.

Paul Hazard. *European Thought in the Eighteenth Century, from Montesquieu to Lessing.* Translated by J. Lewis May. 2nd printing. Cleveland: Meridian Books, Inc., 1965.°

Arthur O. Lovejoy. *Great Chain of Being: A Study of the History of an Idea.* New York: Harper and Row, Inc., 1960.°

Kingsley Martin. *French Liberal Thought in the Eighteenth Century: A Study of Political Ideas from Bayle to Condorcet.* New York: Harper and Row, Inc., 1963.°

Robert R. Palmer. *Catholics and Unbelievers in Eighteenth-Century France.* New York: Cooper Square Publishers, 1961.°

Robert Shackleton. *Montesquieu: A Critical Biography.* New York: Oxford University Press, 1961.

Preserved Smith. *A History of Modern Culture.* Vol. 2, *The Enlightenment, 1687–1776.* New York: The Macmillan Company, 1962.°

Charles Vereker. *Eighteenth Century Optimism: A Study of the Interrelations of Moral and Social Theory in English and French Thought between 1689 and 1789.* Liverpool: Liverpool University Press, 1967.

Arthur M. Wilson. *Diderot: A Man for Our Time.* New York: Oxford University Press, 1972.

CHAPTER FIVE: *"A New Nation Conceived in Liberty"*

Peter Amann, ed. *The Eighteenth Century Revolution: French or Western?* Boston: D. C. Heath & Company, 1963.°

Bernard Bailyn. *The Ideological Origins of the American Revolution.* Cambridge, Mass.: Harvard University Press, 1967.°

Samuel F. Bemis. *Diplomacy of the American Revolution.* 3rd. ed. Bloomington: Indiana University Press, 1957.°

Cedric B. Conway. *The Great Awakening and the American Revolution: Colonial Thought in the 18th Century.* Chicago: Rand McNally and Co., 1971.°

Lawrence A. Cremin. *American Education: The Colonial Experience, 1607–1787.* New York: Harper and Row, Inc., 1970.

Philip G. Davidson. *Propaganda and the American Revolution.* Chapel Hill: University of North Carolina Press, 1967.°

Lawrence H. Gipson. *The Coming of the Revolution: 1763–1775.* New York: Harper and Row, Inc., 1954.°

Jack P. Greene, ed. *The Ambiguity of the American Revolution.* New York: Harper and Row, Inc., 1968.°

J. Franklin Jameson. *The American Revolution Considered as a Social Movement.* Princeton: Princeton University Press, 1967.°

Lawrence S. Kaplan. *Colonies into Nation: American Diplomacy, 1763–1801.* New York: The Macmillan Company, 1972.

Dumas Malone. *Jefferson and the Ordeal of Liberty.* Boston: Little, Brown and Co., 1969.°

Forrest McDonald. *Formation of the American Republic, 1776–1790.* New York: Penguin Books, 1965.°

Richard B. Morris. *American Revolution Reconsidered.* New York: Harper and Row, Inc., 1967.°

Max Savelle. *Seeds of Liberty: The Genesis of the American Mind.* Seattle: University of Washington Press, 1965.°

Arthur M. Schlesinger [Sr.]. *The Birth of a Nation: A Portrait of the American People on the Eve of Independence.* New York: Alfred A. Knopf, Inc., 1968.

James Morton Smith, ed. *The Constitution.* New York: Harper and Row, Inc., 1971.°

CHAPTER SIX: *Europe on the Eve of Revolution*

T. C. Blanning. *Joseph II and Enlightened Despotism*. London: Longmans, 1970.°

J. F. Bosher. *French Finances, 1770–1795: From Business to Bureaucracy.* New York: Cambridge University Press, 1970.

Edward Crankshaw. *Maria Theresa.* New York: The Viking Press, Inc., 1970.

John G. Gagliardo. *Enlightened Despotism.* New York: Thomas Y. Crowell, 1967.°

Leo Gershoy. *From Despotism to Revolution: 1763–1789.* William L. Langer, ed. "Rise of Modern Europe." New York: Harper and Row, Inc., 1944.°

Bentley Glass *et al.*, eds. *Forerunners of Darwin, 1754–1859.* Baltimore: Johns Hopkins Press, 1959.

Albert Goodman, ed. *European Nobility in the Eighteenth Century: Studies of the Nobilities of the Major European States in the Pre-Reform Era.* New York: Harper and Row, Inc., 1967.°

Louis Gottschalk. *Lafayette between the American and the French Revolution.* 2nd impression (with corrections). Chicago: University of Chicago Press, 1965.

Henry Guerlac. *Lavoisier—The Crucial Year: The Background and Origin of His First Experiments on Combustion in 1772.* Ithaca, N.Y.: Cornell University Press, 1961.

A. R. Hall. *The Scientific Revolution, 1500–1800: The Formation of the Modern Scientific Attitude.* 2nd printing. Boston: Beacon Press, 1957.°

Norman Hampson. *A Cultural History of the Enlightenment.* London and New York: Pantheon Books, Inc., 1969.

Thomas L. Hankins. *Jean d'Alembert: Science and the Enlightenment.* New York: Oxford University Press, 1970.

Richard Herr. *The Eighteenth-Century Revolution in Spain.* Princeton: Princeton University Press, 1958.°

Arthur Hertzberg. *The French Enlightenment and the Jews: The Origins of Modern Anti-Semitism.* New York: Schocken Press, 1968.

James A. Leith. *The Idea of Art as Propaganda in France 1750–1799: A Study in the History of Ideas.* Toronto: University of Toronto Press, 1965.

Paul Mantoux. *The Industrial Revolution in the Eighteenth Century: An Outline of the Beginnings of the Modern Factory System in England.* New York: Harper and Row, Inc., 1962.°

S. T. McCloy. *The Humanitarian Movement in Eighteenth-Century France.* Lexington, Ky.: University of Kentucky Press, 1957.

Nancy Mitford. *Frederick the Great.* London: Hamilton, 1970.

Charles Petrie. *King Charles III of Spain: An Enlightened Despot.* New York: John Day, 1971.

Thomas Riha, ed. *Readings in Russian Civilization.* Vol. 2, *Imperial Russia, 1700–1917.* Chicago: University of Chicago Press, 1969.°

Caroline Robbins. *The Eighteenth-Century Commonwealthman: Studies in the Transmission, Development and Circumstance of English Liberal Thought from the Restoration of Charles II until the War with the Thirteen Colonies.* Cambridge, Mass.: Harvard University Press, 1959.°

Charles Singer, E. J. Holmyard, *et al.*, eds. *A History of Technology.* Vol. 4, *The Industrial Revolution, c. 1750–1850.* Oxford: Oxford University Press, 1958.

Gladys S. Thomson. *Catherine the Great and the Expansion of Russia.* New York: The Macmillan Company, 1962.

Abraham Wolf. *A History of Science, Technology, and Philosophy in the Eighteenth Century.* 2 vols. New York: Harper and Row, Inc., 1961.

CHAPTER SEVEN: *Epilogue*

William F. Church, ed. *The Influence of the Enlightenment on the French Revolution.* Boston: D. C. Heath and Co., 1964.°

Lester Crocker, ed. *The Age of the Enlightenment.* New York: Harper and Row, Inc., 1968.

D. K. Fieldhouse. *The Colonial Empires: A Comparative Survey from the Eighteenth Century.* London: Weidenfeld and Nicolson, 1966.

Jacques Godechot. *France and the Atlantic Revolution of the Eighteenth Century.* Translated by Herbert H. Rowen. New York: The Free Press, 1965.

Norman Hampson. *The First European Revolution, 1776–1815.* New York: Harcourt Brace Jovanovich, 1969.°

Robert B. Holtman. *Napoleonic Revolution.* Philadelphia: J. B. Lippincott Co., 1967.°

Georges Lefebvre. *The Coming of the French Revolution.* Translated by Robert R. Palmer. Princeton: Princeton University Press, 1967.°

Frank E. Manuel. *The Prophets of Paris: Turgot, Condorcet, Saint Simon, Fourier, Comte.* New York: Harper and Row, Inc., 1965.°

Leonard M. Marsak, ed. *French Philosophers from Descartes to Sartre.* Cleveland: Meridian Books, Inc., 1961.°

Louis T. Milic, ed. *The Modernity of the Eighteenth Century.* Vol. 1 of the *Proceedings of the American Society for Eighteenth-Century Studies.* Cleveland: Press of the Case Western Reserve University, 1971.

Robert R. Palmer. *The Age of the Democratic Revolution: A Political History of Europe and America 1760–1800.* 2 vols. Princeton: Princeton University Press, 1969–70.°

——*The World of the French Revolution.* New York: Harper and Row, Inc., 1971.

Arthur P. Whitaker, ed. *Latin America and the Enlightenment.* 2nd ed. Ithaca, N.Y.: Cornell University Press, 1961.°